Political Thought in
Early Fourteenth-Century England:
Treatises by Walter of Milemete,
William of Pagula, and William of Ockham

───────────────

Medieval and Renaissance Texts and Studies

Volume 250

Arizona Studies in the Middle Ages
and the Renaissance

Volume 10

Political Thought in Early Fourteenth-Century England:
Treatises by Walter of Milemete, William of Pagula, and William of Ockham

Edited and Translated

by

CARY J. NEDERMAN

Arizona Center for Medieval and Renaissance Studies
Tempe, Arizona
in collaboration with
BREPOLS
2002

Dust jacket image: Folio 21v, Christ Church MS 92,
Christ Church College, St. Aldate's, Oxford.

© Copyright 2002
Arizona Board of Regents for Arizona State University
and Brepols Publishers n.v., Turnhout, Belgium

ASMAR Volume 10: ISBN 2-503-51439-1 and D/2003/0095/70

All rights reserved. No part of this publication may be reproduced, stored in a retrieval system, or transmitted, in any form or by any means, electronic, mechanical, photocopying, recording, or otherwise, without the prior permission of the publishers.

Library of Congress Cataloging-in-Publication Data
Political thought in early fourteenth-century England : treatises by Walter of Milemete, William of Pagula, and William of Ockham / edited and translated by Cary J. Nederman.
    p. cm. — (Medieval and Renaissance texts and studies ; v. 250)
    Contents: General introduction : varieties of English political thought, c. 1250–c. 1350 — Walter of Milemete, On the nobility of wisdom, and prudence of kings — William of Pagula, The mirror of King Edward III — William of Ockham, Whether the ruler can accept church property for his own needs, namely, in the case of war, even against the wishes of the Pope.
    Includes bibliographical references and index.
    ISBN 0-86698-291-4 (alk. paper)
    1. Political science — Great Britain — History — To 1500. 2. Political science — Early works to 1800. I. Nederman, Cary J. II. Walter, of Milemete. De nobilitatibus, sapientiis, et prudentiis regum. English. III. William, of Pagula, ca. 1290–1332. De speculo regis Edwardi III. English. IV. William, of Ockham, ca. 1285–ca. 1349. An princeps pro suo succursu, scilicet guerrae, possit recipere bona ecclesiarum, etiam invito papa. English. V. Medieval & Renaissance Texts and Studies (Series) ; v. 250.
    JA84.G7 P685 2002
    321.6--dc21   2002074370

This book is made to last.
It is set in Garamond Antiqua typeface, smythe-sewn and
printed on acid-free paper to library specifications.
Printed in the United States of America

For

James Muldoon & Paul E. Sigmund

Table of Contents

Preface   ix

A Note on Texts and Translations   xiii

General Introduction: Varieties of English Political Thought, c.1250–c.1350   1

1. Walter of Milemete, *On the Nobility, Wisdom, and Prudence of Kings*
    - Introduction   15
    - Translation   24

2. William of Pagula, *Mirror of King Edward III*
    - Introduction   63
    - Translation, Version A   73
    - Translation, Version B   105

3. William of Ockham, *Whether a Prince Can Receive the Goods of the Church for His Own Needs, Namely, in Case of War, Even Against the Wishes of the Pope*
    - Introduction   141
    - Translation   153

Table of Biblical Citations   199

Index of Names   207

Preface

The early fourteenth century was an especially explosive period in English history. Its convulsions were marked by the final years of Edward I's reign, followed by the precarious rule and fall of Edward II, and then the open conflict between the future Edward III and his mother, Isabella, along with her lover, Mortimer. These events, not to mention the international intrigues in which successive kings of England were implicated, made for an anxious and uncertain political climate. In this highly charged atmosphere, it is hardly surprising that philosophers, clerics, and clerks would find it appropriate to comment on public affairs and to offer advice to the royal house about how to conduct itself. The changing fortunes of the Plantagenet dynasty afforded considerable grist for the mill of political punditry and theoretical reflection.

A few of the political treatises dating to the early 1300s — such as the *Modus Tenendi Parliamentum* and the *Speculum Justiciariorum* — have been edited and translated, receiving wide attention. But many more have languished unread and unappreciated, perhaps mainly due to their unavailability in print. The present volume seeks to remedy this situation by publishing for the first time in English translation several important commentaries on the political scene in early fourteenth-century England: Walter of Milemete's *On the Nobility, Wisdom, and Prudence of Kings* (1327); the two versions of William of Pagula's *Mirror of King Edward III* (1331 and 1332); and William of Ockham's *Whether the Ruler Can Accept Church Property for His Own Needs, Namely, in the Case of War, Even Against the Wishes of the Pope* (1338). Although all of these works date from the early years of Edward III's reign, they address issues that were pertinent to his immediate predecessors as well. While the tracts are certainly of interest for their commentaries on current issues, they also afford the reader fascinating insights into the multi-faceted nature of political theory in the fourteenth century. In particular, they demonstrate how the available source materials of political thought — legal, philosophical, and theological — might be brought to bear on the pressing problems of the age, such as the extent and limits of the king's power, the legitimacy of royal taxation, the relationship between church and state, and the particular duties of the ruler towards various of his subjects.

The genesis of this collection of texts may be ascribed to the convergence of several different sources. My interest in Ockham's *Whether the Ruler* ... was stimulated by my study of that work for a chapter of my 1983 York University doctoral dissertation. Although I published a paper on the treatise in 1986, I set it largely aside in the intervening years. But I have been disappointed that it is the only major political work by Ockham that has not been translated. William of Pagula's two mirrors for Edward III have been a recurring object of my scholarly investigation during the past fifteen years, from a variety of perspectives — as commentaries on social and economic events in the 1330s, as distinctive additions to medieval thinking about rights, and as contributions to the *speculum* genre that achieved such popularity during the late Middle Ages. I had long entertained the idea of publishing a translation of the writings of the two Williams, if only to satisfy occasional requests from fellow political theorists who lacked Latin but whose interest was piqued by reports of the ideas contained in these writings. The inclusion of Walter of Milemete's tract on kingship came at the suggestion of Kate Forhan, who had previously worked on the iconographical program of its manuscript illuminations. Upon reading Milemete for the first time in early 1999, I was impressed with the sophistication and innovation of his doctrines and happily acceded to undertake the translation of the work. The General Introduction derives from materials that I first explored in my dissertation and expanded upon in several chapters of an unpublished book manuscript upon which I labored in the late 1980s.

A project that occupies one's energies off and on for nearly two decades is necessarily indebted to many scholars who nourished and nudged it along the way. I wish to single out for thanks (in strictly alphabetical order) Professors Janet Coleman, Kate Langdon Forhan, Cynthia J. Neville, and Neal Wood. Professor Forhan and Professor James M. Blythe served as reviewers for the manuscript and saved me from numerous errors and infelicities. Dr. Leslie S. B. MacCoull copyedited the volume with a thoroughness and professional precision that I have seldom encountered. I would be remiss if I did not express gratitude to Bob Bjork, the general editor of Medieval and Renaissance Texts and Studies, for his enthusiastic insistence that this text must be published by his imprint. Much of the translation work was undertaken in scenic and luxurious surroundings at South Lake Tahoe, Nevada, provided by my dear friend Edd Whetmore, whose only expectation in exchange was that I occasionally forego the joys of translating fourteenth-century Latin in order to join him in watching a televised baseball game or in sampling an excellent bottle of wine. Donnalee Dox is, as ever, a fount of support for my scholarly forays, more so than she is ever likely to understand or accept.

The academic climate for the study of the far recesses of medieval political thought remains a chilly one, in North America at least. Thus, I register my thanks, by way of dedication, to two scholars who not only kept the flame burning but who found myriad ways over the years to ignite the scholarly endeavors of others, the present author included. During his years at the Camden campus of Rutgers University, Jim Muldoon never had the opportunity to supervise his own graduate students, but he nevertheless inspired and stimulated many junior scholars with his superior scholarship, as well as his personal charm and keen wit. Paul Sigmund of Princeton University bore a large share of the responsibility for keeping the study of medieval political ideas alive in the American political science discipline for a generation, and he sought out and encouraged younger scholars in the field when they appeared. Some of my most cherished memories involve conversations — often over a meal or a cup of libation — with Jim or Paul. To both of these generous scholars and human beings, I owe a huge personal as well as professional debt, which the dedication of the present volume does not so much repay as simply acknowledge.

Tucson, Arizona
January 2000

A Note on Texts and Translations

There is a single manuscript, a sumptuously illustrated presentation copy, of Walter of Milemete's treatise, which is now located at Christ Church, Oxford. M. R. James produced a facsimile edition of *On the Nobility, Wisdom, and Prudence of the King* (Oxford, 1913), which includes a thorough description of the manuscript. A critical transcription of the text was undertaken by S. J. Bird in an unpublished University of North Carolina Master's thesis in History entitled *A Speculum Principis for Edward III* (Chapel Hill, 1975). No translation of the text into English (or any other language) has ever been published, to my knowledge.

The two recensions of the *Mirror of King Edward III* (designated A and B) were edited by Joseph Moisant (Paris, 1891), although misattributed to Archbishop Simon Islip. Moisant's critical edition is based on a single manuscript of each version, corrected and collated on the basis of the four other extant manuscripts of each work: A is derived from Oxford Bodleian Digby 172, fols. 134v–141r, B from Oxford Bodleian 624. Moisant's introduction provides a careful account of the manuscript evidence. A short excerpt of Version A was translated into English by Cary J. Nederman in *Medieval Political Theory — A Reader*, ed. C. J. Nederman and Kate Langdon Forhan (London, 1993; repr. as *Readings in Medieval Political Theory 1100–1400* [Indianapolis, 2000]), 201–206.

Ockham's *Whether the Ruler*... was edited by H. S. Offler in volume 1 of his *Guillelmi de Ockham, Opera Politica* (Manchester, 1940; 2nd ed., 1974). Two manuscripts are extant: a full text in Vatican Library, Codex Vaticanus Latinus 4115, and a partial version in Balliol College, Oxford, MS. 165B. Offler's introduction describes the manuscript tradition of the work. A small selection from it was translated into English by Nederman in *Medieval Political Theory — A Reader*, ed. Nederman and Forhan, 208–220.

General Introduction:
Varieties of English Political Thought,
c.1250–c.1350

THE MEDIEVAL POLITICAL TRADITION: SOURCES AND GENRES

All of the treatises that are translated in the following volume were written by English authors and were in some measure informed by current events in England. It is reasonable, therefore, to inquire whether they may be fitted into some larger picture of the development of a uniquely English understanding of political life. However, the interpretation of political thought during the Middle Ages organized around local or "national" political identities is largely out of vogue at present. The tendency of recent textbooks and scholarly monographs is instead to treat medieval writings from a broader, trans-European perspective suggested by the cosmopolitanism of most Christian schoolmen as well as the universalism of the Christian faith. Yet the neglect of territorial or regional variations in medieval political thought is not entirely warranted. In England, for example, a clear sense of an insular identity informing a self-conscious political tradition has long been observed. In the closing chapter of the *Second Treatise of Government*, John Locke directs the attention of his "Reader to *Bracton*, *Fortescue*, and the Author of the Mirrour, and others; writers, who cannot be suspected to be ignorant of our Government, or Enemies."[1] For Locke's own particular purpose — validation of the claim that amongst the English it has always

---

[1] John Locke, *Two Treatises of Government*, ed. Peter Laslett (Cambridge: Cambridge University Press, 1988), 475.

been held that subjects may rightfully remove their prince — these medieval figures may not provide the most solid underpinning.[2] But Locke's recommendation of such authorities in the *Second Treatise*, and in other of his writings,[3] demonstrates that already in the seventeenth century Englishmen recognized and valued a tradition of political thought peculiar to their nation that dated to the Middle Ages. Indeed, Locke's implicit view regarding the distinct and exceptional character of English political life has been reaffirmed by more recent social scientists and historians.[4]

The appropriate question for the scholar of medieval political thought to pose, then, is: What ideas or doctrines were so widely asserted in the texts of English provenance from the later Middle Ages that we may speak of a coherent and unified tradition of thought? In turn, it also becomes necessary to ask: How did the core concepts of this tradition relate to the special qualities of medieval England's political, legal, and social practices and institutions? Replies to these questions are hampered by the wide variety of genres through which political expression and debate occurred in English culture. On initial inspection, there might seem to be little common ground among the law books and the chronicles, the philosophical tomes and the administrative manuals, that form the legacy of English political thinking during the thirteenth and fourteenth centuries. Yet careful examination discloses, I believe, that the historically distinctive condition of political life in medieval England in fact yielded a ground shared by the full array of English political texts and authors to the extent that we may begin to identify the salient features of a definite intellectual tradition.

Given that medieval writers were especially aware of the need to cloak their work in the mantle of textual authority, it is always important to take note of the source materials at their disposal. English authors, just like their continental counterparts, cited holy scripture and patristic writings, the texts of canon law (and, to a lesser extent, civil law), the pagan classical phi-

---

[2] The wide range of uses to which medieval sources were put in English political argument during the seventeenth century has been examined by Cary J. Nederman, "Bracton on Kingship First Visited: The Idea of Sovereignty and Bractonian Political Thought in Seventeenth-Century England," *Political Science* 40 (1988): 49–66.

[3] The same or a similar list appears in at least three other of Locke's writings: *Thoughts on Reading and Study*, *Thoughts Concerning Education*, and a private letter to the Rev. Richard King; see his *Collected Works*, 10th ed. (London: T. Longman, 1801), 3: 272; 9: 177; and 11: 306.

[4] See Kenneth Dyson, *The State Tradition in Western Europe* (Oxford: Martin Robertson, 1980), 36–44, 51–53, and 71; and Philip Corrigan and Derek Sayer, *The Great Arch: English State Formation as Cultural Revolution* (Oxford: Basil Blackwell, 1985).

losophers and historians, and the most revered figures among more recent Christian thinkers (such as Bernard of Clairvaux and Thomas Aquinas). In addition, however, political writers in medieval England showed a special sensitivity to the elements of the so-called English constitution, namely, common law and the statutory proclamations and legislative documents associated with royal government. This was not limited solely to treatises with an overtly legal and administrative content. Even English authors whose sources were primarily scholastic in character made reference to the laws and charters as well as the judicial processes that bound both Englishmen and their kings. Thus, these political commentators may have spoken in the universal discourses shared with other literate men in medieval Christendom, but they did so with a distinctly English accent.

As a consequence, English authors evolved or perfected forms of political expression that had few counterparts elsewhere in Europe. For instance, following the banishment of Roman civil law from England during the time of King Stephen, repeated attempts were made to codify the legal structures and institutions of the common law by means of collections recording customary practices and royal decrees. Perhaps the most famous such work is *De legibus et consuetudinibus Angliae*, long supposed to have been composed during the mid-thirteenth century and attributed to the hand of Henry de Bracton, a Chief Justice during the reign of King Henry III. It now seems certain that this lengthy tome was in fact produced by a series of authors and compilers over a period of several decades, possibly beginning as early as about 1220; Bracton was primarily the beneficiary of his predecessors' knowledge, rather than a substantial contributor to the authorship of the work.[5] Embedded in the copious compendium of common law materials are important discussions of the king's relationship to law, the nature of royal power, and the relationship between the crown and the constituent parts of the kingdom.[6] The success of *De legibus et consuetudinibus Angliae* inspired the preparation of similar legal texts, such as *Fleta* and *Britton*, that could be used to instruct public officials and attorneys in the statutes and procedures of English justice, as well as to explain the foundations of com-

---

[5] This discovery is explained and defended by the modern editor of the text, Samuel E. Thorne, in his introduction to the third volume of *De legibus et consuetudinibus Angliae* (Cambridge, MA: Harvard University Press, 1968-1977), 3: xiii-lii.

[6] Cary J. Nederman, "Bracton on Kingship Revisited," *History of Political Thought* 5 (1984): 61-77, and idem, "The Royal Will and the Baronial Bridle: The *Addicio de cartis* in Bractonian Political Thought," *History of Political Thought* 9 (1988): 415-429.

mon law in light of the unique constitution of the realm.[7] Such treatises, one must realize, never aimed simply to reproduce the legal system that they surveyed. Instead, each sought to rationalize and to improve the delivery of the king's justice, and hence each constructs an idealized image of the judicial process.

At times, such idealization could be carried well beyond the confines of conventional legal and political practice. Two medieval political works that have proven most resistant to classification — the *Speculum Justiciariorum* and the *Modus Tenendi Parliamentum* — appear to build upon the widespread English tendency to intermingle documented statutes and procedures with wholly imaginary customs and traditions. The anonymous *Speculum Justiciariorum* (the work to which Locke refers as "the Mirrour"), composed early in the fourteenth century, purports to be a law book in the manner of the Bractonian text. In fact, the tract incorporates entirely novel legal and political dictates (such as the susceptibility of the king and his family to judgment by Parliament) in the guise of longstanding conventions extending back to the earliest times of English government.[8] Likewise, the *Modus Tenendi Parliamentum*, also an anonymous work of early fourteenth-century provenance, claims to be simply an account of the procedures for summoning, holding, and dismissing a parliamentary assembly. Whatever its origins (which have been hotly contested), the tract does not document any particular English parliament of the late Middle Ages, rather depicting an idealized vision of how a representative gathering ought to be constituted and to operate.[9] While historians have often dismissed the *Speculum Justiciariorum* and the *Modus Tenendi Parliamentum* as "historical curiosities," they follow very naturally from the general tenor of medieval English political and legal theorizing, which integrates established practice with normative aspirations.

---

[7] Noel Denholm-Young, "Who Wrote *Fleta*?," *English Historical Review* 58 (1943): 1–12; E. H. Kantorowicz, "The Prologue to *Fleta* and the School of Petrus de Vinea," *Speculum* 32 (1957): 231–249, repr. in idem, *Selected Studies* (Locust Valley, NY: J. J. Augustin, 1965), 167–183. The texts are: H. G. Richardson and G. O. Sayles, ed., *Fleta*, 2 vols. (London: Quaritch for the Selden Society, 1955); F. M. Nichols, ed., *Britton*, 2 vols. (Oxford: Oxford University Press, 1865).

[8] H. G. Rueschlein, "Who Wrote *The Mirror of Justices*?," *Law Quarterly Review* 42 (1958): 265–279; Cary J. Nederman, "The Mirror Crack'd: The *Speculum Principum* as Social and Political Criticism," *The European Legacy: Toward New Paradigms* 3 (1998): 18–38. The text is: W. J. Wittaker, ed., *Speculum Justiciariorum* (London: Quaritch for the Selden Society, 1895).

[9] Nicholas Pronay and John Taylor, *Parliamentary Texts of the Late Middle Ages* (Oxford: Clarendon Press, 1980), 13–63.

Implicitly contained in idealized representations of English institutions and conventions may be found veiled criticism of the shortcomings of the status quo, and particularly of the failings of the monarchy to live up to its lofty purposes.[10] On occasion, this subdued critique broke out into overt hostility toward the actions or personalities of the king and members of his curia. Medieval England had a proud tradition of popular and semi-popular political protest literature, often composed in verse form.[11] Even among the best-educated segments of the population, grievances about and resistance to royal misconduct — often couched in terms derived from the mainstream of the English political tradition — were given public expression. One of the most famous cases of a protest tract fully conversant with the intellectual terrain traversed by English legal and political authors was the *Carmen de Bello Lewensi*, an anonymous song written sometime during the early 1260s in defense of Simon de Montfort's rebellion against Henry III. The work clearly repeats ideas found in the Bractonian *De legibus et consuetudinibus Angliae* or some other legal text derived therefrom, but it turns those doctrines into the basis for justification of de Montfort's revolt against the crown.[12] It is the rebels, says the author of the *Carmen de Bello Lewensi*, who are the upholders of the dignity of the English crown, in contrast with the king and his counselors, who debase the honor of the royal office with their evil deeds. The author himself thus claims that the followers of de Montfort are the true patriots and lovers of the realm and its monarchy, which have been undermined by an unworthy occupant of the throne. Henry III is advised by the poem to rule in cooperation and peace with his barons — a counsel that enjoyed a long history in English political thought both before and after the de Montfort uprising. Similar criticism of another weak king, Edward II, is advanced in the *Vita Edwardi Secundi*, an anonymous chronicle containing a considerable amount of political reflection that was completed in 1326 or soon thereafter.[13] Clearly, the learned elite of later medieval England was not shy about making public its dissatisfaction with the kingdom's rulers.

For the most part, English political writing during the late Middle Ages

---

[10] A similar point is made about fifteenth-century English "mirror-for-princes" works by Judith Ferster, *Fictions of Advice: The Literature and Politics of Counsel in Late Medieval England* (Philadelphia: University of Pennsylvania Press, 1996).

[11] The standard collection of these works is Thomas Wright, ed., *The Political Songs of England* (London: Camden Society, 1839).

[12] C. L. Kingsford, ed., *Carmen de Bello Lewensi* (Oxford: Clarendon Press, 1890).

[13] Noel Denholm-Young, ed., *Vita Edwardi Secundi* (Edinburgh: Thomas Nelson and Sons, 1957).

emanated from legal and clerical origins rather than from the schools. This, too, sets England apart from the continent, where a large body of scholastic political thought emerged from the University of Paris and the other centers of formal instruction. Famed schoolmen associated with Oxford, such as Roger Bacon in the thirteenth century and Duns Scotus in the early fourteenth century, had little to say about political topics, even in the oblique form of glosses on works of ancient political philosophy. William of Ockham, as we shall see in a subsequent chapter, became embroiled in political controversy only after he left England. Among English scholastics of our period, Walter Burley, another Oxford Master, seems to have been alone in producing a commentary on Aristotle's *Politics*, which was completed around 1340. Although such commentaries tended to be quite literal restatements and expositions of the original, with little direct contemporary relevance, Burley's treatise deserves a definite place in the political tradition we are discussing as a result of its repeated references to conditions in England.[14] Burley, who apparently enjoyed the patronage of Edward III's court, whittled down many of the examples given by Aristotle derived from Greek constitutional systems. Instead, he praised the form of kingship that he observed in his native land, but also incorporated into the work a discussion of parliament's role in governing the realm. With at least forty extant manuscripts, Burley's commentary may be counted one of the more popular explanations of Aristotle's political ideas, perhaps in some measure because it drew direct connections to a political landscape more familiar to its audience.

THE IDENTITY OF THE MEDIEVAL ENGLISH TRADITION

The sheer range in the genre and style of the political writings that may be found in later medieval England is truly daunting. So is it even possible to speak of something like a coherent "tradition" of political thought there? An affirmative reply depends, first, upon the delineation of the historical issues that were of primary concern to England's politically-minded writers during the thirteenth and fourteenth centuries. Scholars who have previously addressed this problem concentrate heavily upon the conflicts between king and barons that rocked England repeatedly from the reign of King

---

[14] Cary J. Nederman, "Kings, Peers, and Parliament: Virtue and Co-rulership in Walter Burley's *Commentarius in VIII Libros Politicorum Aristotelis*," *Albion* 24 (1992): 391–407.

John to that of Richard II.¹⁵ It is supposed that these conflicts generated two competing and incommensurable conceptions of royal government: one of which treats the king as "absolute," the other of which posits royal power as "limited."¹⁶ The most complete and detailed articulation of this interpretation of the medieval English political tradition has been offered by Donald W. Hanson in a much-neglected work, *From Kingdom to Commonwealth*. Hanson argues that "the particular collisions of king and barons" may be held primarily responsible for shaping the unique "development and meaning" of English political thought from the thirteenth century onward.¹⁷ Specifically, royal and baronial doctrines respectively appear in the English tradition by way of the "persistent conception of the nature of political authority ... that legitimate authority was vested in both the king and the great magnates independently."¹⁸ In other words, the key idea of English thought was "divided sovereignty," according to which the constituent elements of governmental power were composed of autonomous and self-subsistent forms of lordship. The king, as one such independent authority, asserted an unencumbered *maiestas* over all the subjects in his realm. The magnates, as a second type of power, claimed their own primacy over the discretionary prerogatives of the crown. And because this dynamic opposition between royalist and baronial conceptions of government was never reconciled historically, Hanson says, medieval thinkers addressing the English framework were trapped within "a characteristic clash and oscillation between alternative principles of political organization," namely, between "absolute" and "limited" forms of rule.¹⁹

Hanson's interpretation of the central thematic of political thought in medieval England — relying upon the presumption of a constant opposition between "Crown" and "Baronage" — stands in need of some revision and qualification. It is true that no English king from the time of William the Conqueror until the War of the Roses reigned immune from the threat of baronial rebellion and open civil war. Yet historians now widely recognize

---

[15] R. F. Treharne, "The Constitutional Problem in Thirteenth-Century England," in *Essays in Medieval History Presented to Bertie Wilkinson*, ed. T. A. Sandquist and M. R. Powicke (Toronto: University of Toronto Press, 1969), 46–78.

[16] Robert Eccleshall, *Order and Reason in Politics: Absolute and Limited Monarchy in Early Modern England* (Oxford: Oxford University Press for Hull University Press, 1978).

[17] Donald W. Hanson, *From Kingdom to Commonwealth: The Development of Civic Consciousness in English Political Thought* (Cambridge, MA: Harvard University Press, 1970), 135.

[18] Hanson, *From Kingdom to Commonwealth*, 24.

[19] Hanson, *From Kingdom to Commonwealth*, 172.

that such political discontent and conflict reflected the English nobility's belief that it was the king's natural and proper partner in government, and thus had a profound political stake in the rule of the realm. Indeed, the English monarchy depended so heavily on the magnates and other lords of the kingdom as the executors of the royal will that its rule is perhaps best characterized in the phrase suggested many years ago by A. H. White: "Self-government at the king's command."[20] Consequently, the English nobility acquired a collective self-image as fully a part of the king's government, and it naturally objected to exclusion from involvement in the political affairs of the crown. No less an authority than Marc Bloch remarked upon "that collaboration of the well-to-do classes in power, so characteristic of the English polity as long ago as the middle ages."[21] More recently, Michael Prestwich has observed, "It makes much more sense to see the normal pattern of political life as one of cooperation and collaboration between" the "Crown" and the "Baronage."[22] The ordinary administration of government, simply stated, was rooted in a regularized "partnership" between the king and the lords of the realm, manifesting a notably cooperative spirit among all parties.[23] When contention arose, it was primarily as the result of a temporary breakdown — whether occasioned by personalities or policies — in this overall structure of collaboration.

As English thought from the *Carmen de Bello Lewensi* to Fortescue emphasized, the highly attuned sense of unity derived from a system of governmental cooperation between the king and his seigneurial colleagues by no means diminished the power and dignity of the crown. In general, the Anglo-Norman and Plantagenet monarchy of England was viewed as the focal point for political authority within the realm. The royal monopoly on such "banal" powers as taxation, high justice, warfare, and castle-building,

---

[20] A. H. White, *Self-Government at the King's Command* (Minneapolis: University of Minnesota Press, 1933).

[21] Marc Bloch, *Feudal Society*, 2 vols., trans. L. A. Manyon (Chicago: University of Chicago Press, 1967), 2: 371.

[22] Michael Prestwich, *The Three Edwards: War and State in England, 1272-1377* (London: Weidenfeld and Nicolson, 1980), 146.

[23] Bertie Wilkinson, "The 'Political Revolution' of the Thirteenth and Fourteenth Centuries in England," *Speculum* 24 (1949): 502-503; Helen Maud Cam, *Liberties and Communities in Medieval England* (London: Merlin Press, 1963), 240; David C. Douglas, *The Norman Achievement, 1050-1100* (Berkeley: University of California Press, 1969), 86, 113-114; Maurice H. Keen, *England in the Later Middle Ages* (London: Methuen, 1973), 12-13; W. M. Ormrod, *The Reign of King Edward III: Crown and Political Society in England 1327-1377* (New Haven: Yale University Press, 1990), 200-202; and G. L. Harriss, "The Formation of Parliament, 1272-1377," in *The English Parliament in the Middle Ages*, ed. R. G. Davies and J. H. Denton (Manchester: Manchester University Press, 1981), 29-60.

not to mention direct control over the feudal institutions of land tenure, knight service, and vassalage, all betokened a crown the authority of which was far more extensive and advanced than elsewhere in Western Europe. Yet underlying the growth of centralized royal government in England was the monarchy's dependence upon the good will and aid of the feudal aristocracy. By the opening decades of the thirteenth century, royal bureaucratic and judicial institutions had become collaborative ventures with the nobility, in the sense that most offices at all levels were occupied not by a coterie of paid professional administrators (as was typically the case on the continent), but by the lords of the realm. From the greatest earl to the most humble knight of the shire, seigneurs provided the effective agency for the *potestas* wielded by royal grant and in the king's name. Moreover, the feudal class enjoyed a forum for the expression of its interests and grievances, first by means of the Curia Regis, then later through Parliament. Thus, the English aristocracy acquired a permanent stake in the centralized governance of the island; nobles participated actively in the formulation as well as implementation of royal policy.

In turn, the uniquely English devolution of the crown's public authority into seigneurial hands can be seen to shape the development of political discourse in the late Middle Ages. In particular, political authors tended to highlight what might be termed "reciprocity," that is, the maintenance of cohesion between the ruler and his cohorts in a fashion that allowed both for royal dignity and for seigneurial loyalty to the central government. Since the emergence of England's cooperative institutions resulted not from a conscious plan, but from largely unrecognized factors, political theorists devoted considerable attention to the foundations upon which the nation's governance was conducted. How did lords acquire their duties and responsibilities within the realm? To what extent and in what manner were members of the nobility to be guided and controlled in discharging their public (as opposed to domestic) obligations? What guarantees existed that the legitimate power of the king would not be diminished or dissipated by the delegation and distribution of authority? What assured that the crown remained in overall charge of governing the realm? Such dilemmas about the nature of self-government at the king's command stimulated the diverse modes of political writing that appeared in England during the later thirteenth and early fourteenth centuries. The special cooperative quality of medieval English politics shaped a distinctive tradition of thought devoted to articulating a "balanced" conception of government, according to which, on the one hand, the assignment of royal powers to nobles would not disintegrate into their independent and uncoordinated exercise and, on the other, the king would not attempt to retain such powers for himself or to abuse the authority of the crown. This weighing informed the salient English theme of the reciprocal and mutual sharing of power among the king and his subjects.

CROWN AND CO-RULERSHIP

English political writings during the thirteenth and fourteenth centuries shared a common assumption regarding the concentration of authority in the crown. Authors were insistent upon the king's retention of a monopoly of control over the use of power in his realm. Even work critical of the conduct of the English monarchy, such as the *Speculum Justiciariorum*, argues that it is a serious crime (specifically, perjury, a form of *lèse majesté*) to "deprive the king of his franchises or other manner of rights appended to the crown, by occupations, appropriations, or in another manner." To this assertion is appended a long list of all the prerogatives (political and legal) that accrue uniquely and exclusively to the crown.[24] No one may possess these rights without royal permission; however, the king may freely grant them to his subjects as liberties within a limited sphere and conditionally. The ceding of a jurisdiction by the king does not entail the elimination of his supervision of its use. As the Bractonian text states, one who holds "liberties by concession of the lord king" cannot in turn remit to another any such rights "any more than he can make a justice under him when he himself is a justice of the lord king in that place, unless the king himself confirms the act and concession of the enfeoffing lord."[25] Franchises granted from the royal reserve of power remain under the control of the king and cannot have their terms or possession altered without his permission.

Consequently, English thinkers insist that the king must exceed in power all others in his realm, having neither superior nor peer. The Bractonian text is clear on the principle of royal supremacy: Kings "have neither peers nor superiors. Under them, there are those who have ordinary [jurisdiction] in many matters, but not as completely (*meram*) as ... the king."[26] The author of the *Modus Tenendi Parliamentum* likewise argues that, among the segments of parliament, "the king is the head, beginning, and end of Parliament, and he has no peer in his grade, and he by virtue of kingship alone is

---

[24] *Speculum Justiciariorum*, 16–17. Similar enumerations of the king's licit powers may be found in *Vita Edwardi Secundi*, 116, and *Fleta*, 2: 36.

[25] *De legibus et consuetudinibus Angliae*, 2: 117.

[26] *De legibus et consuetudinibus Angliae*, 4: 281.

the primary grade."[27] Walter Burley asserts that every subject should "love" his royal master and submit to him, since each occupies, and must be content with, an inferior "grade under the king."[28] The logic of this view is clear-cut: If jurisdiction resides primarily and originally with the crown, then the royal ruler is set apart by virtue of his unique status. Any lord who would challenge this principle would undermine the foundation for his own possession of rights and powers within the kingdom. Thus, even the most vehement of pro-baronial writings, the *Carmen de Bello Lewensi*, claims that it "devises nothing against, nor seeks anything contrary to, the honor of the king; instead, it is zealous to reform and magnify the royal station (*status*)."[29] In precisely this sense, the authority of the English monarchy is coextensive with and inseparable from the powers enjoyed by the nobility (and increasingly, the other politically relevant members of the body politic).

Therefore, alongside their postulation of the monopoly of authority pertaining to the crown, English authors commonly incorporated a conception of what Burley termed "co-rulership," according to which subjects of the crown possess a duty to assist the king actively in ruling the realm. "Co-rulership" presumes that at least certain groups of subjects have been delegated some of the functions of royal administration in order to promote the common good more efficiently. The Bractonian text distinguishes two forms of such co-rulership. The first, "delegated jurisdiction," includes those prerogatives that the crown assigns directly to a magistrate for a particular period of time and for which the official is immediately an agent of the crown. This includes all officials of the royal curia as well as circuit judges, sheriffs, bailiffs, and other royal servants outside the court, every one of whom holds office strictly at the king's pleasure.[30] It would be impossible, the author says, for royal government to be made effective without such offices: "It is expedient that magistrates of the republic are constituted, because, by those who are called prominent in right, matters acquire effect. For little justice exists in the community (*civitate*) unless there is someone who can enforce right."[31] The second form of co-rulership stems from the titles and prerogatives of the nobility, whose jurisdiction, while by no means autonomous, is less directly under royal supervision. The Bractonian

---

[27] *Modus Tenendi Parliamentum*, sec. 26, 78.
[28] MS. Balliol 95, fol. 184r.
[29] *Carmen de Bello Lewensi*, ll. 535–538.
[30] *De legibus et consuetudinibus Angliae*, 2: 167.
[31] *De legibus et consuetudinibus Angliae*, 2: 26.

text explains, "Kings associate these [ranks] with themselves for ruling God's people, ordaining them with great honor and power and name when equipping them with swords ... The sword signifies defense of the realm and the country."[32] Earls, barons, vavasors and the like are the king's companions and associates, and though they are subject to his judgment, they are not as fully constrained in their exercise of co-rulership as possessors of delegated jurisdiction. Indeed, in certain cases — specifically, where *lèse majesté* is charged — the great men of the realm may be called upon to replace the king on the seat of justice, since no one can be both plaintiff and judge in the same case.[33] The *De legibus et consuetudinibus Angliae* thus posits royal servants and associates as essential participants in a process of self-government mediated and coordinated through the crown. This cooperative principle transcends mere feudal *consilium et auxilium*; it suggests that much of the regular operation of royal rule is transferred by delegation and commission from the king to his co-rulers. Yet one ought to understand this as consonant with the maintenance of a strong and unified system of kingship, not as a challenge to the authority of the crown.

By around 1300, the locus for the cooperative arrangements between crown and subjects came to be recognized as Parliament. Well into the fourteenth century, the word "Parliament" conveyed ambiguous meaning, applying in both administrative documents and political writings to councils of the great lay and spiritual nobles as well as to larger assemblies additionally containing representatives of the lesser ecclesiastical and secular estates.[34] The Bractonian text does not speak of Parliament at all, nor does the *Carmen de Bello Lewensi*. A generation later, the author of the *Speculum Justiciariorum* refers to Parliament as a meeting of the king with the great lords. The monarch ought "to assemble his earls ... at London in order to hold Parliament about the guidance of God's people, how men should protect themselves from sin, should live quietly, and should receive right by regular practices and sacred judgments."[35] Moreover, the treatise claims that legal charges against or involving the king and the royal family should be tried in Parliament by his "companions."[36] Such "companions" become, in the Aristotle-tinged phraseology of Walter Burley, his "co-rulers"

---

[32] *De legibus et consuetudinibus Angliae*, 2: 32–33.

[33] *De legibus et consuetudinibus Angliae*, 2: 337.

[34] J. C. Holt, "The Prehistory of Parliament," in *The English Parliament in the Middle Ages*, ed. Davies and Denton, 1–28.

[35] *Speculum Justiciariorum*, 8.

[36] *Speculum Justiciariorum*, 7.

(*comprincipantes* or *comregnantes*), whom kings "create for themselves" and each of whom "perceives himself that he co-rules in the king and with the king."[37] The mechanism for this co-ruling function, according to Burley, is Parliament: "In a kingdom, a multitude, constituted by the king and the nobles and the wise of the kingdom, in a certain measure rules. Consequently, such a multitude rules as much or more than the king alone, on account of which the king convokes Parliament for considering arduous business."[38] Here the composition of Parliament is left somewhat ambiguous; it may or may not contain representatives of the non-noble classes, depending upon one's reading of "the wise of the kingdom." But the justification of a parliamentary assembly is unambiguous, following directly from need for the realm to be ruled in a cooperative manner. Any ambiguity is entirely erased, however, in the *Modus Tenendi Parliamentum*, which stipulates that not only the magnates of the church and the temporal sphere, but also the lesser seigneurs and delegates from the towns and dioceses of the kingdom, are necessary to compose a properly constituted Parliament.[39] Indeed, at least when Parliament is considering issues of taxation, "two knights, who came to Parliament for their county, have a greater voice in conceding and contradicting than the great English counts." The absence of representation from the "community of the realm," namely, the knights, citizens, burghers, and clerics, is sufficient reason to conclude that no Parliament has occurred; but the same cannot be said for the absence of lay and spiritual magnates, so long as they have been properly summoned.[40] The author of the work thus introduces a check to ensure that taxation will not occur without full and proper representation of the entire kingdom — a recognition, perhaps, that the stake in the governance of England was felt very widely indeed by the fourteenth century. However one interprets this inclusion, it is evident that Parliament had come to be seen as a sort of national body for mutual coordination and cooperation on the part of the politically influential classes in conjunction with the crown. And over the course of time, some authors at least were prepared to cast the net widely to identify who deserved to participate in the process of reciprocal collaboration between king and community.

One finds, then, in the plethora of political writings generated in England during the thirteenth and fourteenth centuries several themes that

---

[37] MS. Balliol 95, fols. 184r, 186r.
[38] MS. Balliol 95, fol. 182r.
[39] *Modus Tenendi Parliamentum*, 68–70.
[40] *Modus Tenedi Parliamentum*, 89–90.

indicate the presence of a coherent tradition of thought. Lawyers and schoolmen, administrators and controversialists — all were seeking to define and institutionalize the basic principles supporting self-government at the king's command. Of course, they found different frameworks and political languages useful in expressing their views. Yet the questions that stimulated them and to which they sought responses — queries arising from the historically distinct patterns of political development characteristic of medieval England — remained essentially the same in all cases. It shall become evident how these questions also shaped the thought of the three authors whose works are included in the present volume.

Introduction to
On the Nobility, Wisdom, and Prudence of Kings
by Walter of Milemete

THE MIRROR GENRE

Among the numerous literary genres pioneered during the Latin Middle Ages, perhaps none was as typical or as pervasive as the so-called "mirror" or *speculum*. The medieval "mirror" was, most essentially, a book of advice addressed to an individual or (more commonly) a group, detailing a code of conduct or set of values appropriate to its addressee's social position or standing.[1] *Specula* contained many different forms of instruction, and almost no category of persons escaped the notice of some "mirror" writer: virgins, wives and widows, priests and laymen, courtiers, lawyers and merchants — all were among the audiences for whom various advice-books were designed. In some cases these *specula* were highly moralistic in tone, while in other instances their subject matter followed a more practical route. Nor did *speculum* literature die out with the waning of the Middle Ages. Works employing some variant of the "mirror" theme and title persisted well into early modern times.[2]

---

[1] An overview of the genre is provided by Einar Már Jónsson, *Le miroir: Naissance d'un genre littéraire* (Paris: Les Belles Lettres, 1995).

[2] For a comprehensive account of the genre, see Herbert Grabes, *The Mutable Glass: Mirror-Imagery in Titles and Texts of the Middle Ages and English Renaissance*, trans. G. Collier (Cambridge: Cambridge University Press, 1982). This is a substantially revised version of the author's *Speculum, Mirror und Looking-Glass: Kontinuität und Originalität der Spiegelmeta-*

Walter of Milemete's *On the Nobility, Wisdom, and Prudence of Kings* is one among many such treatises of counsel, falling into a popular subset of advice writing commonly called the *speculum principum* (otherwise known as the *Fürstenspiegel* or "Mirror-for-Princes"). The *speculum principum* seems to have made its initial appearance during the Carolingian epoch, and became a fixture of political discourse after the middle of the twelfth century.[3] The scholarly fortune of the princely mirror has waxed and waned during the twentieth century. A flurry of important studies appeared (primarily in German and English) during the years between the World Wars.[4] This research had the central aim of charting the main contours of the political "mirror" tradition and cataloguing the texts properly belonging to it. Thereafter, a period of pronounced lack of intellectual interest occurred, as historians of medieval thought became "discouraged ... by works thought to be stereotyped and conventional, with no visible relation to concrete political life."[5] Most recently, however, scholars have directed renewed attention to the genre, although this time in an attempt to understand how the *speculum principum* reflected *mentalités* of medieval life and why it retained such vast appeal throughout the Middle Ages and into the Renaissance.[6] One of the most promising consequences of these latest examinations of such "mirror" writings is the recognition that they contain a rich and com-

---

pher in den Buchtiteln des Mittelalters und der englischen Literatur des 13. bis 17. Jahrhunderts (Tübingen: Max Niemeyer, 1973).

[3] In the classic study of the subject, Wilhelm Berges argues against a direct connection between Carolingian and later medieval *specula*, taking the view that the genre was reinvented after c. 1150 (*Die Fürstenspiegel des hohen und späten Mittelalters* [Stuttgart: Hiersemann, 1938], 3–8). This view has been convincingly challenged, however, by Dora M. Bell, *L'Idéal Éthique de la Royauté en France au Moyen Age* (Geneva: Droz, 1962), 8–13; Sverre Bagge, *The Political Thought of the King's Mirror* (Odense: Odense University Press, 1987), 19 ff.; and Harry R. Dosher, "The Concept of the Ideal Prince in French Political Thought, 800–1760" (Ph.D. diss., University of North Carolina, 1969), 43–138.

[4] In addition to the work of Berges, *Fürstenspiegel*, see Lester K. Born, "The Perfect Prince: A Study in Thirteenth- and Fourteenth-Century Ideals," *Speculum* 3 (1928): 470–504; J. Röder, *Das Fürstenbild in den mittelalterlichen Furstenspiegeln auf französischen Boden* (Emsdetten: Lechte, 1933); Wilhelm Kleineke, *Englische Fürstenspiegel vom Policraticus Johanns von Salisbury bis zum Basilikon Doron König Jakobs I* (Halle: Max Niemeyer, 1937); Allan H. Gilbert, *Machiavelli's Prince and Its Forerunners: The Prince as a Typical Book de Regimine Principum* (Durham: Duke University Press, 1938).

[5] Bernard Guenée, *States and Rulers in Late Medieval Europe*, trans. J. Vale (Oxford: Basil Blackwell, 1985), 70.

[6] For example, Guenée, *States and Rulers*, 69–74, 86–88; Jacques Krynnen, *Idéal du prince et pouvoir royal en France à la fin du Moyen Age* (Paris: Picard, 1981); Diane Bornstein, "Reflections of Political Theory and Political Fact in Fifteenth-Century Mirrors for the Prince," in *Medieval Studies for Lillian Herlands Hornstein*, ed. J. B. Bessinger and R. R. Rayno (New York: New York University Press, 1976), 77–85.

plex discourse about political affairs, the significance of which was far more apparent to medieval and Renaissance readers than to modern ones. Rather than dwelling on the sameness and abstractness of the tracts, current scholarship stresses their diversity, recognizing that *specula* were not universally written in the Latin language, nor were they exclusively prose works, nor did they always address the same audience or offer identical advice about the ruler and his office.[7]

It seems likely that one factor contributing to the longevity of the genre was its adaptability as a tool to criticize the faults of particular rulers. Judith Ferster has recently detected telling ambiguities in even the most rigidly conventional *specula* — ambiguities that suggest a submerged level of criticism even while such works embrace and affirm the traditional language of the medieval "mirror." She argues that "the manuals' dullness is a disguise necessitated by the danger of writing frankly about contemporary political issues, but not a total avoidance of them. The mirrors for princes are not only more topical than they appear to be but also more critical of the powerful than we might expect."[8] Although she concentrates on late fourteenth-and fifteenth-century England, Ferster believes that such camouflaged criticism was an enduring feature of the *speculum principum*, explaining its wide audience up through the 1500s. Indeed, she claims that Machiavelli's *Il Principe* was highly conventional in this regard — not a subversion of the "mirror" genre, as some have suggested, but a continuation of a long-standing tension within the tradition itself.[9]

The textual and intellectual sources of medieval *specula* were diverse and eclectic. An early example of the genre, such as John of Salisbury's mid-twelfth century *Policraticus*, cobbles together scriptural and patristic source materials with pagan Roman sources such as Cicero, Vegetius, Frontinus, and other Latin historians, poets, and playwrights, throwing into the mix what he knew of Greek philosophy and literature as well.[10] Once Aristotle's *Nicomachean Ethics* and *Politics* began to circulate in Latin translation in the

---

[7] Kate Langdon Forhan, "Introduction" to Christine de Pizan, *The Book of the Body Politic* (Cambridge: Cambridge University Press, 1994), xvii–xx; Jean-Philippe Genet, "General Introduction" to *Four English Political Tracts of the Later Middle Ages* (London: Royal Historical Society, 1977), ix–xviii.

[8] Ferster, *Fictions of Advice*, 3.

[9] Contrast Mark Hulliung, *Citizen Machiavelli* (Princeton: Princeton University Press, 1983), 24 with Ferster, *Fictions of Advice*, 16–73.

[10] Janet Martin, "John of Salisbury as Classical Scholar," in *The World of John of Salisbury*, ed. Michael Wilks (Oxford: Basil Blackwell, 1984), 179–201; Cary J. Nederman and J. Brückmann, "Aristotelianism in John of Salisbury's *Policraticus*," *Journal of the History of Philosophy* 21 (1983): 203–229.

middle of the thirteenth century, princely mirrors came to take on a systematically Aristotelian cast. The archetype of the Aristotelian *speculum principum* was Giles of Rome's *De regimine principum*, a huge tome (about 155,000 words) destined to become the single most popular mirror composed during the Middle Ages; approximately three hundred fifty manuscripts of it — three hundred in the original Latin, the rest in various vernacular translations — have been identified.[11] Perhaps the most influential source for the medieval *speculum principum* genre, however, was neither Christian nor classical pagan in origin. It was instead the Arabic *Kitâb sirr al-asrâr*, translated into Latin under the title *Secreta* (or *Secretum*) *secretorum* and circulated as an authentic work by Aristotle. The product of an anonymous ninth-century Arabic hand, the *Secreta secretorum* purports to be a letter of instruction from Aristotle to Alexander, advising the young king on an array of topics ranging from the virtues necessary for a ruler to the machinations of royal courtiers to the curriculum for an appropriate princely education. The tract was popularized by, among others, the Oxford Franciscan Roger Bacon, and became a mainstay of European political writing into the fifteenth century. In its two Latin translations, some four hundred manuscripts exist; there are countless partial or complete vernacular translations and adaptations.[12] Given such an extensive assortment of sources, it is hardly surprising that scholars share little agreement about the nature of the genre (or even whether it can be defined *as* a genre).[13]

---

[11] James M. Blythe, *Ideal Government and the Mixed Constitution in the Middle Ages* (Princeton: Princeton University Press, 1992), 59–63; Charles F. Briggs, *Giles of Rome's "De Regimine Principum"* (Cambridge: Cambridge University Press, 1999).

[12] The best overview of the original *Kitâb sirr al-asrâr* is Mahmoud Manzalaoui, "The Pseudo-Aristotelian *Kitâb sirr al-asrâr*: Facts and Problems," *Oriens* 23/24 (1974): 147–257. On the Western reception of the text, see M. A. Manzalaoui, ed., *Secretum Secretorum: Nine English Versions*, vol. 1 (Oxford: Oxford University Press for the Early English Text Society, 1977), ix–l; Steven J. Williams, "Roger Bacon and His Edition of the Pseudo-Aristotelian *Secretum secretorum*," *Speculum* 69 (1994): 57–73; idem, "Defining the *Corpus Aristotelicum*: Scholastic Awareness of Aristotelian Spuria in the High Middle Ages," *Journal of the Warburg and Courtauld Institutes* 58 (1995): 29–51; W. F. Ryan and Charles B. Schmitt, *Pseudo-Aristotle, Secret of Secrets: Sources and Influences* (London: Warburg Institute, 1982); and Charles B. Schmitt and D. Knox, *Pseudo-Aristoteles Latinus* (London: Warburg Institute, 1985), 54–75. On vernacular versions, in addition to Manzalaoui, see Oliver A. Beckerlegge, ed., *Le Secré de Secrez* (Oxford: Basil Blackwell for the Anglo-Norman Text Society, 1944), xi–lviii; Philip B. Jones, ed., *The "Secreto de los Secretos": A Castilian Version* (Potomac, MD: Scripta Humanistica, 1995), 1–58; Ferster, *Fictions of Advice*, 39–66.

[13] Compare Genet, *Four English Political Tracts*, xv–xvi with Nederman, "The Mirror Crack'd: The *Speculum Principum* as Political and Social Criticism," 19–20.

Walter of Milemete and His Mirror

The author of *On the Nobility, Wisdom, and Prudence of Kings* is almost entirely unknown to us. In the text, he refers to himself as a *clericus*; M. R. James, who produced a facsimile text of the manuscript, located a 1328 document identifying one "Master Walter de Milemete" as the "King's clerk" and assigning to him a prebend in Cornwall.[14] As no records of the institution in question are extant, we shall never discover whether Walter ever occupied the position. Beyond this, biographical knowledge of Walter must be a matter of speculation. We are certainly dealing with an individual of wide learning, as references in *On the Nobility, Wisdom, and Prudence of Kings* to canon and civil law, not to mention classical philosophy and history, attest. Advanced studies at Oxford (or even Paris) appear likely. Only a man of considerable means could have endowed the production of the sumptuous decoration of the manuscript (assuming, as seems plausible, that Walter himself was behind the illumination program). Absent further documentation, however, the best and most complete testimony we have to Walter's life must be his treatise itself.

On the Nobility, Wisdom, and Prudence of Kings provides us with considerable internal evidence about the circumstances of its composition. In its opening paragraph, Walter explains that it was written "in honor of the illustrious Lord Edward, King of England by the grace of God, beginning his rule in A.D. 1326." Although Edward III did not take the throne until January 1327, the dating is accurate, since the calendar then in use would have included the first three months of (our) 1327 in 1326. The text also indicates that *On the Nobility, Wisdom, and Prudence of Kings* was intended as a companion piece to a copy of the Pseudo-Aristotle *Secreta secretorum*, the production of which Walter had commissioned and which appears to have been completed and sent ahead prior to the composition of its complement.[15] Indeed, Walter seems to have meant *On the Nobility, Wisdom, and Prudence of Kings* to be a sort of commentary on the Pseudo-Aristotle, a view confirmed by the fact that the former work adapts many of its chapter titles from the latter, but does not simply parrot the language of the *Secreta secretorum*.

---

[14] M. R. James, ed., *The Treatise of Walter de Milemete: De nobilitatibus, sapientiis, et prudentiis regum* (Oxford: The Roxburghe Club, 1913), xi–xii. Some further biography details are provided by A. B. Emden, *A Biographical Register of the University of Cambridge to A.D. 1500* (Cambridge: Cambridge University Press, 1963), 406.

[15] It survives as London British Library MS add. 47680. See Lucy Freeman Sandler, *Gothic Manuscripts 1285–1385*, 2 vols. (Oxford: Harvey Miller, 1986), 2: 93–94.

In addition to the *Secreta secretorum*, Walter demonstrates familiarity with a number of classical and medieval sources. The opening chapter, for instance, contains quotations from or citations of the *Corpus Juris Civilis*, Gratian's *Decretum*, and Plato's *Timaeus*. Martin of Braga's little tract entitled *Formula honestae vitae* is employed in the course of Walter's discussion of the salient moral qualities of the king. And Vegetius's popular *De re militari* forms the basis for nearly the entire final chapter of *On the Nobility, Wisdom, and Prudence of Kings*. Interestingly, Walter evinces no awareness of Aristotle's *Ethics* and *Politics*, works that were by the 1320s a standard part of the advanced university curriculum. Whether we ought to conclude much from this silence is debatable, however, since it parallels that of many other medieval *specula* and similar political treatises, including those by William of Pagula and William of Ockham published in the present volume.

WALTER'S POLITICAL IDEAS

The fame of *On the Nobility, Wisdom, and Prudence of Kings* perhaps rests primarily on the magnificent illuminations that accompany the text.[16] While there is certainly justification for focusing attention upon the decoration program of the manuscript, this should not distract us from the ideas that Walter propounds in his treatise. As Kate Forhan has stressed, the illustrations are present in order to reinforce and enhance the teachings set out in the written portion of the manuscript.[17]

The treatise commences in a conventional manner, praising the recently crowned Edward and offering good wishes for the state of his soul in the sight of God. By Chapter 3, however, Walter begins to announce the more practical, earth-bound themes that will guide the course of the argument: namely, kings have a responsibility to acquire an education in those fields of knowledge that are useful in the governance of their people (and thus, in the attainment of honor and glory for themselves), and subjects possess a reciprocal duty to instruct and guide their rulers for the sake of the republic (and hence, the advantage of its inhabitants). *On the Nobility, Wisdom, and Prudence of Kings* announces itself to be a manual on how to succeed in

---

[16] Sandler, *Gothic Manuscripts*, 2: 91–93.
[17] Kate Langdon Forhan, "Visual and Verbal Interplay in Walter de Milemete's *The Noble, the Wise, and the Prudent Prince*" (paper presented at the International Congress of Medieval Studies, Kalamazoo, Michigan, May 1991).

kingship (and also, not incidentally, how subjects contribute to this success). The message of the handbook, consequently, is not merely that a king ought to be good or virtuous (though it is obviously important for the ruler to possess a morally upstanding character). Rather, the lesson is that the king must acquire certain skills (included under the rubric of "liberal and legal" learning) in order to rule effectively in times of war and peace.

This instructional emphasis, though hardly surprising, has a particularly hard-edged and practical cast in Walter's hands. For instance, he expands considerably upon the advice given in the *Secreta secretorum* regarding the treatment of counselors and courtiers. He suggests in Chapters 9 and 10 quite specific, and somewhat devious, stratagems for testing the veracity and loyalty of those advisors upon whom a king must rely, clearly in the belief that men should not be trusted with secret business except when some prior proof exists of their reliability. Walter's recommendations to Edward in Chapter 7 about deliberation and in Chapter 8 about gratitude are couched pragmatically to encourage the ruler to employ his authority and largesse in a manner most likely to produce obedient and compliant subjects, especially among members of the noble class. In a similar vein, the advice proffered in Chapter 17 (drawn from Vegetius) concerning military affairs is united by the purely utilitarian criterion of what actions on the part of the king have the greatest probability of producing victory (even if this may involve telling a lie to one's own troops). The author of *On the Nobility, Wisdom, and Prudence of Kings* is evidently a man of some worldly experience who is unafraid of stating frankly the stark realities involved in the use of political power. Walter is no Machiavelli, but neither is he merely an impractical moralizer.

One of the most pressing issues addressed by Walter is the maintenance of peace and harmony among the magnates of the realm — a concern that probably stems from the disputes that wracked the later years of Edward I's reign and that ultimately resulted in the deposition of Edward II. Chapter 6 admonishes the king to ensure that conflicts among members of the nobility are quickly mediated, and warns him not to play favorites. Moreover, a good ruler ought to formulate his policies openly in cooperation with his nobles "in the context of parliaments and other royal councils," taking care that he act promptly on expressions of grievance and explain his decisions clearly and completely. Walter also stresses in Chapter 13 that the great men must be consulted about and must approve any plans for warfare, at least in the case of offensive forays to vanquish enemies or for the sake of conquest. In Chapter 12, Walter cautions that the king's intimates should not include men who are covetous, avaricious, or jealous, since such persons generate discord and resentment among the rest of the populace. Surely it is not too implausible to detect in such warning a thinly veiled criticism of the poor judgment exercised by Edward II regarding the royal favorites Piers Gaveston and the Dispensers, father and son.

On the Nobility, Wisdom, and Prudence of Kings also addresses another contemporary issue about which one hears much more in the tracts by William of Pagula and William of Ockham reproduced in subsequent chapters of the present volume, namely, whether the king can legitimately demand material support for his military endeavors from religious communities by requisitioning supplies from them (a practice that seems to have been widespread during the reigns of Edward's father and grandfather). In Chapter 13, Walter sides decisively with the crown on this question. He argues, first, that the churches and religious establishments of the realm are known to be wealthy far in excess of their immediate needs, and thus will not suffer from such exactions. Second, the properties and persons of the religious are protected by means of royal troops, without whom they would be subject to every manner of depredation; hence, a principle of simple equity pertains, in the sense that burdens as well as benefits should be shared by those party to a cooperative scheme. Provision must be made for the king's soldiers, lest the kingdom be unprepared when necessity demands military action.

It would stretch credulity to claim for *On the Nobility, Wisdom, and Prudence of Kings* the status of an unacknowledged "classic" of political theory. Walter's doctrines are too derivative, and his arguments too underdeveloped, to be included within the first tier of political reflection. Yet his treatise is revealing and intriguing for several reasons. First, it affords insight into the ways in which a professional civil servant of the fourteenth century balanced the salient moral principles of classical and Christian learning against the exigencies of everyday politics. In contrast with so many other volumes within the same genre, *On the Nobility, Wisdom, and Prudence of Kings* does not simply provide a litany of princely virtues — cardinal as well as scriptural — but instead recognizes that the most important qualities of the king are those that contribute to his earthly success.

Second, the text illustrates Ferster's point that even very mainstream and superficially conventional mirrors for princes might well contain implicit — or even more overt — criticism of royal behavior. As Walter's tract makes evident, it remained possible to comment on many of the raging political controversies of the day without the author's endangering his own position. In part, this may be why writers of such works cloaked their teachings in the authority of an Aristotle or some other venerable source, even when they departed from the original: it was an effective means of deflecting blame for the expression of uncomfortable or unpopular opinions and judgments.

Finally, *On the Nobility, Wisdom, and Prudence of Kings* signals an emerging trend in late medieval thought toward considering the king as a public steward or administrator, responsible for maintaining and enhancing the prosperity and material welfare of the realm. While Walter by no means overlooks the moral and spiritual significance of rulership, he concentrates primarily on the effects that government exercises upon the temporal order. "The greatest comforts of the king," he declares in Chapter 11, are to be found "in the glorious praiseworthiness of a prosperous realm, and in attending to the utility of his subjects and kingdom . . ." Such remarks suggest an orientation toward political affairs (quite consistent with the pragmatism evinced by Walter) that emphasizes the ruler's function as the chief source of legal protection and public tranquility, and thus indicates how carefully a prince must gauge the impact of his policies and decrees upon the subjects over whom he rules. Specification of the king's reciprocal duties toward the inhabitants of his kingdom, particularly as concerns their physical wellbeing, becomes a *leitmotif* of later medieval political thought in England, culminating in the work of Sir John Fortescue in the second half of the fifteenth century.

On the Nobility, Wisdom, and Prudence of Kings

Walter of Milemete

Here begins the chapter summary of this book, *On the Nobility, Wisdom, and Prudence of Kings*, composed in honor of the illustrious Lord Edward, King of England by the grace of God, beginning his rule in A.D. 1326 after the Incarnation:

1. On the prayers and divine supplications suitable for the king; and on the histories of the deeds of our Creator for the king to behold. [There is no chapter in the manuscript corresponding to this rubric.]
2. On the invocation of the name of God at the beginning of every work.
3. A letter inviting the Lord King to education in royal knowledge.
4. On the religion of the king and the hope for divine power in [royal] affairs.
5. On the nobility of the king and the prosperity of his rule; and on the sources of his procurement of them.
6. On the wisdom of the king.
7. On the deliberation of the king.
8. On the gratitude of the king.
9. On the advancement of royal education.
10. On not revealing the counsels and secret plans of the king; and on trials to be established by him for his counselors.
11. On the comforts of the king and the music to be performed in the presence of the king.
12. That everyone who is covetous, avaricious, or jealous is properly to be removed from the councils and companionship of the king.
13. On the provision of the king for his fighting men.

14. On the clarification of the letter sent by King Alexander to the philosopher Aristotle; and on the response he received.
15. On the four cardinal moral virtues pertaining to the king; that is to say, on the justice, prudence, courage, and temperance of the king.
16. On the gentleness and mercy of the king.
17. On the battles of the king and his prudence in conducting war; and on the training of his knights and other men-at-arms, etc.

Chapter 2
On the Invocation of the Name of God at the Beginning of Every Work

In the name of the Father and the Son and the Holy Spirit. Amen.

At the beginning of every work the name of the holy and indivisible Trinity is to be invoked: Father and Son and Holy Spirit; this is shown in the *Codex, de officio prefecti pretorio Affrice*, law *In nomine Domini*.[1] We must believe that this name designates "one deity under equal majesty and pious Trinity," as is shown in the *Codex, de summa Trinitate et de Fide Catholica*, first law.[2] And the *Decretum* says: "There cannot exist a good beginning of a work where Christ is not considered the foundation," as is shown in question one, chapter one, *Cum Paulus*.[3] "And truly the most influential part of anything is the beginning," as the *Digest* shows, *De origine iuris*, second law.[4] And "everything is performed rightly and well if the beginning is suitable and pleasing to God"; this is shown in the writing, "How bishops and other clerics ought to be directed toward ordination," first paragraph, ninth collation.[5]

It is meritorious, therefore, that at the beginning of good works there is to be an invocation of the name of God, "from whom proceeded the creation of the whole world and its elements, and who brought forth their arrangement into the world," as is stated in the *Codex, de veteri iure enucleando*, first law, at the beginning;[6] and this is more clearly expressed in Plato's book, *Timaeus*, near the middle.[7]

---

[1] *Corpus Juris Civilis, Codex*, 1.27.
[2] *Corpus Juris Civilis, Codex*, 1.1.
[3] Gratian, *Decretum*, 1, q. 1, chap. 26.
[4] *Corpus Juris Civilis, Digest*, 1.2.
[5] *Corpus Juris Civilis, Novellae*, VI, coll. 1, title 6, preface.
[6] *Corpus Juris Civilis, Codex*, 1.17.
[7] Plato, *Timaeus* 28B–29A. (cf. 27C)

Wherefore, it is agreed that there is power in the name of God, to whom every heavenly, earthly, and infernal knee bows (Philippians 2:10). For this reason, the name of Almighty God is especially to be invoked in human activities, because all good gifts and all perfect gifts are derived from above from the Lord Himself, who is Father of Lights (James 1:17). This is shown in the document, "That the freed are not to be denied the golden ring," at the beginning of the sixth collation;[8] also in the *Decretum*, q. 1, c. 2, *Quam pio*;[9] and in the twenty-third distinction in the chapter *In nomine Domini*.[10] And elsewhere in the *Decretum*, it is said: "Whether we eat, or drink, or do anything else at all, we ought to do it in the name of the Lord (1 Corinthians 10:31), in whom we live, and move, and exist (Acts 17:28)," as is shown in q. 26, c. 6, *Non observetis*, at the end.[11]

Truly this is admonished to us by the Lord Emperor Justinian, who said: "We should invoke our great God and Savior Jesus Christ and the grace of the Holy Spirit in all our deeds, so that by the invocation of the name of the supreme God, we may anticipate that God will become author and defender of all our works."[12] This is demonstrated in the writing, *De armis*, at the beginning of the sixth collation.[13] And again the Emperor Justinian says in another place: "Let us always, with God's aid, make every provision that the subjects entrusted to us by his indulgence are preserved from harm," as is shown in the document, *De questore*, at the beginning of the sixth collation.[14] Elsewhere the Emperor says this: "Under God our maker governing our empire that he has entrusted to us by his celestial majesty, we successfully fight wars and pay homage to peace; and we uphold the condition (*statum*) of the republic; and we lift up our souls to Almighty God as our helper to such a degree that we trust neither in arms, nor in our soldiers, nor in military leaders, nor in our own skills; but rather we rest all hope solely in the supreme providence of the Trinity," as is shown in the *Codex*, *De veteri iure enucleando*, first law, the beginning.[15]

For these reasons, on the authority of the foregoing, I invoke at my beginning Almighty God our Savior, from whom proceed all wisdom and vir-

---

[8] *Corpus Juris Civilis*, *Novellae*, LXXVIII, coll. 6, title 6, preface.
[9] Gratian, *Decretum*, 1, q. 2, chap. 2.
[10] Gratian, *Decretum*, dist. 23, chap. 1.
[11] Gratian, *Decretum*, 26, q. 7, chap. 16.
[12] This text is not in the *Corpus Juris Civilis*.
[13] *Corpus Juris Civilis*, *Novellae*, LXXXV, coll. 6, title 13, preface.
[14] *Corpus Juris Civilis*, *Novellae*, LXXX, coll. 6, title 8, preface.
[15] *Corpus Juris Civilis*, *Codex*, 1.17.

tue, humbly imploring his aid. And I have devoutly thought it right to pray for the intercession of the glorious Virgin Mary and all the company of heaven in order that God Himself, out of His superior grace and goodness, might consider me worthy to understand some of the moral affairs of the human race, especially of kings, and to abridge them in writing for useful comprehension. May this work redound to the profit (*commodum*) and honor of our venerable lord, Lord Edward, duke of Aquitaine, count of Chester and Ponthieu, for whose love this tract was created.

In order that the most glorious God may favor our lord, the duke and count of Chester, the first-born son and heir of our illustrious lord, Lord Edward, by grace of God King of England (whom may the Most High help and conserve in all his good and useful acts, by the fullness of His grace), for this reason may He concede to him the wisdom to understand the writing in this book, to retain in memory what he has understood, and to act prudently according to this in conducting his business, so that through the examples handed out below he will be able to abound in all the virtues. And may he attain earthly honor in this world, as well as eternal glory and joy in the world to come. May this be conceded by God, who lives and rules in an infinite world without end.

CHAPTER 3
A Letter Inviting the Lord King to Education in Royal Knowledge

To his Most Excellent and Illustrious Lordship, Lord Edward, King of England by divine provision, lord of Ireland, and duke of Aquitaine. His humble and devoted clerk, Walter of Milemete, sends reverence and honor and the most faithful service of devotion, averring that he and all that is his are ready to furnish all precepts and teachings with alacrity. May Almighty God, the heavenly king, whose infinite goodness always supports those whom He loves, who is the dispenser of all virtues and the bestower of all gifts, impart to you His divine grace and affection, and concede to you triumphant success in your vigorous actions.

Your Revered Lordship knows that royal honor and royal nobility precede all other forms of nobility and honor on earth. And the subjects of lords should provide watchful care and also diligent study, and they should reflect continually in their hearts how they may fruitfully augment the honor, profit, and advantage of their lords by their faithful counsel and aid, since the augmentation of the honor and military success of their lords often tends to the profit of the republic and to the advantage of all subjects.

Thus it is, Most Revered Lord, that I, your subject, have undertaken a proper study in the composition of the present book, for the sake, I hope, of immeasurable utility to you and, I think, of augmenting your honor by the grace of God, also drawing on the book of the philosopher Aristotle, in which is contained a great measure of human prudence and discernment, just as will become quite evident in diverse chapters below.

Wherefore it brings continual joy to human hearts, and the entire kingdom of England is properly joyful, that you, lord, king, duke, and count, first-born son and heir of the illustrious lord, our recent king of England (whom may the supreme God favor in seeing his deeds through to completion and grant always the grace of dong well), have become educated, through the providence of God, as I truly believe, and are instructed by me in the liberal and legal branches of knowledge, whence will arise mature fruit; and thereafter will emerge inestimable progress on the part of the people. For learning and the teachings gleaned from the formal branches of knowledge will in future events be useful to the highest degree for governing the people in your realm, for vanquishing the enemy, and for conquering territories by force, as will be satisfactorily demonstrated in this tract. And thus I find it written in diverse books that in ancient times the sons of great men generally — including knights, barons, counts, dukes and princes, kings and emperors — were accustomed to instruction in the liberal branches of knowledge and were prudently trained in such disciplines by approved teachers of discernment. For advanced knowledge shapes human character. When one acts according to it, a human being is rendered wise in actions, prudent in escaping dangers, temperate in spurning vices, just in judging, courageous and bold in the face of what is frightening, liberal in the largesse of gifts, gentle and merciful in acquiescing to just requests, agreeable in rewarding those who serve him, humble and subservient in submitting to one's father and mother, benevolent to good men, and replete with all forms of goodness. And, beyond this, following moral doctrine makes a person pure, kind, humble, affable, gracious, compliant, strong, and full of all the types of virtue, beloved by all humanity, and pleasing and acceptable before God.

Wherefore it is agreed that the king or duke who would purposefully will his actions according to philosophical industriousness will without doubt be able to overwhelm his enemies easily; to acquire for his lordship various and diverse kingdoms and provinces; to subjugate to himself many foreign peoples and nations; and to reign over them well and usefully with peaceful tranquillity; and, in times of war or peace, rightly to triumph in all territories subject to him over the people subject to him; and also to act sensibly and prudently in all his royal deeds.

For there is a clear example of this in the noble King Alexander of Macedon, who once acquired many lands and foreign provinces under his lordship by the counsel and teachings of the philosopher Aristotle, the wisest philosopher, who long ago compiled for King Alexander a book which is called *Aristotle's Book of the Secret of Secrets*. Since the philosopher Aristotle was very old and his body was infirm, on account of which age and infirmity he could not remain at the royal court for personal consultation, he composed this book for the use, and at the request, of the king; from this book, King Alexander learned the teachings of the philosopher for ruling himself and his empire happily in times of peace and in the face of aggressive acts of war. Through this counsel, he overwhelmed his enemies, won wars, blockaded castles and cities, acquired diverse lands and peoples under his lordship, and subjugated a great empire under himself; and he achieved triumph in every conflict and occupied himself energetically in all royal actions.

Hence, Most Revered Lord, I have commissioned the copying of this same book, word for word, for your use, so that, Lord, you might have his teachings, along with other supplements and excellent examples that pertain to royal majesty, which I have drawn up from careful thought and have added to this book for the sake, I hope, of advancing your dignity.

Wherefore as a result of the industriousness which the philosopher Aristotle passed on to King Alexander (and which you will possess, as has been already indicated), he profited to such a great extent that, in every conflict and in all other acts of war and peace with which he was personally concerned, he held the superior hand. And just as it is advised in legal affairs that "Like is to be judged alike," and "Where there are similar cases, the same law is to be imposed," so, Lord, when you have attained the state of manhood and, by the grace of God, to a state of greater power and dignity, you will (as it seems likely to me, and as I firmly believe and proclaim indubitably) attain your purpose in the conduct of all your good and honorable business and your lawful deeds, if you are educated according to the lessons given to King Alexander (along with the erudition offered here) and if you make a firm effort to conduct yourself and your acts according to them. And you will be able to enjoy triumph in all your actions, whether in matters of war or peace.

There are further reasons why you ought to act in accordance with the examples found below in this book (as is fitting and as you have the ability to do well): first, to please God with kindness in all your actions; to subdue enemies; to retain your friends in friendship; to gain money, possessions, and treasure; to avoid dangers and hazards; to win battles; to defeat castles and cities; to subject diverse kingdoms and foreign peoples to your authority (*imperium*); to pacify prudently the discords that arise among nobles, whenever they occur, and to bring them back to concord and restore peace among them; to reward the merits of the meritorious; to punish the mistakes of transgressors; to possess always the ardent love and benevolent affection of the counts, barons, and all the nobles of the land, as is necessary, and to foster continually peace and concord among them without interruption; to live virtuously in accordance with all forms of virtue; to reign happily over peoples; to achieve conquest wherever it pleases you; to have grace and assistance from the glorious God in all your enterprises; and finally, after exiting this life, to wear the crown of glory in the celestial kingdom and to abide in eternal joy without end, reigning in that same kingdom and with all the celestial host.

And so that this may be, whoever reads this chapter or has it read to him should say with devotion, three times, the Lord's Prayer and the Hail Mary to the praise and honor of Almighty God and the Blessed Virgin Mary.

Chapter 4
On the Religion of the King and the Hope for Divine Power in [Royal] Affairs

Most Revered Lord King, I do not want your lordship to be uninformed, but sincerely desire you to know that there exists on earth no conduct as profitable, as beneficial, or as pleasing or acceptable to God, as the observance of true faith and divine law among kings, dukes, and princes.

Wherefore, just as legal and divine writings testify, it is necessary that the duke or prince who ascends to royalty is above all to love God perfectly; to believe indubitably in God in all his business; to place his hope firmly in divine power at the beginning and end of all he does in matters of war and peace; to comply with the precepts and commands of God in himself, and to enjoin them to be observed by others, from which the augmentation of divine worship is evident.

Because that which one learns in youth may be recalled from memory in old age, and one seldom forsakes in later years that to which one has become accustomed when one is young (as it is exceedingly difficult to relinquish old habits [*consueta*]), it is thus that a duke and prince who attains to royalty should acquire useful habits in childhood and adolescence, and should be correctly instructed in the law of God and the Catholic faith, as well as in a knowledge of the law of his land. Wherefore he will more readily maintain unharmed the rights and liberties of the church, and also will preserve the kingdom and republic undamaged, by which he promotes the advantage of his subjects. Thereby the lordship of the king will be exalted and his kingdom will be prosperous.

So the king should preserve the liberties of the church unharmed, and by his deeds he is to extol divine worship. Wherefore it is proper for him to take regular part in the divine offices and devoutly to hear at least one mass daily; to distribute alms to the poor; to punish those who commit injuries; to assist the oppressed; to exercise mercy toward subjects in accordance with place and time; and to perform frequently other works of charity. It also agrees with goodness that the king command and require all the religious subject to his lordship, and that he exhort them, to make special memory of the king, the queen, their offspring, and their ancestors in their devotions, sermons, and masses, and to implore divine aid frequently in order that the heavenly God may give grace and virtue to the earthly king, so that he can govern his kingdom well and usefully in order that God may be pleased and all the people may be improved; and may he be granted triumphal success in his royal business. Wherefore it is well known that the prayers and merits of the good offered to God often lead to a favorable outcome where otherwise damage and misfortune might result.

From this, it will appear evidently that the prince loves God and advances divine worship, which is shown inasmuch as the best sign of loving is doing good works. For may Your Nobility know that, although every Christian is obliged to this as a result of the benefits received from God, still it is especially required for the king above others to devote his ardent love to the supreme God. Regardless of the honor to which God raises a person on earth, He intends, if one serves Him, to exalt one more greatly in heaven; and one who is greater on earth should love Him who is greater in heaven. And there is another reason why it benefits the king to love God, inasmuch as he who loves the Lord perfectly in all his affairs always accomplishes matters usefully; one who serves God in all things is not permitted by God to perish, but He supports and advises him in all his deeds. For whoever loves God has his love returned to him by God; and whomever God loves He does not desert without support. And who can put up resistance against one to whom God has granted His supreme aid? No one. Wherefore he can be secure that in all his affairs divine protection will keep him within the proper limits and will make him proceed usefully. For then, without doubt, the subjects in the lands of the king or duke, and all those others in foreign lands, will love the king, duke, or prince more and [not wish] to offend him, or to initiate war (heaven forbid!) or conflict or some other irritation; but they will be afraid to pursue any quarrel or make war against him. And they will manifest toward him greater reverence, obedience, and deeply ardent love.

And there is this reason: for perhaps when there occurs dissension among the king and barons or among subjects, there will be subjects on each side speaking in like manner when they assemble in their councils: "Behold, our lord (whether he be king, duke, or prince) is a good Christian, loving God and the holy church, and accordingly he will have divine protection. Far be it from any of us if he would do offense to or stand against the ruler! For there is no doubt: if one were to attempt something against him, one cannot avoid confusion and destruction as a result of divine vengeance. Rather, since it is the condition of a wise person to procure for himself better counsel, therefore we should improve the soundness of our will and counsel for the better. And we should wish to imitate our Lord in all matters with the entirety of our strength, and, if anyone among us offends or causes damage to others in his realm, we will persevere in his judgment and correction. And if we or any among us have done any harm toward him or have considered being of less service, then we repent our deeds; and we shall devoutly implore his grace and mercy. For our Lord is kind and merciful and gracious to those who beseech him; wherefore, we should have complete confidence in his mercy."

And subjects will frequently put aside their malice and preconceived enmity, and there will be harmony and unity among them; and as a result of this approach, peace and tranquility will be predominant in your kingdom, where otherwise there might perhaps be war, discord, and iniquity.

CHAPTER 5
ON THE NOBILITY OF THE KING AND THE PROSPERITY OF HIS RULE; AND ON THE SOURCES OF HIS PROCUREMENT OF THEM

May Almighty God, King of kings and Lord of lords (Revelation 19:16), who is the distributor of grace and the fount of virtue, deem it worthy to bestow grace and a superabundance of virtues upon you, Most Excellent Lord King, in whom human goodness abounds and a richness of morals is brought forth, as is clear to any observer.

I desire to show Your Revered Lordship, lest it not be brought to your attention, that the best and primary foundation for triumphant success and tranquility in any kingdom whatsoever is that, first of all, the king is to settle justly in his own mind, according to his wisdom, the deeds to be undertaken; second, his determination is to please God; and third, divine aid is to be invoked in each of his actions. For the perfection of everything good descends from glorious God above, and God always favors pleas for aid from just petitioners. But what enemy shall he to whom God furnishes refuge on high fear? None, to be sure. Rest assured that He subjugates all of His adversaries under His lordship. And he whom God wills to be destroyed for his faults and sins can be defended from destruction by no one on earth.

There is another related form of assistance for kings: that the king's subjects — especially the great men, but also the common people of his kingdom — universally love, fear, and obey the king. This occurs when they see that he is just, wise, virtuous, and God-fearing. And by frequent application of royal power, he should punish those worthy of punishment, reward those deserving of reward, hand out justice to everyone and iniquity to no one, and exercise mercy by sparing many. And also he should repay their love reciprocally through protecting and defending them, and rewarding them according to their merits, so that he generates simultaneously love and fear in the hearts of his subjects.

The third useful lesson follows the previous ones: that the fame and nobility of the king in his laudable wisdom is to be spread across the entire earth, so that he may be held among all peoples to be wise, vigorous, virtuous, and fully excellent in all things. For then other kings and other dukes and foreign princes will be moved to honor and fear him more and to rise up against him more rarely, but instead will obey him and offer subjection to his lordship. These qualities being found in him, he can peacefully exercise lordship over his subjects, easily vanquish rebels against him, and achieve conquests in the lands of his adversaries and subject all his enemies to his majesty.

You should also, Most Noble Lord King, by adopting the previously mentioned virtues and, in accordance with the foregoing method, relying upon the virtuous actions of your illustrious character, take studious care to fulfill and maintain three conditions through your noble character (the ways and methods of which can be achieved well and more easily, as has been stated previously): namely, that your actions, with the invocation of God's aid, will be pleasing to God; that your subjects adhere to you in affection and love you with perfect love; and that the commendable fame of your nobility and wisdom is to be noted and spread throughout the many regions of the world.

Truly, if you were to act thus, I entertain a firm trust that you will have laudable success and will triumphantly conquer many locales. Moreover, you can and should ascend through the grace of God to the heights of lordship on earth and attain to the perfection of eternal glory in heaven.

Chapter 6
On the Wisdom of the King

Just as the wisdom of the king is exceedingly commendable, incomparable to all treasure because of its nobility, so it is the perfection of the kingdom and the glory of the regime. For it brings about the utility of the entire kingdom itself. And it expels all iniquity. It recalls the past, deliberates the present, and contemplates the future long before it arrives. It provides everything advantageous to the kingdom, and it avoids the damages of loss.

Wherefore it is to be known that wisdom is the discerning disposition (*habitus*) of the mind, through which everyone discovers and knows effects as a result of past, present, or future causes. And it is agreed that all effects in the natural world proceed from their certain and fixed causes. And whoever wishes to produce some effect or to impede its production ought to consider diligently its cause, so that, if they wish to create the effect, the cause may be ordained and set in motion. And if he wishes to impede the effect, the cause is to be hindered.

For one who is wise in practical matters pays attention to the causes of future effects before their occurrence, and to probable contrary causes by which effects of this kind can be impeded; and one always strives for that which is better and more useful, and tries to achieve one's intention. For example, victory on the battlefield proceeds from these causes: the boldness, courage, constancy, and faithfulness of the combatants, along with deliberately well planned orders and the arousal of warlike sentiments by the field commander, as well as other precautions and provisions that deprive the enemy of strength and induce victory. And therefore, whoever desires victory prepares the causes of victory; from the latter he arrives ultimately at the proper and desired end.

Likewise, that effect which constitutes the peace and tranquility of the kingdom proceeds from the harmony of the great men, not principally from the lesser sorts, since the lesser are regulated and ruled by the greater. And all are nevertheless subject to the prince. Wherefore contrary causes produce contrary effects, and the harmony of the great men is the cause of the peace of the kingdom; as a consequence, discord among them produces war and conflict. For that reason, the wise king rightfully governs in times both of war and of peace. For in time of war, the wisdom of the king considers all causes and disposes the circumstances out of which victory can follow; and removing impediments to causes, he obtains victory, while among the great men of the land he reprimands errors and nourishes harmony. Neither does he permit their disagreements to persevere, but he guides antagonists back to love.

It is not fitting for the king to take the part of one great man against another, since from this enmity increases among his subjects; discord is invigorated. But the wisdom of the king is to bind them together in the love of peace and judge justly among them in accordance with equity (Psalms 67:4, 96:10). If he thus wills, he compels his subjects to be peaceful by the strength and rigor of his lordly power, so that fear of the king should restrict the conduct of people and often subvert their iniquitous intentions.

The wisdom of the king considers the causes of all actions in the context of parliaments and other royal councils. The king in his vigorous wisdom should openly propose articles to be touched upon there, along with reasons and arguments lending weight to each point of view. And he pronounces the business to be handled among the nobles with promptness; he desires justice; he restrains injury; he rewards those keeping faith with him; he torments infidels and rebels. And he always preserves his majesty from damage. And therefore, the aforementioned philosopher labels such a king wise, whom God grants the grace of His support. For such a king upholds vigorous leadership and his lordship will prosper continuously.

Chapter 7
On the Deliberation of the King

Most Noble Lord Emperor, Most Vigorous Conqueror, you who are the gem of virtue and the fount of goodness, Your Sublime Nobility should know that it greatly benefits the royal majesty for all royal business to be expedited and completed wisely and with discretion. As a result, it befits your dignity to do everything discreetly and with counsel and to conclude nothing finally without your fullest deliberation.

Wherefore it is understood to be sufficiently known that barons, counts, knights, vassals, and ecclesiastical prelates, and other greater and lesser people of the land will often come to Your Majesty and devoutly speak to you in regard to their various affairs, in connection with the concession of liberties and escheats, wardships, marital rights, lands and rents to be held in mortmain. And they will request from Your Dignity immunities and privileges of place and person, and innumerable other favors.

Wherefore it is right that when any favor (as is stated above) requested by a subject is conceded by the king or duke, it is to be such that it ought to be conceded out of equity or another just and reasonable cause. But it is not fitting for the king or duke to concede instantaneously a petition and plea when someone asks a favor of him, lest (heaven forbid) he appear to be impetuous and to act without deliberation and without counsel. But it befits royal majesty to respond to a petitioner thus: "We have understood your petition and we will deliberate regarding it both with our council and by ourselves, and ultimately we will do that which it seems to us ought to be done." And as much as possible your Privy Council should approve consensually what sort of favors are to be granted and what sort are not to be granted. Still, Your Discretion should deliberate diligently with yourself regarding the causes and circumstances of the favors; and, having deliberated whether it seems to you expedient or at least not prejudicial, you should concede the petition of the subject if this is profitable to you. If the contrary is the case, it should be denied, without giving expression to the reason why it is displeasing, or with the reason for the displeasure, if this is sensible to Your Highness. And you should always kindly acquiesce to the petitions of great men and nobles whenever such petitions yield no damage or prejudice to you.

Wherefore, Your Contemplativeness should take regular note to handle and arrange the business of great men, nobles, and especially illustrious men neither too quickly nor too slowly, lest you be regarded by the people to be either impetuous or negligent and remiss. But rather [follow] the middle way, wisely bringing business to a close with all promptness and deliberation in the manner of virtuous lords, since human virtue holds a middle place between the opposing extremes of the vices.

And it especially suits the noble to act in this way, so that he may be reputed by the subjects to be prudent and discerning and entirely full of wisdom. For then his subjects will fear him all the more; they will more humbly obey him; they will observe his ordinances and precepts more firmly; and they will adhere to him with greater love admixed with fear. And from this, the praise of the prince will grow and he will be the glory of the regime.

Chapter 8
On the Gratitude of the King

Most Beloved Lord King, Your Sublime Nobility should know that kings, dukes, princes, and great men ought to exercise a certain graciousness toward subjects, so that the meritorious are rightly rendered the profits of their merits.

Wherefore you ought to know that people for the most part serve great men, in whatever type of service, for three reasons: sometimes on account of a certain natural inclination from which emerges a voluntary sentiment of love; sometimes because of the hope of future rewards; and sometimes compelled by the strength and power of lordship. And in all cases they are to be rewarded according to the weight of their merits. And I will demonstrate to you reasons that persuade in a rationally satisfactory manner.

Wherefore you ought first to know that sometimes a subject serves a lord and adheres to him due to a voluntary and loving sentiment, merely for the reason that he thinks the lord to be virtuous and abounding in diverse types of virtues. For such a subject loves his lord perfectly and serves him faithfully. He frequently prays devoutly to God that divine grace may save and assist his lord; that which he believes pleasing to his lord, he bestows upon the lord, to the extent that his resources permit the giving of gifts; for the sake of the love of his lord he exposes himself to many dangers; in whatever location he may be, he promotes the advantage and honor of the lord, as much as he can. A lord may place firm confidence in such a client regarding counsels about private and personal actions that touch upon the improvement or prejudice of the lord.

Wherefore, although such a person does not serve his lord on the pretext that he will receive reward from the lord, still nevertheless he is to be rewarded with the value of his merit on account of the virtue of gratitude. Wherefore, because he is devoted to his lord from a spirit of affection, he is far more deserving than others; and that intrinsic sentiment of benevolence and love, whenever it endures for a gracious lord, ought to be accepted and greeted more than any other gift whatsoever that can be given by a subject to a lord. And thus it is understood that this is to be discovered in Scripture. For God loves the soul and heart, the sentiments and love, of human beings more than any of the temporal possessions possessed by humans that could be offered by humans to Him.

But human beings can scarcely be certain of the love of another except by probable conjecture and opinions that are derived from gratuitous human works, for example, if one person were to reveal his secret counsel to one near to him; and when a greater person does a gracious act for a lesser person, where it is not presumed that he hopes for some future reward from a benefactor (and the extent of a friend's gratitude is best tested in a case of necessity); also when a lesser man yields courteously to a greater man without any aforementioned hope, by means of gracious gifts, faithful service, humble speech, and other declarations of human love and affection. For one ought to trust human deeds and works, and only rarely words, since the best sign of love is the performance of works.

Likewise, in the second case, take someone who enters voluntarily of his own free will into the service of some lord, in the hope of future remuneration: for example, if foreign vassals, mercenaries from another province, or worthy subjects of his own land who are uncoerced (such as *schanaldores*)[16] serve a lord in war or conquest. Their duty discharged and their service finished, the lord, if he acts wisely, should call them all before him and hand over to each, in accordance with his merits and status, a substantial and appropriate reward, while kindly thanking them for their labors and services with a smiling face. And equity advises this, since "the laborer is worthy of his hire" (Luke 10:7).

For by acting in this way the lord will uplift the hearts of his subjects and attract their ardent love to him, since a great benefit is the foundation of love and gratitude; and the subjects and vassals will thereafter be benevolent toward their lord. And when they are assembled together, they will say to one another: "Behold, this noble lord, to whom we have offered our service, has conferred gifts upon us from his largesse and has shown courteous regard for our labors; for he has liberally given his gifts to us according to what we deserve. There are none among us who do not feel his largesse, and every one of us is well contented with his portion of the reward. And so we wish to please him; we are willing to attack his hostile enemies and others rebelling against him, wheresoever in the world they be; we shall vanquish injuries done to him; and we shall oppress his adversaries, wheresoever they may be. This lord is indeed very distinguished: abundant, liberal, gracious, vigorous, and kind. If he should happen to need our service henceforth, we shall serve him before anyone else in the world; and we shall be ready for his precepts and commands, and we shall be prepared to pursue his advantage and honor in our hearts. For this is a prudent and noble lord, whom may the Most High preserve. He knows how to distribute his riches and acquired possessions wisely among meritorious subjects, saving for himself only that which it is fitting to retain under his lordship. Such a lord ought rightfully to have lordship over peoples: he is meant to be a conqueror of kingdoms and foreign lands. And we should enthusiastically support the growth of his lordship and majesty — so long as we are

---

[16] I have been unable to trace the meaning of this term. *Scandile* is a stirrup; perhaps the term connotes those who hold the king's stirrups.

strong and our power suffices; all the more, we should offer our aid in perpetuity to him and his whenever and wherever it is required of us. In no way shall we abandon him on account of fear of death; we shall expose ourselves to all threats for the sake of saving his honor from danger, for his success is identical to ours."

With this said, the lord can place bold confidence in the aid of subjects; and he will have the superior hand in his wars and other hostile actions. Wherefore you should know that such subjects will bravely vanquish the enemies of their lord and will boldly attack his antagonists, on account of their ardent love of their lord; they would prefer to die on the field of battle rather than to flee. And then they will always be ready to fight well, and their lord will attain his goal.

Wherefore it is found in the deeds of old that the noble King Alexander of Macedon, who was the conqueror of many lands through the virtues and power of his subjects, did thus. And he courteously distributed lands acquired by conquest among his brave subjects on their merits, reserving to himself royal lordship; and he exercised his great liberality among his subjects regarding acquired riches, and he augmented his lordship and majesty continually right up to the very final moments of his life. In no land could anyone resist strength of his army, on account of the aforementioned reasons. And consequently, he subjugated all the lands that were attacked by him. And thus, by operating in a similar fashion, by the grace of God, you will have similar success.

Furthermore, in the third case, of those who are bound to the service of great men, the principle remains: the work having been completed, if they have proven meritorious, justice requires that they are to be rewarded for their merits; and thereafter they will be beholden on account of the gratitude weighed out to them by the lord. Wherefore you should know that gratitude is a praiseworthy virtue pleasing to God and humanity, through which one is taught that one is to reimburse the value of a favor accepted. And therefore the lord ought to treat each one of his servants (as has been shown above) according to the value of their merits, and to render his kind thanks to each one for his labors. And unless the lord does this, he stands accused of the vice of ingratitude (which is the contrary of the previous virtue), by not taking consideration of the benefits accepted from others and not rewarding the meritorious. And it is noteworthy that the vice of ingratitude is highly absurd to God and odious to human beings. Wherefore it is said in the ancient histories: "There is to be found no penalty which can sufficiently punish the vice of ingratitude." For it is said in verse:

> Law and nature,
> Christ and every right,
> Condemn the ingrate.
> His birth is to be lamented.[17]

And the servants of such a lord, who has acquired the reputation of ingratitude, will remark amongst themselves when they are together: "Behold, we have labored for our lord and we are poorly remunerated. He has no respect for our labors: we have spent sleepless nights for his love; it is now our regret that we were in his service. Wherefore we repute him to be ungrateful. We have no desire to serve him in future." And such subjects, although they may be with their lord and in his service in body, are not his in mind; and however much they perhaps appear splendid in their expression, their heart is far removed from him. For from the previously stated cause, their ...[18]

Chapter 9
On the Advancement of Royal Education

May Glorious God, who encourages those who love Him, and who through His grace instructed His Apostles on this earth in the disciplines of knowledge and directed their laudable actions along the path of truth and virtue, extend His love to you. May He, through His power, make Your Kind Lordship efficacious in all your affairs; and may He carry on your illustrious actions from good to better; and may He illuminate your intellect, fortify your inclinations, and increase your education in learning.

Most Revered Lord, Your Laudable Lordship should know that it is very expedient for a noble and sublime person to become knowledgeable about the fields of human learning, to know, understand, and read the Scriptures and writings in French and Latin; and above all else to have the knowledge to write documents. Wherefore truly one ought to rejoice and give thanks to the Most High that these virtues flourish in your person. And because it does little good to possess knowledge and virtue and to desist from using them at all, and although it may be difficult for them to be employed always and constantly (nor perhaps is this required of great men), still it is very useful to put the preceding into effect at the appropriate

---

[17] I have been unable to identify the source of this verse.
[18] The text breaks off abruptly.

place and time. Therefore, if it please Your Clemency, I intend to show you that the aforementioned are useful to you, and how and when it is necessary for them to be used by you.

For you should direct yourself often, Your Discerningness, to how, as was previously stated, it may be useful to you to know and understand, and also, among other things, especially to write, documents. There is a way to show this satisfactorily. Recall often to mind one teaching: that all business and plans to be carried out expediently have a start in good and faithful counsel, and therefrom the effect is achieved. When someone acts wisely according to useful counsel, his secret intentions must nevertheless rather remain hidden. But in order that an illustrious man's counsels may be secret and his intentions in a given case kept hidden, it is advantageous for him to write letters in his own hand and send them to friends, wherever they may be, at least in case of arduous business, whenever and wherever it becomes necessary and the loftiness of the business demands, as in cases that happen when there would be a danger in revealing one's plans to someone else. And unless an illustrious person knows how to write documents in his own hand, it will be necessary for him to speak his counsel to a secretary and hence to express his counsel and plan to another. Such might be dangerous in a given case, since the secretary could then, unless he be very constant in such affairs, betray the illustrious person's confidence regarding his counsels. And seldom may there be found a man who is so reliably stable that a noble can confide regarding his secrets in business of great danger and difficulty; indeed, he will become aware that he has been injured and deceived in the end, because the Devil, by promising to people worldly honors and riches, suggests to them unlawful deeds, drives them to perversity, and makes them evil, except for those such who may be proven constant and faithful. Therefore, the wise person says: "Let one in a thousand be your counselor" (Ecclesiasticus 6:6). Thus it is that all regions and everywhere on earth many illustrious persons are deceived in their secrets through human fraud. Wherefore one is to be sorrowful: for they will suffer infinite damage.

And Your Nobility should know that the more danger is perceived, for prudence's sake the more readily counsel is taken, that it can often happen in times of war and conflict that the king, duke, or other illustrious person who is faced with a war started by another, or who has made war for just cause upon another, will greatly need the aid and succor of friends living in remote locales and will wish to pass on to them his concealed counsels by means of messages and letters in order that they may come quickly to his aid. Truly, then, if the lord or illustrious person knew how to write such a document to them, he could recount all his counsels and plans in various letters and transmit them rapidly to his designated friends under his secret seal. Nor could his intent be known by any one of his adversaries or antagonists, since his intent would be related to no one. And thus, in wars and conflicts where there exist great threats, he will succeed in his plans and will dominate and triumph in victory. And unless he should do thus, his intent might perhaps be frustrated and subverted by treachery. Consequently, it is consonant with sufficient reason that so long as your secret plans remain hidden in your mind, they are known to no one nor is there any doubt about this. But once it is related by you to another — a dictationist or secretary — then your secret depends upon the power of another and his arbitrary will, such that it may be secret or (heaven forbid) it may be passed on to another and, as a result, betrayed. And then, of course, there is greater uncertainty about your secret; for it is agreed: that which remains in two or three mouths is hardly counsel, and could be damaging.

Consequently, it is not a little useful to keep your counsels hidden, at least as far as the faculty of reason permits. It is of the greatest advantage in cases when times of war and conflict are at hand; and it is also to a great extent useful at various points arising not in wartime but from peacetime that your plans should be known by no one until they are brought to effect. Hence it is, Most Beloved Lord, that your noble discretion, acting prudently in your business [and] often considering future threats, will appropriately conceal your plans (when it is necessary and in cases where it is necessary, where it could accrue to your advantage), the detection of which would be harmful. Nevertheless, when your prudence dictates that it would be useful and opportune, your secret is to be made known, still hiding your more secret plans from others; and, as stated above, you may wisely reveal them to your friends by means of documents written in your own hand, signed with your seal, whenever circumstances require. For written documents are signs and indicators of the soul's passions, and in them a great or noble man can secretly manifest to his absent friend the true intent of his mind, and whatever else that he would wish to tell him if he were present with him holding a discussion. And this is at least true if sufficient caution and foresight is taken regarding the loyalty and constancy of the messenger.

And this is the manner in which I find it written that the noble conqueror King Alexander of Macedon often acted. In a similar way, you, Most Revered Lord, will maintain a perfect end and glorious success, by providing for discretion in your actions (in accordance with the previously mentioned outline of circumstances) and disposing of your secret business in such an admirable way. For then the great men of the land and all the people of the region will love you and will fear you more; and you will be among peoples by the grace of God like a flower of the field (Song of Songs 2:1) and the light of heaven, making useful plans for your affairs and upholding peaceful lordship; and through this your majesty will be extended to the praise of God [and] the profit of the people.

CHAPTER 10
ON NOT REVEALING THE COUNSELS AND SECRET PLANS
OF THE KING; AND ON
TRIALS TO BE ESTABLISHED BY HIM FOR HIS COUNSELORS

May Omnipotent God, who fashioned human beings in His own image (Genesis 1:27) and endowed the human race with knowledge and prudence, augment your honor and the usefulness of your lordship and bestow upon you faithful counsel.

Your Wisdom should know that you must often be very cautious lest you reveal your counsel which, if detected, could perhaps lead to your harm. The only exception to this is those close advisors (*secretarii*) whose fidelity has been demonstrated by experience and whose stable conscience and firm character have been proven by your diligence. For extreme danger occurs when the counsel of another person is betrayed. From this, great damage often hinders the one seeking counsel, and his plan is frequently ruined. For you should shrewdly place your trust in those to whom you reveal your secrets, lest perhaps such a person may be (may God prevent it) of the sort that he causes harm to you, should through him your secret be divulged to someone feeling jealousy and hatred toward you. And from this no small damage (heaven forbid) could happen to you.

Wherefore you should know truly that from the revealing of a secret there arises the source of malice among people. For from this friendships are dissolved, harmony is dissipated, anger springs up, animosity emerges, jealousy is nourished, and malice takes root. It creates discord, encourages rancor, and perpetrates many wrongful things. On account of this, the inward conditions of close advisors are to be considered, since he who is now a close advisor might later be an adversary, due to some unknown reason; and then an enemy knows what your friend previously knew, and he possesses the materials on the basis of which he can provoke trouble for you.

And rarely is a person to be found who always keeps safely hidden within himself and preserves undetected whatever counsel he knows about someone else. And therefore conduct a test, if you can, whereby, if there is some one of your intimates to whom you wish to reveal a secret, you can make some judgment about him in this way before you make the intimate a close advisor and he knows your secret.

Your Shrewdness, during the intervening time, should be making prudent inquiries of others about who is his faithful and special friend (unless you otherwise know). And then you should pose questions to your future counselor wisely and covertly about the private deeds and counsels of his absent friend, about whom you might enter into a discussion regarding his private deeds and plans. Moreover, Your Industriousness should clandestinely be praising his friend in all things and suggesting in various ways that this person has a reputation for wisdom [or] prudence, pretending that if you had known about his prudence and industry, you would have been wiser. And if your future counselor discusses anything private, you should move cautiously in the direction of the absent friend's private counsels. Wherefore, if from the start he refuses to say anything about his absent friend, nevertheless try him many times — hungry, fed, drunk, and in various states — alleging that he does not love you unless he discloses to you every secret that he knows. And if he should expose and disclose to you the secrets of another person, do not rush to censure him immediately, but settle in your mind that you cannot place trust in him; nor in any case should you inform him of your secret, because, just as he has disclosed to you the secret of someone else, so likewise he might reveal your counsel to another, perhaps envious and hostile, outsider, which could turn out to be counterproductive and harmful for you.

Perhaps, however, in the face of many requests, he always remains stable in his will, refusing to expose the secret of another person regardless of enticing promises and serious threats, maybe claiming: "Lord, in other matters I would freely satisfy your desires, but what you desire is neither proper nor permissible. For I would humbly submit to the harshest pain rather than reveal the counsels of another person. Therefore, if it please you, you ought not to desire what it is not proper for anyone to do." And then you should consider in the judgment of your mind whether his words proceed from his true conscience. Then faith may be placed in him. Yet if he presents himself to be constant and faithful in a false and deceptive way, Your Industry should reject totally his deception and fraud.

And there are a great many other deceitful people full of iniquity. Although they are not invited, they will come to you and, so that they might please you, they will reveal to you the secrets of other people they know under pretense that you be secured from threats. Yet in relating their speech, they deceitfully mix many lies with it. And while you show them a pleasant countenance as you thank them (as is required), take care lest they know your counsels, since they lack the worth to be anyone's close advisors, as they are the purveyors of deceit.

Nonetheless, it can be useful in many instances that you know the secret plans of other people, so that whether they are open or hidden enemies, Your Providence may be able to injure your enemies since you know their evils in advance, to look out for yourself against them, to eradicate their plans, and to reduce to ruins the machinations of your adversaries. And it is expedient for you that your secret counsels be hidden away from such people, lest they be handed over to those jealous of you and to your enemies, lest having prepared themselves against you (heaven forbid) they harm you and disturb you. For one who guards against another is less likely to be hurt by him.

Consequently, Your Illustrious Person should know that there are many perverse, naturally jealous people, bearing honey in their mouths, but deceit and cupidity in their minds; these search for such information about the good counsels of their excellent lord from which they have cause to harm him. And Your Nobility should know that, on account of the goodness and virtue found in a man of nobility, reprobates harbor jealousy of him, since only misery lacks jealousy. And evil jealousy often lies within the heart among those who are equals in dignity and honor, from which there frequently arises great loss.

And one is to act cautiously wherever the greatest danger is imminent. Therefore, it is prudent to be cautious, so that your secrets remain hidden, inasmuch as they can, lest they might be in any way relayed by your close advisors to jealous rivals of yours who have a hatred of you. And unless a lord acts thus (as stated before), and has probed his close advisors in accordance with the aforementioned outline, and according to the ways and means by which human industry tests human character and conditions, he will often be tricked out of his secrets and deceived by those in whom he confides, since human nature is prone to lapse and illicitness. And there are few people who conceal hidden inside themselves what they hear secretly from others. On the contrary, that which is most detrimental they reveal to enemies; and many (as seems evident) are unable to hide their own acts, although base, dishonorable, and contrary to good morals. And how would one who freely exposes his own vice hide away the counsels of someone else?

Truly, Your Excellency should know that he who reveals the counsels of other people that he was bound to keep hidden becomes a traitor, since he betrays another. And he incurs divine indignation, and he will suffer serious vengeance from God for his enormous fault. And one must always prudently beware human frauds. However, through astrological knowledge a true judgment may be possessed (which it would be needlessly prolix to include here) as to how a person can come to know the difference between the false and the loyal, and to whom his counsel can securely be handed, about which matter it will be touched on more fully in a different place and shown for your learning in another way.

Nevertheless, Your Most Loved Lordship, by acting circumspectly and prudently providing for future contingencies, and by refusing to manifest your secrets except when the counsel of another person need be sought regarding your secret, you can most likely bring about advantage to yourself and to those persons alone on whom Your Prudence has rightly relied, as long as these are faithful and have been strictly sworn to reveal nothing and are men of good repute and are reputed faithful by the common people. And then, although it should not be presumed that anyone is unmindful of his own well-being, it is sufficiently safe to accord them your trust; and your secret counsels (may God permit) will always bring you profit and never harm.

Chapter 11
On the Comforts of the King and the Music to be Performed in the Presence of the King

Most Noble Lord King, let me acquaint Your Prudence with the sorts of comforts that ought rightly to pertain to your royal nobility.

It is indeed fitting in the extreme that the king has honorable comforts. Wherefore it is well known that, according to place and time, it is especially suitable that royal majesty be comforted by delighting in birds, hunting with dogs, and exercising with arms and horses for the purpose of enhancing military honor. And also it is suitable for the king to see delightful books, to hear temperate songs, and to perceive visually proportionate objects; and it is permissible to bring before the king, at the right place and time, all sorts of instruments by which the human senses can be beneficially and honorably comforted, as well as other honorable diversions which are suitable and do not diminish his reverence or honor. For as a result the king's senses are comforted, his intellect is fortified, his mind is delighted, his constitution is invigorated, and his sense perception is enhanced. For every sensible and proportionate object works to the improvement of his senses. And the improvement of his senses is the direct and generative cause of intellectual penetration. Thereafter, the king can better discern and dispose of all the business pertinent to his majesty in any way whatsoever.

Heaven forbid that the king should take delight in or become accustomed to vicious and vile activities incompatible with his dignity. For by this he would disgrace himself and thrust aside his honor. For then his subjects will regard him less highly, and his enemies will rejoice.

But the greatest comforts of the king ought rather to be in the glorious praiseworthiness of a prosperous regime, and in attending to the utility of his subjects and kingdom by means of conquering land and using arms; in the promotion of military improvements and the putting down of enemies; and in the practice of the virtues. For from these things his praise will fly across diverse kingdoms, and he brings honor and glory upon himself.

Chapter 12
That Everyone Who Is Covetous, Avaricious, or Jealous Is Properly To Be Removed from among the Councils and Companionship of the King

Most Noble Lord, I strive to explain to Your Nobility what sorts of human conditions a king ought to decline lest devotees of vice be retained in his service. Wherefore Your Venerable Lordship should know that the belly of these people is covetous and avaricious; and neither is a jealous person worthy to be a counselor of the king nor in his service, and he ought not to remain at the royal court. For the covetous are always grasping, and they cling to gifts and the acquisition of money, and they are never sated, because the more they possess, the more they desire. And there is in them an insatiable appetite and an interminable desire; and one who desires everything in excess often loses what he possesses. And rarely may there be found cupidity when there is not also found avarice.

Nor has such a person any respect for the honor and profit of his lord, but only for himself and his own advantage; and he always looks toward gathering treasure for himself. And when other vices desert a person in old age, covetousness and avarice are reinvigorated in the covetous. And it is presumed that such a covetous and avaricious person is willing to betray his lord for the love of treasure or money given or promised to him by an enemy of his lord; and from his treason (which is to be grieved) detestable damage can happen to the lord.

An envious person is properly reproved and removed from the royal court, because he always betrays the just and those meriting their gifts, and he desires to harm them; he condemns the praiseworthy and vilifies the wretched, since misery alone lacks jealousy. He supposes himself superior to those greater than he; he accounts no one his equal; he often solicits honor disgracefully; he disseminates evil words behind one's back; he generates discord among the peaceful. He frequently objects to the prosperity of others; just as frequently, he rejoices in bad things happening to good people; he makes people faithful to their lord to hate their lord, and induces the bad and the unfaithful to enter the court in service of the lord. From this, whenever there are such occurrences, great discord arises and considerable evil results.

Wherefore it is to be known that it is prudent to beware the covetous, the avaricious, and the jealous, as well as their counsels and companionship. For if there should be any such, their counsel is not be believed, since they are engaged in vice, exerting themselves excessively for their own advantage and dissenting from the moral virtues. Their companionship is to be disdained. But the faithful, the just, the knowledgeable, and those of resplendent character are, according to philosophical teachings, to assist in the business of the king and offer their faithful labor for the king; and by means of their counsel and faithful service, there will be honor and praise for the lord and prosperity for the whole people.

Chapter 13
On the Provision of the King for His Fighting Men

Most Kind Lord King, I shall inform Your Clemency in what manner it would be expedient that Your Nobility provide for your valiant yet indigent vassals, in light of your own need for military forces. For Your Nobility should regularly recall to memory that the royal person is but one, composed of a soul and a body, whose bodily vigor is one, while triumphant victory arises from many. For this reason, you will notice that the courage of the king is constituted by the strength of the people in his army.

And a benefit received or wished for renders people in all grades of labor solicitous and attentive. And the person who provides for himself long before the advent of necessity quickly rejoices. Therefore, it is fitting and useful to the republic that the king introduce measures for his valiant men to arrange for their sufficient provision. And then, as often as he needs them, he may confidently put his trust in them, since a benefit once received is to be forever kept in memory. And we recognize that is it known, and it is approved by Scripture, that it pertains to the king and benefits the royal majesty when the king provides in times of peace for the sustenance of his indigent fighting men, in order that he can have greater confidence in them during times of necessity.

For it is appropriate that a king might wish to vindicate himself against his enemies, or subject some land or province to his lordship, through the power of his people and by conquest. For first, the great men having reached a consensus, the king should make inquiry with deliberate counsel throughout his kingdom to determine the whereabouts of indigent young men (*iuvenes homines*), who, although of non-noble origin, still are sound of body, well-disposed in limbs, ferocious in appearance, honorable in character, fearless in facing terrible dangers, and fit for warfare. And he should provide them with the ways and means by which they may be honorably prepared for deployment.

And unless this can be done in a better way, he should honorably arrange sufficient victuals and garments for them by means of royal requests and documents addressed to abbeys, priories, and other religious places. Nor does this seem to bring about any prejudice to the religious, since they are known in every part of the kingdom to abound in lands and incomes that are beyond their sustenance and needs. And armed men ought to defend them and their possessions whenever the threat of war arises; and they are judged to deserve advantage [in return for] advantage. And those who have gained ought to sustain the burden.

Moreover, the king should direct that men of this sort are to be instructed formally and well practiced in military activities performed with bows and ballista, lances, and other instruments of war; and when he needs their strength, he may take them along with his army. And then the king will know through experience that, on account of their instruction and practice in arms, and on account of their ardent love for the king (because he will have provided for them), one of them will be worth six other rude and uneducated men in battle; and, as a result of their constancy and fortitude, the king will very often achieve his goal, which would perhaps have been frustrated otherwise.

And also in the case of those who have previously served the king many times in war or other services, and have been rendered disabled through mayhem, infirmity, or old age, it is proper that royal benevolence should provide them with the necessities of life and garments in the aforementioned manner, so that other courageous men, hoping for the same if something of the same sort befalls them, will adhere more fervently to the king and be more constantly devoted to him. And on account of such things, the king will very often prevail in war, where otherwise ruin might strike him.

Therefore, it is expeditious that the king sometimes is seen to put on his arms and visit and inspect his army, and recall to the memory of his people how he has provided for some of them and intends to provide for the rest. For the king's pleasing speech and promises of benefits very often attracts the hearts of people to the king and compels their bodies to be put at risk for the sake of the royal honor. And the king should always admonish subjects to maintain the royal honor and to destroy his enemies with all their strength.

And the king should always furnish a just cause for a war that has been fought or is being fought on his behalf. He should remove fear from the hearts of his people and transform it into boldness. And then he will have a prosperous result and will confound his enemies. And he will be a conqueror dominating and triumphing over peoples.

CHAPTER 14
ON THE CLARIFICATION OF THE LETTER SENT BY KING ALEXANDER TO THE PHILOSOPHER ARISTOTLE

Most Wise Lord King, immense in majesty and prudent in circumspection, Your Most Illustrious Sublimeness should recall from memory that any person who is born and nourished in some land has, in respect to his basic character (*complexio*), a natural inclination toward the land from which he draws his origin, on account of the nature of, and a similarity with, the elements of his land (namely, water, air, earth, and fire, of which the human body is composed). And men who are dispossessed of such natural land and houses by the strength and power of a conqueror have haughty hearts and tumultuous souls, often fancifully scheming amongst themselves initially and hoping to acquire once again their lost possessions.

And yet the conquering lord's pleasing speech, his honorable patience, his toleration (*tollerati*) of their feelings to some extent, together with the gifts and pleasing promises given them by the lord, as far as the quality and condition of his person are concerned, soothe the instinct of their souls and ardently attract to the conquering king the emotions and love of the people of a foreign land. For thus had King Alexander of Macedon once acted, after having subjugated the Persians to him, as I find written in the counsel of the wise philosopher Aristotle given to him. And thereafter he acquired many lands through the strength and power of the Persians.

In a similar way, you, Lord, will attract the affection and love of great men of foreign lands that you will subjugate in the future through power and conquest, by your grant of your benefits to them; and then they will submit to you well and faithfully in your business, and by the grace of God you can dominate over them usefully. And through their aid and the vigor of their bodies you will possess greater principalities and honors. May God, who disposes and governs all things, concede this.

CHAPTER 15
ON THE MORAL VIRTUES PERTAINING TO THE KING

May the laudable God, the heavenly King full of every virtue, pour into you, Sweetest Lord King, the moral virtues, since it is fitting for a noble king to possess virtue far above other people in the world (for whenever a higher degree of honor or dignity is found in anyone at all, greater perfection of virtue and goodness is required in him), and since regal honor and royal dignity surpass every other excellence on earth and ought to adhere to perfect virtue.

Therefore, Sweetest Lord King, I intend to treat for you (with all due brevity) of the various royal virtues as they rightly pertain to royal majesty. For Your Illustrious Excellency should know that in a noble king there ought properly to abound all good morals and moral virtues, and among others especially the cardinal ones, which are: justice, prudence, courage, and temperance.

For it is fitting for royal majesty to observe justice. For justice is the discretionary virtue of the soul, judging rightly among conflicting parties, discerning and rendering to each what is his. Truly, justice pertains to the greatest extent to the king: through it quarrels are ended, discord is settled, malefactors are restrained, and right judgments among litigants are given in the royal court. And also through royal justice, wrongdoers are punished, rebels are suppressed, and the oppressed poor are aided. Furthermore, one who possesses the virtue of justice is kind to just people, wheedling to no one, familiar with few, equitable to all, in no way believing rumors and slanders, opposed to slanderers, resistant to anger, slow to vengeance, and quick to mercy.

By means of the virtue of justice, it is fitting for the king to direct the great men of his land that they should not destroy their tenants nor extort their goods through unjust lordship, because, regardless of whose tenants they are, they are the king's subjects and bound to royal services; and because it is known to be useful for the king and productive for the republic that the king has rich subjects, inasmuch as the greater the amount of the riches subjects possess, the better they are able to serve the king in all royal business. Therefore, the virtue of justice (which it is fitting for the king to possess) dictates that the king ought to curb the great men by subjection lest they presume to wicked harshness against their tenants.

Truly, it pertains to royal justice to punish despoilers and transgressors for their crimes, since it is useful to the republic that human malice be restrained and that the region be purged of malicious people, so that the punishment of some may create fear and an example for others. And therefore royal justice is a laudable and supremely commendable virtue.

Prudence is the disposition and virtue of the soul that disposes matters, something very necessary for the king; through it, he recalls the past, deliberates about the present, and conjectures about future probabilities. For the virtue of prudence empowers the king in many ways, and particularly in time of battle to provide for future events.

For it is characteristic of the prudent person to examine a counsel and not proceed with it in facile credulity. He enters into doubtful matters with hesitance, rather upholding a suspension of judgment for a while. One who desires to be prudent extends his gaze into the future, and he visualizes in his mind everything that could possibly occur. Nothing will be a surprise to one who has been on the lookout for everything in advance. For one who is prudent does not say: "I did not ever think that would come to pass," since he is not in doubt, but rather expects it; nor does he surmise about the occurrence of things, but he is forewarned. He delves into the cause of every event and deed; when he discovers beginnings, he will consider conclusions. For a prudent person does not wish to deceive; he cannot be deceived.

The words of a prudent person are not inane, since he either persuades or moves or consoles or teaches. He seldom praises; he finds fault even less. He makes promises with care; he carries out more than he has promised. The mind of the prudent person is disposed in three ways: it orders the present, foresees the future, and recollects the past. Wherefore one who has no forethought for the future is often weighed down by an unforeseen event. It is clear from what was stated above, therefore, that the virtue of prudence is extremely useful to the royal dignity in taking precautions against future threats.

Temperance is the moral virtue of direction, consisting in those things that are necessary for life; through it one possesses honorable continence. For one who is continent abstains from excess victuals, and restrains his desire. Through it, he considers how much nature requires, not how much pleasure he desires. If one truly is continent, one will be content with what one has, regardless of how little. And whoever is satisfied with what one has is born with riches. Such a person places the bridle upon concupiscence; he refuses for himself every flattering pleasure; he eats just short of sating enjoyment; he drinks just short of inebriation; he is caused to eat by his hunger, not by sensuality; he flees from everything evil; he takes delight in perfection; he is afraid of no one more than himself; he loves useful words more than witty or charming ones, and straightforward language more than obsequious talk, since it is rough words, rather than smooth ones (that are often mixed with deceit), that are to be dreaded the more. The continent person has an honorable laugh, without clamor, and a sense of humor without meanness. His movements occur without tumult; he speaks kindly with a merry countenance. He avoids flattering; he does not care to be flattered. He responds readily to an inquirer; he quickly yields to one who objects. He gives of himself generously to his equals; he does not disdain inferiors. In adversity, he stands firmly; in prosperity, he is cautious. He despises the prudence of no one; he is sparse with words, desirous of wisdom, endowed with good character, and proper in every deed. Wherefore it is apparent that the goodness of this sort of virtue belongs to the nobility of royal dignity.

Courage, inasmuch as it is a moral virtue, is not bodily strength, but is the perfecting virtue of the soul, through which one confronts terrible things on account of a good end. And the virtue of courage is connected to the virtue of magnanimity, since these virtues are inseparable from one another.

For a person is courageous and magnanimous who is not afraid of threats, like one who is timid; nor is he vindictive, but upstanding in equity. For one who is magnanimous does not turn off the path of truth, neither for a supplication nor for a price, neither for love nor for hatred. Of an enemy, he says: "He did not injure me, he had the mind to do harm." And when he sees an enemy in his power, he will deem it to be sufficient vindication that he could have exacted vengeance. Whoever is magnanimous lives freely, actively, and intrepidly. And one who is perfect shows the most mercy, does not back down from death, confronts terrible things, follows constancy, seeks to benefit everyone, and wishes to hurt no one. Consequently, the virtue of courage rightly belongs at the pinnacle of royal majesty.

Likewise, it is extremely necessary for the king to be liberal; for royal liberality is the preparatory cause of a good regime and triumphant success. Wherefore it should be understood that liberality is a moral virtue consisting in a middle point between two extreme vices, which are prodigality and avarice.

For the prodigal person gives all that he has, including what should be held back as well as what may rightfully be given. And also he gives at inappropriate times and to non-needy and unmerited people. And since he consumes all his things, he is always poor and needs the goods of other people. An avaricious person is one who bestows nothing; he parts with none of his goods. He retains all his things, what should be held back as well as what should rightfully be given. He does not return benefits accepted; he does not repay rewards to the well-deserving, nor does he offer aid to the needy. But he continually embraces the vices of avarice and cupidity. And consequently, he renders himself detestable to many people, and he gives up a great deal for the sake of a little.

Truly, a lord of illustrious liberality maintains a middle position between these two wrongs, spurning each of these preceding vices. For liberality is the moral virtue through which he gives those of his goods that should be given and retains those that should be retained. And also it rewards the well-deserving; it assists the worthy and the needy. For the liberal person considers both time (as is appropriate) and the merit of persons whenever he wishes to confer a gift. And he also investigates how much and when he is to give, and he contemplates the character, merit, and condition of people upon whom he wishes to bestow a gift. Furthermore, a liberal person does not give everything, but only what should be given; and he retains what of his should be retained. And also he gives to those to whom things are to be given, at a time when it is appropriate to give. Subjects are more accustomed to loving, revering, and fearing such a liberal and kind lord, on account of the virtue of liberality.

Wherefore it is explicitly clear that liberality and, especially, the four cardinal virtues ought rightly to pertain to the royal majesty, inasmuch as by exercising them at the suitable place and time the king acquires the people's love and destroys the strength of enemies; the king's praise will be carried through diverse kingdoms; and his honor and glory will increase.

Consequently, Gracious Lord, Your Illustrious Person should become habituated to the previously stated virtues, so that you can lead a life of virtue on earth and, by the grace of God, can have the most gracious success in a glorious regime to the praise of God and to the utility of the entire kingdom.

Chapter 16
On the Mercy of the King

Most Pious Lord King, fount of piety and stream of gentleness, I touch in brief compass for Your Presence, if it pleases, on royal grace, gentleness, and mercy.

Hence it is extremely proper and useful for the king to exercise mercy and to show gentleness toward captives and prisoners. For it is said to be a great abuse when the king is without mercy. And even though it may be by mere right that transgressors are to be punished for their faults and the demerits of men are to be assailed by penalties, and he may seem to harm the good who spares the evil, still it is pious to be kind to captives and prisoners and to pardon their injuries; therefore, the virtue of gentleness requires that the king from his mercy pardon offenses and grant indulgence to his subjects, especially the great men, who (although they transgress) are humble petitioners for forgiveness, unless they are convicted of treason or grave sins. For in the exercise of mercy, the king shows his royal power for the good of subjects, and also demonstrates himself to have power over their life, death, and limbs.

And an earthly king who spares his subjects follows the will of the supreme Creator in his gentle compassion. For one who is too vindictive is sure to suffer from the vengeance of another. But mercy will follow to one who has merciful compassion toward another. Therefore, the mercy of the king is the perfection of law and the goodness of the regime.

For mercy is a great virtue [when] usefully conjoined to royal power; through it the whole earth is created, the human race is saved, vengeance is softened, and anger is dampened. Through it injury is pardoned and grace is attained. Inasmuch as the royal will, regulated by right reason, is observed as law, whatever he graciously forgives is relieved by law. Therefore, whoever enters into the king's presence and devoutly asks for his kind mercy ought to experience royal gentleness and have royal mercy. Through this the king will be seen by all to be kind, illustrious, gracious and merciful; for from this, he acquires divine grace and love in the hearts of all subjects.

Thus also you, most pious lord king, having inspected the magnitude of the crimes and the condition of the persons wishing to request mercy, ought graciously to give your royal grace and gentleness to each one with all good measure and speed. And then everyone on earth will more freely obey your precepts and subject themselves to your royal lordship. And you will have the pleasure of God and the love of the masses (*vulgi*), as well as the superior hand all the more rapidly in your vigorous actions. May this be conceded by merciful God who bestows His mercy in everything.

Chapter 17
On the Battles of the King and His Prudence in Conducting War; and on the Training of His Knights and Other Men-at-Arms

Most Compassionate Lord, Most Noble King, I seek to demonstrate to you certain useful things that are somewhat necessary, things which usually happen in battle. For when other legal remedies do nothing to subjugate enemies, mutineers, and rebels, one has ultimately to turn to war.[19]

For battle is the foundation of peace, since many preserve the peace on account of their fear of war. Therefore, one who desires peace prepares for war; and one who desires victory diligently instructs his knights; and one who wishes for a successful outcome fights by art and not chance. Wherefore Your Clemency should know that no one dares to provoke or to offend either a noble or a non-noble whom he discerns to be a superior fighter.

For there is nothing more stable or happier or more laudable than a republic in which there abound skilled knights in an experienced army. For it is not guardians of the wardrobe, or keepers of gold or silver or hoarded gems, who turn enemies toward the reverence and grace of the king. Rather, they are subjected to royal lordship solely by the fear of arms and the power of soldiers. This is why, Most Learned King, I endeavor to expound for Your Highness regarding the exercise of knights and the condition of soldiers, as well as the points according to which knights may be examined and the exercise of arms in which they are to be instructed.

Wherefore Your Nobility should know that exercise and practice in arms for knights is a large cause of fighting and vanquishing enemies in war (as is sufficiently clear). For it seems that the Roman people would never have subjugated the whole world except for their exercise in arms, discipline in the camps, and practice in military service. For how would a small number of Romans prevail against a multitude of Gauls? For how could the diminutive Romans have resisted against the tall Germans? Certainly, it was through practice in arms, knowledge of warfare by knights, and constancy in conquering enemies.

For military practice nourishes firm boldness in combat, both because no one is entitled to do what he is not confident he has learned well and because wise men of expertise perform more surely than pretenders. Hence it

---

[19] This chapter relies heavily on a compilation of passages from Vegetius, *De re militari*.

is that in the making of war, a small number of trained individuals is better suited and more effective for victory than a rude and uneducated multitude, which is always exposed to slaughter. Therefore, it is expedient that your knights and others who fight in wars are to have exercise and practice in arms before they are led into battle.

Truly, Most Excellent Lord King, I inform Your Prudence that people (for the most part) whose nations are close to the sun are naturally timid. In matters of counsel, they are indeed discreet, and this is because they have a somewhat temperate character. And since they are dried out by the excessive heat of the sun, they therefore have less blood, which they are afraid of losing. For this reason, they dread injury; consequently, they have no constancy in fighting.

Regarding the conditions of armed people on foot and horseback, it should not escape the notice of Your Lordship whether those from the countryside or from cities are more useful fighters. For it is found in many places and demonstrated in Scripture that the rustic masses (*plebs*) are better at arms than city-dwellers. For I believe that the rural masses are best adapted to arms, since they are nourished in constant labor, they are plagued with strenuous activity: enduring the sun, neglecting shade, unfamiliar with baths, ignorant of luxury, simple of mind, content with little food, their limbs tolerant of endurance in all labors. They turn away less from death. They more greatly hold to constancy. For one is less afraid of death who is not familiar with the gifts of luxury in life. Therefore, it is seemly to recruit the elite of trainees from the countryside.

And also it is advantageous that youths are to be selected for knights and instructed prudently in the practice of arms, because that which is learned in youth is imparted not only more rapidly but also more perfectly. Furthermore, it is better that a young trainee laments that the age of fighting has not yet arrived rather than that he grieves in old age the fact that it has passed. Truly, practice and exercise in youth results in a vigorous fighter. Consequently, once soldiers have enlisted, learning is to be provided to them through daily exercise in arms.

And continual practice is necessary during times of peace in those things that ought to be retained in the confusion of battle. For those who have not seen people wounded or killed for a long time, or ever at all, are horrified or confused with panic when they first look upon such things; and they start to think more about fleeing than about the conflict.

And it is easier to instruct newcomers in the virtue of boldness than to restore it to those who have panicked. And therefore fighting is sweet to the inexperienced. Nor is one to be entirely confident of a knight, although he may affect the word "battle," since many portray themselves as bold who are naturally timid and, gripped with fear, are entirely crippled in battle. And it behooves you to know that a soldier is never to be brought up to the line of battle unless you have already obtained experience of his boldness. And whenever Your Laudable Industry seeks to ascertain the condition of knights for battle, you should often pay attention to their faces, their words, their bearing and their movement, from which you may make sufficient determination. And it is to be noted by you that honor renders a knight suitable. Moreover, modesty prevents him from fleeing, while it causes him to be victorious.

And in every conflict, place and time are wont to be better than strength in war. And the virtue of combatants makes for better results than their numbers. For nature creates few courageous men, and good arrangement in an orderly battle renders more of them; and the hope of victory in their expeditions and the promise of rewards makes knights better. And also industrious training is enhanced through labor and degenerates through inactivity. Hence, you should note that the captains, magistrates, and commanders whose labor and practice have instituted modesty in your army are more praiseworthy and more loving toward you than those whose troops are coerced into obedience from fear of punishment.

Nevertheless, when you wish to move forward into battle, take care to provide circumspectly that your army is well ordered, each in his ordained grade and place. Truly, there is nothing greater to be watched over on the march or the line of battle than that all soldiers observe the order of advance, which cannot otherwise happen except if they learn in training to walk the same and to ride swiftly and evenly. For there is nothing so difficult that continual preparation by exercise does not render it easy. For a divided and disordered army always sustains the gravest harm from enemies.

For the author Sallust recounts the following regarding the military practice of Pompey the Great: "He had contended with the energetic in jumping, with the swift in racing, and with the strong in riding."[20] And he could not have otherwise prepared himself for Sertorius unless he had prepared himself and his soldiers for battle by frequent exercises. For this reason, frequent exercise is to be desired in soldiers.

And before you fight, you should arrange your army in secure positions. Also, the warriors of your army should become accustomed to seeing and knowing the enemy. Furthermore, the enemy should begin to be terrified when they see the battle lines arranged against them. And you ought to

---

[20] Sallust, *Histories*, frag. 2.19, quoted by Vegetius, *De re militari*, 1.9.8–9.

terrify and disturb your enemy by throwing blazing objects and [making] horrible sounds, since a large part of victory is terrifying enemies and inducing fear, and this in the extreme when you wish to begin to fight.

And you should have in your army a full range of types of arms, namely, offensive and defensive arms. For it is necessary that one will assume a more ardent boldness for combat who, fortified on head, chest, and other limbs (as appropriate), is not afraid to fight his adversary. And because a king can place more confidence in his vassals than in foreigners, it is better to educate his own subjects in arms than to hire foreign mercenaries.

And he whose armed forces excel in the greatness of their size and strength should himself fight at the front of the marching column. One who relies on cavalry should seek positions more apt for knights; moreover, one who relies on large numbers of infantry should seek positions more convenient for foot soldiers. And among the ancients, an army infantry was called a wall, for just as a wall protects the castle and the city, so does the army infantry support the strength of the cavalry and defend them from the enemy. And therefore a strong infantry force should be dear and beloved to you, although the cavalry may be of greater dignity and nobility.

Also, you should have with you wooden towers to be built into the sky in order to besiege cities and castles, from which you can spy on what the enemies are doing or preparing in their besieged castles or villages; and there should be other sorts of instruments: large rocks and boulders to be projected for the destruction of houses and walls of cities. In fact, in certain lands, there are elephants carrying wooden towers from which armed men are accustomed to make a great assault.

And you should wish to know that it is sound management and rational determination to pressure the enemy with hunger rather than vanquish him with the sword, since through this your men are spared from harm.

When you take counsel in battle, Your Illustrious Excellency should know that the better counsels are those which are hidden from the adversary. And also beware of the disclosure of counsels. And when you become aware that your counsel has been betrayed to the adversary (heaven forbid), it is appropriate to change your arrangements immediately. And believe the counsel of those who love you and cherish your prosperity (whom you will know from the prior writing; for where there is pain, the finger touches; and where there is constant love, the eye is there).

Indeed, you should consult with many regarding what ought to be done in your wars; yet about what you are going to do, with very few and the most trusted. As I reckon it, what you intend to do is to be disposed in many of these cases by your deliberative mind and is to be revealed to no one. Nonetheless, you should diligently observe that salutary and necessary teaching shown to you in the writing above: that you should possess the love and affection of the great men and people of the whole army (to the extent you can), so that they might cherish you and adhere to you in fervent love.

And it is expedient that you regularly visit your army fully armed before a battle, and that you recite to refresh their memories how you have provided preferments for certain of them and intend to provide sufficiently still better for them, as well as for the rest. And you should promise them gifts, preferments, titles, riches, and honors, because, although Your Illustrious Person may not be giving such things in the future, through such promises the love of people is carefully attracted and their minds are more strongly inclined toward the affection of benevolence. And thereafter they will seek more vigorously after the success of victory and the strong suppression of the enemy. And by your visit to them, you will show your kindness and the virtue of familiarity, entreating them that they maintain your honor for the sake of their own prosperous advantage in future events.

For from this you can draw their love to you, remove fear from them, and powerfully stimulate them to desire battle, and wisely make them constant and bold. And then they will always do well, since they would more freely prefer to die than to flee. And then you will have victory over your enemy and a triumphant campaign.

And you should uphold a firm hope of conquering your antagonists, and also maintain a stable resolution in vanquishing your enemies. For resolve in the king is a great part of victory, since by his hope and resolution fears are removed from his subjects and all the people in his army; and errors in battle, where they would cause great harm, are avoided before they achieve an effect. In other matters where there may be damage, the errors and damage can be corrected afterwards; but harm in battle does not admit of emendation, since bodily wounds may follow immediately from errors. And since no monetary value can be placed on the human body, and the least bodily wound is greater than all remuneration, thus it is that errors in battle are uncorrectable.

And know that it is necessary that those who see their leader despair and who sense the desolation of their captains are prepared to flee. Therefore, it is praiseworthy for the king to be resolute, as it stimulates his warriors in battle and renders them more audacious.

And so, in order that you may act more surely, always afford your army with a just cause for fighting and vanquishing the enemy on your behalf. And you should provide the army sufficient victuals on land and sea.

And do not remain for a long time in the same place once the enemy has been defeated or turned to flight. And nocturnal vigils are necessary, lest you be unguarded and unprepared, and the enemy comes up at an unexpected time. And you should have secret agents among the enemy (and, if you can, they are to be of the adversary's nationality) revealing to you the counsels and plans of the antagonist.

And if you perceive your warriors to be panicked with fear, hesitating, despairing, or scattering, you have to address and comfort them for the sake of integrity; and you should stimulate them to boldness by calling to mind (as was stated already) the benefits you have bestowed on them. And offer to remunerate them fittingly later on, and vehemently assert having a just cause for fighting and destroying the enemy (as was advised previously), so that the enemy does injury and sustains an iniquitous quarrel; and you should frequently declare to them that you are certain of the enemy's defeat. And through this you can restore them to their initial state of courage.

And on the precise day when you wish to fight, you should instruct that each soldier in your army is to eat a small amount, not to full satiety, and to drink once or twice of a good wine. For through this, each one is made bolder and his bodily strength more powerful.

And above all, you should observe in Your Illustrious Person the generous nobility and royal integrity properly pertaining to your majesty, so that ultimately, your enemies being vanquished, you will freely divide amongst your subjects the treasures, possessions, incomes, and lands acquired through conquest — reserving your royal lordship — by conferring on each one a portion according to the merit of his labors and the condition and state of his person. And displaying the kindness of your pleasing countenance, you ought to express gratitude to them in a most familiar manner, with propriety and goodness, for strenuously expending their labors in your campaigns. For through this you will manifest your integrity and the virtue of a liberal soul, you will attract the love of your army, and you will acquire greater praise and honor.

Wherefore, most noble lord, if you will observe the foregoing writing regarding war and conflict and other things about fighting and the character of kings once taught to the noble King Alexander of Macedon, conqueror of the earth, by the philosopher Aristotle, the prince of philosophers (which are contained more fully in the *Book of the Secret of Secrets and the Prudence of Kings* and are sent by me to you), I entertain a firm trust that you will enjoy conquest, honor, and grace on earth, and in heaven, reigning with God and all the celestial host, you will have eternal glory. May God, who lives and reigns without end, concede this. Amen.

Introduction to the *Mirror of King Edward III* (Versions A and B) by William of Pagula

THE POLITICS OF ROYAL FINANCE

The most pressing concern, not to mention consuming passion, of the medieval English monarchy was warfare. Perhaps to a greater extent than any of their continental counterparts, the Plantagenet kings of England were continually engaged in bellicose enterprises, whether in the British Isles (as in the border wars with Scotland and Wales) or overseas (as in the struggle for the French crown).[1] At times, it was even necessary to turn the king's might against the aggression of overly powerful internal rebels. Even when royal troops were not actively fighting an enemy, the English monarchy was generally occupied with strategic operations preparatory to the next phase of its military pursuits.

Concomitant with the Plantagenet obsession with warfare was the inescapable question of how to fund it.[2] By the fourteenth century, warfare had become an expensive affair, the result of repeated technological innovations in military hardware. Moreover, the traditional means of populating the army and financing war — the feudal array — had been displaced over the

---

[1] The indispensable study is Michael Prestwich, *The Three Edwards: War and State in England 1272-1377* (London: Weidenfeld and Nicolson, 1980).

[2] See Michael Prestwich, *War, Politics, and Finance under Edward I* (London: Faber and Faber, 1971), and G. L. Harriss, *King, Parliament, and Public Finance in Medieval England to 1369* (Oxford: Clarendon Press, 1975).

years, a victim of noble resistance to personal service as a means of demonstrating fealty to the crown, as well as of royal recognition that soldering itself had become more professionalized. The cash payments that replaced annual obligations of service proved, however, inadequate to support the mounting costs of war. The levy of direct subsidies upon commons and clerics could not be imposed unilaterally; their consent was required, whether in a formal parliamentary assembly or through local negotiation. And the inhabitants of the realm were disinclined to finance the king's military adventures, especially when no imminent danger of attack and invasion loomed.

The English crown was thus compelled to squeeze income from every one of its customary rights and prerogatives, such as customs imposts and royal monopolies — a practice that came to be known as the monarchy "living on its own." Among the methods of indirect taxation widely employed by the royal household in the fourteenth century to support itself and its military aspirations was purveyance, that is, the right of the king and his immediate family to provide for themselves when touring the realm by confiscating local goods or purchasing them at a fixed, non-negotiable price. Purveyance had its roots in the long-standing liberties associated with banal lordship — the customary power of the ban[3] — but it was seldom invoked by the English monarchy until around 1300. Edward I seems to have pioneered the practice, which was raised to a fine art under Edward II during the years 1314–1316. Desperately in need of resources to support his campaign against the Scots, Edward II together with his agents ruthlessly commandeered the goods of his subjects.[4] In 1316 alone, upwards of thirty commissions of purveyance were issues to royal servants on behalf of the king's household and the office of the marshal.[5] Edward III renewed this intense program of enforced purchasing during the spring of 1333 in preparation for his own campaign against the Scots.[6] Only exceptionally did recorded commissions of purveyance enumerate how much was to be taken and at what rates. Normally, such writs of aid were general in nature, permitting the appointee to buy at will any amount of goods anywhere in the

---

[3] Georges Duby, *The Early Growth of the European Economy*, trans. H. B. Clarke (Ithaca: Cornell University Press, 1974), 172.
[4] J. R. Maddicott, *The English Peasantry and the Demands of the Crown 1294–1341* (Oxford: Past and Present Society, 1975), 17.
[5] *Calendar of the Patent Rolls Preserved in the Public Record Office, 1313–1317* (London: Stationery Office, 1894–1904), 448, 452, 468, 477, 484, 486, 510, 543.
[6] R. Nicholson, *Edward III and the Scots* (Oxford: Oxford University Press, 1965), 109–115.

kingdom. The legitimacy of royal authority to purvey went unchallenged. As late as 1331, parliament itself acknowledged the crown's right to purchase unilaterally goods for use by the royal household.[7]

Not surprisingly, opposition to purveyance during the reigns of Edward II and Edward III was widespread and pronounced. Under Edward II, calls for reform of the practice were made by the Lords Ordainer, and numerous complaints were recorded on parliamentary rolls.[8] The chronicle entitled *The Life of Edward the Second* records the existence of a document, supposedly sent in 1316 to the king's confessor by "a certain well-known and religious author," that laments how "as our king passes through the land, he seizes the goods of men, and he pays nothing or only a little or badly." Fearing lack of any payment whatsoever, the letter continues, those to whom payment is owed "make an agreement to remit a certain amount so that the rest may be paid to them more quickly." So far from rejoicing in the arrival of their king, "his departure rather is preferred and at his leaving they pray that he may never return again."[9] Resistance to purveyance seems to have stemmed from several factors, including the uneven geographic impact of the prises, the abuse of the privilege, the corruption of officials, the failure of royal agents to make good on their promises to pay, and the arbitrariness with which the appropriations were conducted. These grievances were voiced in the Commons time and again during the early fourteenth century.[10] Striking primarily at the poorest of the crown's subjects, purveyance allowed the king to supplement the slow and uncertain processes of seeking parliamentary or clerical subvention for the costs of his government, in particular, of his wars.

THE *MIRROR OF KING EDWARD III*:
DATING AND AUTHORSHIP

The issue of purveyance forms the central theme of the *Mirror of King Edward III*, a title conventionally employed to encompass two related works

---

[7] *Rotuli Parliamentorum*, 6 vols. (London: Record Commission, 1783), 2: 62. For more on purveyance, see H. J. Hewitt, "The Organization of War," in *The Wars of Edward III*, ed. C. J. Rogers (Woodbridge: Boydell Press, 1999), 285–302, esp. 290–291.

[8] Maddicott, *The English Peasantry and the Demands of the Crown*, 23.

[9] Denholm-Young, *Vita Edwardi Secundi*, 75. This passage is discussed at length by Cary J. Nederman and Cynthia J. Neville, "The Origins of the *Speculum Regis Edwardi III* of William of Pagula," *Studi Medievali*, 3rd ser., 38 (1997): 326–328.

[10] *Rotuli Parliamentorum*, 1: 374, 377, 378, 381, 382, 387, 391, 392, 396, 400, 401, 408.

by the same hand, composed in the early 1330s in order to alert the royal court of the circumstances of the rural poor. Beginning with Joseph Moisant, the editor of the two treatises, it has become customary to refer to them as the "A" and "B" versions.[11] It should be noted, however, that the second recension is not a lightly edited version of the first. Rather, B forms an entirely new treatise that restates essentially the same grievances as its predecessor, but does so in less scholarly and more direct language that suggests an urgency to the expression of its grievances.

The author of the *Mirror of King Edward III* was unquestionably a learned man, well read in theology and canon law and familiar with the conventions of Latin political literature. Because of the titles that are prefixed to some of the manuscripts, Moisant had proposed the hand of Simon Islip, Archbishop of Canterbury, but internal evidence disproves this attribution. James Tait, who offered a reliable dating of A to 1331 and B to 1332, proposed another Archbishop of Canterbury, Simon Meopham, as the real author.[12] This ascription, too, is problematic, since the author of both treatises clearly identifies himself as a parish priest in the vicinity of Windsor. The mystery of authorship was finally solved by Leonard Boyle in a pair of papers: the *Mirror of King Edward III* may safely be attributed to William of Pagula, an Oxford-trained canonist and theologian who spent much of his career as vicar of Winkfield, Berkshire.[13]

The details of William's life are spotty. He probably hailed from Paull, near Hull, Yorkshire. The first safe recorded evidence for him comes in a 1313 grant of letters dimissory, followed in 1314 by his institution as perpetual vicar of the church of Winkfield, near Windsor, just inside the boundary of the Salisbury archdiocese. Ordained priest at Canterbury Cathedral during the same year, William seems to have resided at Winkfield only intermittently during the next few years, as he pursued studies toward a doctorate in canon law at Oxford. Completing his degree sometime between 1319 and 1323, he received further appointments in Reading and London, but does not seem to have sought further ecclesiastical preferment, instead settling into the life of a rural parish priest. He most probably died in the summer or early autumn of 1332.

---

[11] *De speculo regis Edwardi III*, ed. Joseph Moisant (Paris: J. Picard, 1891).

[12] James Tait, "On the Date and Authorship of the *Speculum Regis Edwardi*," *English Historical Review* 16 (1901): 110–115.

[13] Leonard E. Boyle, "The *Oculus Sacerdotis* and Some Other Works of William of Pagula," *Transactions of the Royal Historical Society*, 5th ser., 5 (1955): 81–110, and idem, "William of Pagula and the *Speculum Regis Edwardi III*," *Mediaeval Studies* 32 (1970): 329–336.

William's move into the position of full-time vicar did not dampen his enthusiasm for scholarly pursuits, but rather stimulated and guided his literary production. His most famous work, the *Eyes of the Priesthood*, a manual of pastoral theology, deals comprehensively with the matters that ought to fall within the "view" of the parochial clergy. Composed of three parts — dealing respectively with confessional practice, morals, and dogma — the *Eyes of the Priesthood* represents an elaboration of the program of pastoral instruction mandated by the Council of Lambeth in 1281 for the Canterbury province.[14] Its various sections were written over the course of the 1320s, and it soon became an influential work. Fifty manuscripts of it survive, and it gained an even wider following in an abridged edition produced later in the fourteenth century; it was also repeatedly printed during the early sixteenth century.

The 1320s also witnessed the composition by William of three other instructional tracts: the *Summary of Summaries*, the *Summary of Prelates*, and the *Mirror of the Religious*. Comprising five books and about 350,000 words, the *Summary of Summaries* surveyed the responsibilities and station of the clergy. Cast in question-and-answer form, the treatise was designed to enumerate the duties pertaining to each office in the ecclesiastical hierarchy, ranging from the parochial clergy to the upper echelons.[15] The *Summary of Prelates* was an even more ambitious work, approaching 700,000 words in length and intended as a definitive source book for parish priests. It contains, among other features, a large collection of church statutes relevant to parish affairs, as well as an extensive set of sermon themes for every Sunday, feast day, and special occasion within the liturgical year. Finally, William produced a severely compressed version of the *Summary of Prelates*, containing some additional material, which he titled the *Mirror of the Religious*. This handbook concentrates on the rudiments of canon law most necessary for pastoral care. While none of these works was as successful as the *Eyes of the Priesthood* (the *Summary of Prelates*, for instance, survives only in a single manuscript), they all indicate the depth of William's commitment to ministering to the souls of parishioners.

Such concern translates directly into the pages of the *Mirror of King*

---

[14] Roy Martin Haynes, *Archbishop John Stratford* (Toronto: Pontifical Institute of Medieval Studies, 1986), 286-287.

[15] Leonard Boyle, "The 'Summa Summarum' and Some Other English Works of Canon Law," in *Proceedings of the Second International Congress of Medieval Canon Law*, ed. Stephan Kuttner and J. Joseph Ryan (Vatican City: Institute of Medieval Canon Law, 1965), 415-456.

Edward III. William describes his own experiences of the devastating effects of purveyance upon the countryside around Windsor. He admits to his own fear of the visitation of royal officials, and that he is scared of their rapacious and abusive practices. In comparison with most works of medieval political thought, the *Mirror of Edward III* is deeply personal in tone, and emphasizes to the king the importance of maintaining popular support amongst the denizens of rural villages. Yet William also advances a highly learned case on behalf of England's peasant population. He draws upon his vast knowledge of scripture and canon law, as well as his learning in the classical tradition, to demonstrate how purveyance is a misguided policy spiritually, morally, and politically. Whether either version of the treatise ever made its way into the hands of members of Edward III's inner circle is unknown; if so, it certainly had no discernable impact, since the year after William's death the king commenced an extensive program of purveyance in aid of renewed warfare upon the Scots.

Even with its authorship securely established, the *Mirror of King Edward III* poses additional conundrums. The timing of its composition is curious, insofar as there was a relative lull in the commissioning of purveyors during the early years of the new king's reign.[16] Perhaps William, mindful of the events of Edward II's troubled rule, feared that a new round of prises was on the horizon as the conflict with Scotland began to heat up once again. But this is purely a matter of speculation. It must also remain an open question why William decided to write a second version of the work so soon after the first. Although they touch upon identical themes, there are clear differences between the two recensions. In particular, the extensive quotations from canon law collections, the Fathers, and the classics that pervade A all but disappear from B. One might say that the former is a case constructed on the basis of law and reason, whereas the former adopts the rhetorical style of the pulpit.[17] It may be that William, who must have known the power of preaching at first hand, concluded that his first effort to condemn purveyance lacked an immediacy and urgency that he deemed to be required. Or did William have two different audiences in mind for his treatises? We are unlikely ever to be sure.

---

[16] Nederman and Neville, "The Origins of the *Speculum Regis Edwardi III*," 323–325.

[17] A useful measure of this may be derived from David L. d'Avray, *Death and the Prince: Memorial Preaching before 1350* (Oxford: Clarendon Press, 1994).

MIRROR OF KING EDWARD III: DOCTRINES

The *Mirror of King Edward III* in many respects fits neatly within the conventions associated with the *speculum principum*, discussed in the introduction to Walter of Milemete's treatise in the previous chapter. The *Mirror of King Edward* explicitly addresses itself to the king, offering praise for his majesty couched in the moral and religious terms that readers of advice books have come to expect: God is to be imitated by the ruler in the justice shown by his judgment and will; the king's office and authority derive from the doing of right; the prince ought to bind himself to the law, as a demonstration of his just intent and will; when the king seems to err, it is the consequence of evil counsel, which ought to be banished from the realm. Yet the *Mirror of King Edward III* has received a somewhat odd reception among scholars. Some have rejected its inclusion within the tradition of *speculum* literature, while others have embraced it as a quintessential mirror.[18] Most of the scholarly literature on medieval political thought, however, has chosen simply to ignore the work.

Certainly, the source materials for the *Mirror of Edward III* are fairly conventional. William's primary resource was, of course, the Bible, although he often strays from precise scriptural quotations, suggesting that he may be quoting from memory. As befits his training, he often cites legal texts and principles. He was well versed in the standard patristic and medieval works that one finds in *specula*, including Saints Gregory, Isidore, Augustine, and Bernard of Clairvaux, as well as treatises that were incorrectly ascribed to these figures. Among non-Christian texts, William shows only a little familiarity with Aristotelian learning, but knowledge of Seneca is evident. Perhaps the most surprising source is a Latin adaptation of Joinville's French *Life of King Louis IX*, a section of which he offers a commentary upon in Version B of the tract.

The unexceptional nature of his source materials aside, the *Mirror of King Edward III* develops the quite unconventional central argument, without precedent in medieval mirror writings, that the king should dispense with purveyance and other exactions by which he maintains himself and his household at the expense of the poor. Part of this case William defends in terms familiar to any advice-book reader. The king is warned that the commission of evil endangers his salvation; and theft, which is taken to be coextensive with purveyance, is precisely the sort of evil about which the king

---

[18] Compare Berges, *Fürstenspiegel*, 343 with Genet, *Four English Political Tracts of the Later Middle Ages*, x–xi.

ought to worry. Indeed, what makes purveyance especially dangerous to the health of the king's soul is that it involves stealing from the poor — whom the ruler should be especially concerned to protect — in order to extend his own holdings, which God has already multiplied many-fold. The king therefore proves himself ungrateful to God and unworthy of salvation. William recurrently invokes the frailty of all human life, including the king's; since no man can predict with certainty when his death will occur, each should remain in a constant state of repentance. Otherwise, should death befall him unexpectedly, damnation and eternal punishment are the prospects for the ruler who has not corrected evils done to his subjects.

If the *Mirror of King Edward III* had confined its attention merely to the moral and religious dimensions of royal misconduct, it would still be a remarkable work, noteworthy for its conscious extension of the king's responsibilities to the peasantry. But William mixes this customary advice with criticisms that reveal a more temporal orientation. He observes that the household supported by the king is more than the royal treasury can bear. Instead of supplementing his already large holdings through forced contracts or confiscation, the monarch should cut back on his retainers and thus his expenditures. William even provides a numerical calculation of the costs arising from the provisioning of a single war-horse.[19] The savings to be obtained by reduced royal expenditures could be used to pay off the king's considerable debts and to support the destitute and disadvantaged. At the same time, more rational management of the kingdom's resources would be achieved by repealing oppressive levies, since one consequence of purveyance is to remove from peasants the stores they require to plant the following year's crops. Hence, they are forced to abandon their lands, and the net agricultural production diminishes. By calling a halt to purveyance, the *Mirror of King Edward III* declares, the sustenance of the king's subjects, and thus the wealth of the realm, is promoted.

On William's account, therefore, the crown is seen to have a direct responsibility for ensuring the temporal welfare of all subjects, even (or especially) those outside of the feudal nexus. Indeed, this at times translates into an assertion of the popular foundations of royal rule. The king acquires no special authority to violate the rights of subjects just because he occupies the royal office. William supports his position with reference to recent

---

[19] On William's appreciation of economic calculation, see Cary J. Nederman, "The Monarch and the Market Place: Economic Policy and Royal Finance in William of Pagula's *Speculum Regis Edward III*," *History of Political Economy* 33 (2001): 51-69.

events, reminding Edward III of his own reliance upon the people in rising to the throne and shaking off the mantle of Isabella and Mortimer. William's message here suggests a principle of reciprocity. The king relies upon the good will of subjects to achieve and maintain his power. In turn, he must demonstrate his worthiness to rule by ensuring that he and his agents respect the economic rights legitimately enjoyed by the people within his jurisdiction. William expresses this reciprocity as a bond of "love" between ruler and people, as a result of which the peace of the realm is assured. Of course, many advice books spoke of how the king must earn the love of his subjects and how they ought to love him. But such love was ordinarily construed to arise from the spiritual and moral rectitude with which the ruler guides his people. By contrast, William consistently equates love with the material welfare of the kingdom. The king merits love and enjoys the fruits of peace when his administration manages its affairs in a manner consonant with the prosperity of subjects.

Concern about the temporal well-being of the realm thus pervades the *Mirror of King Edward III*, reflected in William's recommendations that the king should curb his expenditures (especially on the instruments of warfare), pay his debts, keep closer watch over his officials, and use his surplus income to look after the poor and the infirm. Yet William is by no means sanguine that simple reasoned argumentation alone will suffice to convince the king and his court to lay aside the prerogative of purveyance. Because he subscribes to the conventional conception of the "mirror" books that no one, short of God, can proclaim final judgment on the prince's wrongdoing, he does not propose institutional remedies for public grievances against the crown. Rather, his criticism of the household contains the thinly veiled threat that continued violation of the rights of subjects will result in danger to Edward's peaceful rule of the realm. The ruler who in effect steals from his people actually makes war on his own people. There is no tranquility in a land whose king condones the unjust practices of royal officials, since the ruler himself causes the disturbance. The inference to be drawn is that a king who makes war on his people, by employing force in order to rob them, may rightfully be opposed, just as one may legitimately repulse the force of a thief in order to protect oneself and one's goods.

Sometimes the justification of rebellion provoked by the conduct of the royal curia is shrouded in vague terms, leaving unspecified the precise nature of the danger to royal safety. William's point is simply that retribution for the king's theft from his subjects need not be confined to the afterlife, but may occur in the present world as well. In other sections of the texts, however, the threat to the unjust king is clearly explicated in terms of popular rebellion.[20] The first version of the treatise likens Edward's position within the kingdom to that of a head which cannot lead its own body. William's lesson is that if the monarch's subjects are not safe from their royal master, then they will not hesitate to replace him with someone who will respect their property. This follows directly from the reciprocal nature of the relationship that binds the people to the ruler. Perhaps William believes that the populace acts as the agent of a divine will in fomenting revolt. But regardless of the source of inspiration for insurrection, his primary point is that kings who steal from their subjects will be punished by the people directly for their deeds. In proof of this point, the *Mirror of King Edward III* makes persistent references to the deposed Edward II, a painful reminder that recent precedent exists for the threats of popular revolt made by William.

For all of its apparent dependence upon the conventions of the "mirror" genre, then, the *Mirror of King Edward III* distinguishes itself as a work of explicit political criticism, thereby inverting or dismantling many of the expectations held by readers of advice books. While referring to dangers to the eternal soul of the king, William concerns himself primarily with the bodily, not the spiritual, welfare of subjects. Edward III stands accused not of threatening the salvation of his people, but of damaging their ability to sustain themselves materially. The majesty and dignity of the crown is identified with economic prosperity rather than moral and religious uplift. Nor does William shroud his criticisms in tales about the deeds of the rulers (good and evil) of biblical and classical (or even mythical pre-Conquest) times. Instead, he refers repeatedly to events that he has himself witnessed, or that occurred within recent memory and formed part of Edward III's family legacy. William's readiness to build his case upon contemporary history means that very little reading "between the lines" is required to grasp the force of his arguments. If the king does not reform his administration of the realm, it will not be possible for him to govern his people in peace. Given the public outcry that arose against Edward II when his ministers invoked the prerogative of purveyance, Edward III should hardly be surprised if similar disturbances disrupt his rule. The unrelenting and unambiguous expression of popular discontent, and of the danger posed to the safety of the king, renders the *Mirror of King Edward III* exceptional as a work claiming to "mirror" the prince.

---

[20] An analysis of the theoretical considerations supporting this position is offered by Cary J. Nederman, "Property and Protest: Political Theory and Subjective Rights in Fourteenth-Century England," *Review of Politics* 58 (1996): 323–344.

Admonition to King Edward III, or *Mirror of the King*

[*Mirror of King Edward III,* First Version]

William of Pagula

---

1. Lord, my King, from the time when the republic was committed to you for governing, you ought to have begun thinking of the many ways and means that will enable you to order its affairs better and more discreetly to the honor of God and the utility of the kingdom, and also in order to acquire the love of the people. In order to do this, I will give you a method so that indeed you may do justice to each individual. And justice is to return to each what is his own. For justice never sells another's goods, but gives to each one what is his own; it neglects its own utility so that it might serve the communal equity. And according to this, justice is owed first to God, second, to the fatherland, third, to parents, and fourth, to all, according to the blessed Ambrose.[1] Likewise, the justice of the king is the peace of the people, the defense of the fatherland, the freedom of the masses, the defense of the race, the care of the sick, the joy of all, the solace of paupers, the inheritance of sons, and the hope for one's own blessedness in the future, and the war with the vices, as Cyprian says.[2] Likewise, whoever does justice is also loved by God, whence the Psalmist: "The Lord loves the just," etc. (Psalms 145:8). And justice knows neither father nor mother; it knows truth, it does not respect the person, it imitates God, as Cassian says about this,[3] and He is moved by justice. Likewise, Lord King, if you desire to pursue justice, first fear and love God, so that you might be loved by

---

[1] St. Ambrose, *Expositio Evangelii secundum Lucam*, 5.76 (PL 15. 1657A).
[2] (ps.-) St. Cyprian, *De duodecim abusivis saeculi tractatus*, 9 (PL 4. 957C).
[3] Possibly a reference to Cassian, *Collationes* 17.25 or 23.4.

God; for you will love God if you imitate Him in this, so that you may be useful to all and may injure none, and then all men who follow you will call you a just man; they will venerate and love you. And so that you might be just, not only should you not injure, but also you should prohibit injuring, as Seneca says.[4] And Gregory says in the Register [of his letters]: "The highest good in kings is to cultivate justice, and to serve to each one his rights, and not to allow to be done to the subjects what is of power, but to keep to what is right."[5] But how is it either justice or equity these days to buy something for a lesser price than the seller wishes to sell them for, and contrary to consent, when buying and selling are fixed by the law of peoples? For where there is no consent, there is no selling but extortion, no justice but seizure, no equity but falsehood and iniquity. And therefore, those from whom goods are taken cry to God. What they cry to God, I cannot express. Indeed, God knows and God freely hears those paupers; wherefore, the Psalmist says, "The Lord has heard the desire of the poor, your ear has heard the hope of his heart" (Psalms 9:17); and elsewhere, "On account of the misery of the weak and the moans of the poor, now I will ascend, says the Lord" (Psalms 11:6); and elsewhere, "This pauper has cried out and the Lord has heard him. ... The cries of the pauper are not cast down" (Psalms 33:7, 9:13); and Ecclesiasticus 21:6 proclaims, "A plea from a poor man's mouth goes straight to the ear of God and the cry of the innocent rises to God." Exodus 3:9 says, "The cry of the Israelites, who have been weighted down under burdens by the Egyptians, ascends to God, and God hears their groans." Wherefore it is read in Job 24:12: "The souls of the wounded cry out to God and God does not allow them to go away unavenged."

2. Therefore, so that justice may be done to each one, nothing may be taken for a lesser price than the seller wishes to sell it for. And if it is said that this is a royal prerogative, I also say to you, King, that it is destructive to your kingdom and against the will of God, since it is a great error, even though the law would allow it. Wherefore Wisdom 14:16 says, "The iniquitous custom became stronger, and is observed as law and is preserved by the command of tyrants." But you, King, pay attention. Understand that you would have nothing except what you have from God, and nevertheless, He does not remove from you what you have, but multiplies it greatly every day. You ought to learn from this to give to your subjects, not to

---

[4] Seneca, *Epistle* 81.7–8.
[5] St. Gregory the Great, *Registrum Epistularum*, 9.116 (PL 77 1047A).

take anything away from them. But take care not to provoke God to anger, since He will give all good things into your hand, as is said in Job 1; but if it should be said that all things are of the prince, understand this to mean "to be defended," not "to be snatched away"; Ecclesiasticus at the end (33:31, 32) says, "If he is your slave, treat him like yourself, ... since he is like your self in blood," that is, it is a danger to your soul "if you ill-treat him." Likewise, it is said in 2 Samuel 7:7 that David was made king to maintain the flock of the people of God, not to despoil it. Ezekiel 46:18 says, "The prince may not take from the goods of the people by violence"; and it is said in Proverbs 22:22-23: "Do not do violence to a pauper, since God judges their causes and punishes those who ill-treat paupers." And this sin is completely hateful to God, since He has prohibited not only violence, but also that evil will of seizure. Exodus 20:17 says, "You shall not covet your neighbor's ox, or his donkey, or any other goods that are his." And, King, you ought to know that whatever seizure of this sort is done, it is murder, for he eats and drinks a pauper who devours those things without which the poor cannot live. Ecclesiasticus 34:26 says, "A man murders his neighbor if he robs him of his livelihood"; and Micah 3:2-3 says, "Those who violently take the good of my people eat the flesh of my people and cut away their skin"; and so forth in the same vein. Since they have acted in tribulation and danger, "They cry out to the Lord, and He does not answer them, and He hides His face from them, because they have done their evil deeds" (Micah 3:4). The Lord said this to princes, kings, and each and every man. Therefore, so that your good fame may be maintained unharmed by others, you should wish to be loved both by God and by the people, and also to be honored, and it seems good and useful that those serving you take nothing against the will of the sellers. And then wherever you go in your kingdom, men will come on all sides and will bring all sorts of victuals to you and your servants and all necessities to your gate.

3. For men did thus in the time of the last King Henry [III]. And if this were to occur at present, where once there was sorrow and sadness, now and in future there will be joy and happiness around your coming. Those men from your household who agree that this should occur are your friends, since they wish your honor. Presume that they are from the household of God. However, those who disagree are not your friends, but enemies, and from the devil's household. For such ones keep four or five horses in their households where they ought not to have but one or two, and they seize the goods of others, and they pay almost nothing. Wherefore, according to Augustine: "Since they seize the goods of others, they are seized by the devil, and by holding to their injustice, they are held by the

devil." Again, according to Augustine: "For the goods of others which they thus seize, they sell themselves to the devil. For often there has been a pauper who has sold his own hand or foot on account of his poverty, but even more poor is he who sells his whole self, both body and soul."[6] For in this way do many from your household behave, seizing the goods of others against their will, and knowing that their servants have committed these sorts of extortions and robberies throughout the land, nor do they apply any remedy. Wherefore, one who does this is guilty when he is able to correct the situation and neglects to amend it (LXXXVI, *De facientis*).[7] And to neglect to act when one can deflect perverse people is nothing else than to favor them, nor is one absolved who by secret agreement with his companions clearly fails to prevent a criminal (LXXXIII, *De nemo error*, etc., *Quid enim*, etc. *Consentire*).[8] And the king would seem to agree to the wrongdoers [when] he does not hasten to correct what ought to be corrected. And on account of these sorts of purchases and pillagings that occur through your ministers, indeed servants of the devil, your status is no little defamed. Therefore, so that your reputation should be good and be preserved unharmed by others, it is necessary that you should act to correct without delay all the things mentioned before, since good reputation yields more than infinite wealth. Wherefore Proverbs 22:1 says: "A good name is better than great riches." And you ought to labor toward this, so that you might have a good reputation, since, according to Augustine, two things are necessary to you, that is, just conscience and honorable reputation: conscience for you, reputation on account of your neighbor.[9] For whoever neglects his reputation is cruel. Again, according to Cassiodorus, whoever pursues the advantages of good reputation disregards the increase of wealth; and the faculty of ruling will then be more potent when one strives to acquire a treasure of good reputation, disregarding the utility of monetary goods.[10] And you, King, if you wish to acquire for yourself the love of the people for your work, should demonstrate this. Wherefore Gregory says, "Our love toward our neighbor accomplishes more good work than words, so that the neighbor may be seen to be loved by you through this good work; and when we are not able to do as much as we would wish to do, the secrets of our heart suffice to Almighty God, ... and through love of God,

---

[6] St. Augustine, *Sermo* 77 (PL 39. 1896).
[7] Gratian, *Decretum*, dist. 87, c. 3.
[8] Gratian, *Decretum*, dist. 83, c. 2, 3.
[9] St. Augustine, *Sermo* 47 (PL 38. 301).
[10] Cassiodorus, *Variae*, 6.9 (PL 69. 691D).

love of our neighbor is born, and through love of neighbor, love of God is sent. For whoever neglects to love his neighbor truly does not know how to love God, his Creator."[11]

4. But it is a wonder — and not wonderment in the sense of admiration — how boldly, how fearlessly members of your household skilled in law, and other men claiming the law of God and the reputation of holy men in such matters, appropriate things for themselves and for their own men against the will of the owners, and dispose of these things at their own pleasure, and eat and drink of these things against what it says in Tobit 2:19–21: "Anna, the wife of Tobit, lived by the labor of her hands and brought to [Tobit] the victuals she could obtain; wherefore [one day] accepting a goat, she brought it home, but when her husband heard its bleat, he said: 'I suppose this goat has been stolen. Return it to its owner, since it is not permitted to us to take and eat what is stolen.'" But now there is a cry almost throughout all of this land that the king and his men live from such robbery, if we dare to say. And those from your household are deaf, since they do not wish to hear this, according to the Psalmist, "They have ears and do not hear" (Psalms 134:17); and Psalms 39:13 says, "My iniquities took hold of me, and I am unable to see them"; and Wisdom 2:21 says, "Their malice has blinded them." They have become like dogs that are not healthy enough to bark, for such men, fearing to lose royal grace, become frightened to speak the truth boldly; and such are certain bishops and prelates in these days. According to the voice of truth, no one is now devoted to the keeping of the flock or to pastoral zeal, but instead to the life of brigands, since they flee from the approaching wolf while they hide themselves in silence. For the Lord rebukes them hence through the prophet, saying in Ezekiel 13:5, "You have never ventured against the adversary, you have never bothered to fortify the house of Israel in order to hold fast in battle on the day of God." Indeed, to rise up against the adversary for the defense of the flock with a free voice is to go against the powers of this world. And to stand in battle on the day of the Lord is to resist those who fight unfairly out of love of justice. For to have been afraid to speak the truth to the shepherds, what else is this but to have turned your backs by keeping silent? Without doubt, if they interpose themselves for the sake the flock, they put up a wall to enemies for the sake of the house of Israel. And it follows: "Cry, do not stop, raise your voice like a trumpet" (Isaiah 58:1). O Lord, my King, you have observed the rights and praiseworthy customs of

---

[11] St. Gregory the Great, *Homiliae in Ezechielem*, 2.5 (PL 76. 988B-C).

the kingdom, and especially [protected] the liberties of the churches from all evil and illicit burdens. For doing this, you took a public oath upon your coronation, and all those acting against the articles contained in the Magna Carta are by that fact excommunicated, which sentence has been confirmed many times by the apostolic see. Therefore, by what foolishness and instigation of the devil do your servants, as they say, and precursors of the devil, take away, consume or injuriously diminish anything from the homes, manors, farms, or other places of bishops, prelates, or of other ecclesiastical persons against their will? For such ones are by this fact excommunicated, and in consequence they are members of the devil, nor may they be absolved until they make satisfactory restitution for the injuries. In the constitution of Lambeth, [Archbishop] Pecham [...][12] in the same times [...][13] they seized horses and carts, and they made the servants of Christ work day and night in your service. Yet they paid them nothing for their service and labor, when they ought to give for a two-horse cart ten denarii a day and for a three-horse cart fourteen denarii a day, as is set forth in the Magna Carta;[14] and since they did not pay in the manner stated in the Magna Carta, they were excommunicated. As is said by James at the end (5:4), "Behold the wages of workers, ... who were cheated by you, they cry out to God and their cries enter the ears of the Lord."

5. Behold, my King, what evil things follow from this robbery. The first evil is the magnitude of this sin, which magnitude first appears through this: that such sin destroys in humanity the foundation of justice and goodness, concerning which foundation Wisdom (12:16) says: the first oath of justice is not to injure anyone. [The primary reason for this is] that it might serve the common utility. Second, by this, [it may be shown] that robbers are worse than the devil. Firstly, regarding the latter, the devil ravages and tortures those who do evil, but robbers ravage those who back away from evil, as is said in Isaiah 59:15: "Whoever departs from evil makes himself prey." And Proverbs 29:10 says, "Bloodthirsty men hate those who are blameless." Wherefore the devil is able to justify himself in comparison to the robbers, for he is able to say that they alone are afflicted who hate you, but the robbers also [hate] those who love you. Third, regarding this, the devil defers to the angel of God deputed to a person for his protection, so that bodily violence should not be inflicted on them; robbers have not done this, since,

---

[12] Lacuna in text.
[13] Lacuna in text.
[14] Magna Carta, sec. 30 (and reissues).

against the will of God, they remove their goods. Fourth, regarding this, the devil tortures men in hell which is "the place of torment" (Luke 16:28). But robbers torture people in this world, whereas people ought to be free to act for themselves and for theirs, according to their wills. Wherefore we can understand that robbers are rightly to be called angels of the devil: "Depart from me, your cursed, into the eternal fire prepared for the devil and his angels" (Matthew 25:41).

6. For there are those sent to do in this world what the devil does in Hell. Fifth, concerning this, they are worse than any beasts, for one robber devours an entire land, just like an evil prince; and a wolf, occasionally, does not devour one man in a single year. Wherefore the prince is to be compared to a lion and a bear, according to Proverbs 28:15: "Like a roaring lion or a hungry bear is a wicked ruler over a poor people." Again, a robber is called a murderer, since it is said in Ecclesiasticus 34:26–27, "A man murders his neighbor if he deprives him of his livelihood." The second evil is the great rudeness that constitutes robbery, for to give is very noble; if, therefore, giving makes a man noble, taking away makes him rude. The third evil is the great stain this sort of sin leaves on [the robber], because scarcely anyone returns things that have been stolen, and a sin is not forgiven unless what was taken is restored, as is said (XIV, q. vi, *Si res aliena*).[15] The fourth evil is the great spiritual damnation which robbers incur while they seize any earthly thing. Wherefore Augustine says: "Wealth in a chest is harm (to the conscience) ... one takes clothing and loses the faith, one acquires wealth and spurns justice."[16] The fifth evil is the little use which robbers have for their seizure. For as far as the body is concerned, it is of little worth since it quickly passes away, as Ecclesiasticus 40:13 says, "The wealth of the impious will dry up like a torrent." But as far as the spirit is concerned, it matters not at all, because thereafter they can give neither alms nor oblations, as is said in Ecclesiasticus 34:24, "Offering a sacrifice from the property of the poor is as bad as slaughtering a son before his father's very eyes." (Also XIV, q. v. c. i, ii and iii, and likewise through the whole section.)[17] The sixth evil is the vengeance that God is ready to take on robbers. And there are four proofs through which it can be shown that God greatly punishes robbers.

7. The first proof is that He strictly judges those who do not distribute

---

[15] Gratian, *Decretum*, 15, q. 6, c. 1.
[16] Pseudo-Augustine, *Sermo* 220 (PL 39. 2152).
[17] Gratian, *Decretum*, 14, q. 5, c. 1, 2, 3.

their own things to paupers. For if He damns those who do not give their own goods to paupers, what would He do about those who take the things of paupers away from them? Wherefore the Gloss on Luke[18] says: "A rich man is not blamed because he robs others, but because he does not distribute his own things." What, therefore, is to be said about one who seizes the property of others? Matthew 25:41 declares, "And the King will say to those at his left hand, 'Depart from me, you cursed ones, into the eternal fire. For I was hungry and you gave me no food,'" etc. But then he is able to say to robbers: "I was hungry and you took from me what I ought to eat." The second proof is the simple curse of widows and orphans whom they have despoiled, as Ecclesiasticus 35:17-19 says, "The Lord does not ignore the orphan's supplication nor the widow's as she pours out her story with groans. Do the widow's tears not run down her cheeks as she cries to God and the Lord listens?" And it follows, "He exacts vengeance" (Ecclesiasticus 35:23), concerning evildoers of this sort, and in the next chapter. What, therefore, is gained if a robber prays, when a pauper cries out to God against him about seizure and injury and the Lord hears his voice? There is no doubt that He would hear the prayer of the injured. The third proof is the love of the Heavenly Judge, which He has for the paupers who are despoiled, concerning which it is said in Matthew 25:40, "As you did it to one of the least of these my brethren," etc. For on account of them, He came into the world. "On account of the wretchedness of the poor and the groans of paupers, I will now rise up, said the Lord" (Psalms 11:6). The fourth proof of this is that the poor whom they have despoiled will be their judges. As Job 36:6 says: "He gives judgment to the poor"; and Wisdom 5:1-9 says, "On that day the righteous, full of confidence, will stand before those who oppressed them and took away their labors. They will be amazed to see them unexpectedly safe and will tremble with terrible fear. Then they will regret what they did, and, groaning in anguish, they will say to one another:" — but too late — "These are the ones we made fun of. We thought they were a joke. We thought they were the crazy ones to live the way they did, and when they died, we did not honor them. And now, here they are, God's own children, with a place of their own among God's own people. We were the ones who wandered off the right road. We never lived in the light of righteousness; the sun of intelligence did not rise on us. All our lives we wandered across unmarked deserts, instead of following the road which the Lord wanted us to travel. And this lawlessness led us to

---

[18] Possibly that of Gregory the Great.

ruin. We were so proud of ourselves. We bragged how rich we were. And now, what good has it done us? All those things are gone now; they have disappeared like a moment's shadow." Again, over and above the aforementioned evils, there is a fourfold punishment for robbers in the present world.

8. The first is poverty, says Proverbs 11:24: "Some people spend their money freely and still grow richer; others are take what is not theirs and yet grow poorer." The reason for their poverty is because, just as they take away, thus it is taken away from them. According to Isaiah 33:1, "Woe to you, destroyer, you will be destroyed." And Habakkuk 2:6, 8 says, "Woe to him who heaps up what is not his own ... Because you have plundered many nations, all the remnants of the people shall plunder you." The second punishment is a hastening of death, says Psalms 54:24: "Man of blood and trickery," etc.; and Proverbs 4:19: "The way of the wicked is as dark as night; they cannot tell where and when they are running"; and Proverbs 5:23, "For lack of discipline, he dies; and he is lost through his own excessive folly." The third punishment is that they frequently die by the sword, and their souls are seized by demons, and sometimes their bodies are not buried, as is said in Jeremiah 19 and 20. Whoever steals visibly, suddenly on the exit of the soul from the body is invisibly seized by the devil. The fourth punishment is that their sons will frequently be beggars and die by the sword. According to Nahum 2:12-13: "The lion filled his caves with spoil for his cubs and his dens with his prey." And it follows: "Behold it is I, the Lord of Hosts, who speaks to you. I mean to send your chariots (*sic*) up in smoke, the sword shall devour your lion cubs; I will wipe the earth clean of your plunder, the voice of your envoys shall be heard no more." If, therefore, so many evil things and so many punishments happen to robbers, what punishments do they deserve who are the authors and promoters of those robbers? He who is ignorant of nothing knows. For the one providing the authority and defense to a criminal sins more greatly than the person doing the act, and he is more worthy of punishment (XXIV, q. iii, *Qui aliorum*).[19]

9. O Lord, my King, behold the kind of deception perpetrated by your court. In these days, a proclamation was made publicly in the marketplace by a certain man of the court that no one should seize any goods from others unless he paid for them and he should be held under heavy penalty [if he did not]. And nevertheless, men of your court — not men, precursors

---

[19] Gratian, *Decretum*, 24, q. 3, c. 32.

of the Antichrist, that is, against Christ — and various servants of your court, that is, servants of the devil and completely bound to him because they are his slaves (wherefore John 8:34 says, "One who commits sin is a slave of sin" and a slave of the devil), seize many goods by violence from the owners of those goods, namely, they seize bread, beer, fowls, cocks, beans, oats and many other things, for which practically nothing is paid. And because of extortions of this kind, many poor people will not have what they need to sow their fields. And behold the malice of these servants. It has been ordered or ordained both tacitly and expressly among those same servants, who have been deputed to one village, that one evildoer (and the worst of them) should carry out robberies of oats, bread, beer, fowls, and cocks; and from these they make their feasts in common and rejoice, and the people are sad. But, certainly, joyful feasts of this kind are changed to sorrowful mourning and wailing, according to Amos 8:10: "I shall turn your feasts into funerals, all your singing into lamentation"; and in Luke 6:25 it says: "Alas, for you who have your fill now; you shall go hungry. Alas for you who laugh now; for you shall mourn and weep." But if a complaint be made in your court concerning this sort of servant, that servant who has taken the aforesaid goods will absent himself and then he will not be found, and the other servants will excuse themselves completely, since all of them have been taking a hand in robberies of this kind. But if only it were ordered in your court that, if one man is thus guilty, all and sundry should be held responsible, since that guilty man does robberies of this kind by the authority and with the defense of the others. Those consenting and acting should be punished with equal penalties; and in the same way their masters should be punished, for he takes on the guilt of the perpetrator who neglects to fix what he can correct; and not only those who act, but those who consent, are judged to be participants, as are those who by secret agreement with their companions neglect to stop this clear crime (LXXXVI, *De facientis*).[20]

10. But it is commonly said that masters do not wish to have servants other than such men, because they know that they live well from robbery, because it is well known throughout the household that the lord is of such a kind; for as is the lord, so is the household. These things are known publicly throughout the land. And unless these aforesaid things are amended quickly, it must be feared for your great damnation, or at least for the damnation of those who allow these things to happen and do not bring any

---

[20] Gratian, *Decretum*, dist. 87, c. 1.

remedy; concerning this damnation, it is said in Ecclesiasticus 10:8, "Kingdoms pass from people to people on account of injuries, injustices, contumacy and diverse harms." And this is clear from Saul 1, 1 Samuel 15 and afterward from Jeroboam 3, 1 Samuel 12, and from many other texts, and also from many great lords formerly governing the kingdom in England. Think, think, and think deeply about the foregoing, and think about the many evils that happened to Eli on that account, because he knew that his sons had committed great evil and he did not correct them, just as it is read in 1 Samuel 3 and 4. Thus, it is feared for you that many evils may happen to you and your kingdom, unless you take steps to amend the aforesaid. And if those men of your household persevere in their malice, and you do not correct them, since you have the power, you and they will perish, as it is said in 1 Samuel 12, in the last chapter [25], where it is said that "if you do things wickedly, you and your king will equally be swept away." And I warn you, King, and all of your household, who consent to robberies of this kind, tacitly or expressly, that when tribulation and anguish come upon you, you will cry to the Lord and He will not hear you. According to Isaiah 1:15, "When you extend your hands to me, I will turn away my eyes from you; and even though you make many prayers, I will not listen to you; your hands are full of blood"; and Proverbs 1:24, 27–30 says: "I have called, and you have refused"; and there follows: "When distress and anguish come upon you, ... then you will cry to God, and He will not hear you; ... because you hated the discipline of God, and did not choose the fear of the Lord, not did you acquiesce in good counsel."

11. O Lord, my King, you must know that your dignity consists in the multitude of the people and your ignominy in the poverty of the masses, as is said in Proverbs 14:28. But those of your household, who seize some goods against the will of the owners, and those consenting to them, in truth are not of the household, although they seem, and are said, to be of your household. This I prove thus. It is said that the faith and the strength of the king are in the multitude of the people. But also the strength of faith is in truth and fear of the Lord, as is said in Proverbs 14:26. Therefore, those seizing the goods of others against their will do not have fear of the Lord, as has been noted above, because "the fear of the Lord expels sins," as is said in Ecclesiasticus 1:27. Therefore, it remains that because they are not of your household, nor of your people, on account of robberies and injustices of this kind, it is as if the whole people sorrows against your coming, wherever you may travel in your kingdom. The people are not of one mind with you, although they seem to be of one body with you, and indeed, if they had another head, they would rise against you, just as they did against

your father, and then, in truth, you will not have a multitude of people with you. But if you have as many as thirty or forty good men of your household with you, and not such men as those who do robberies of this kind, then you will have the whole land with you, and you will hold the multitude of the people in love, and in no way otherwise. And you, King, look diligently, and understand what happened to King Nebuchadnezzar and his son Belshazzar (Daniel 3 and 5).

12. O Lord, my King, hear now the kind of iniquity and falsehood that exists in these days through the servants of your court. If they find oats anywhere, they say that they wish to pay for one bushel of oats only three pennies, even if it is worth five pennies; and if they do not find oats, but barley, they seize from the unwilling owner one bushel of barley for three pennies, even if it is worth nine pennies. If, however, they do not find barley, but beans, they seize one bushel of beans for three pennies, even if one bushel is worth twelve pennies. What justice is this? It is not justice, but robbery, as was noted above. O Lord, my King, in certain deeds you are similar to a leader of robbers, who has under himself many thieves and robbers: one who wishes to make his crossing safely through a place where there are many robbers gives something to the leader of the robbers or to one of his men, so that he may be able to have a safe passage through that dangerous place, and then he [the leader] gives signs and letters, so that none of his men will seize anything from that person. Thus it is, Lord King, in those parts of your lands which you traverse, because if a man wishes to keep his possessions safe, it is necessary that he obtain friends for himself in your court through his wealth, so that he may obtain from you a sort of letter. Yet the letter merely restates the common law, because by the common law no one should seize another person's goods if the owner is unwilling, without just cause. And even if the king orders anyone to seize the goods of another man unjustly, one must not obey the lord in this case; and whoever in this case does not obey the king acquires a great reward for himself, etc. (c. *Imperium*).[21] And you, King, understand what Augustine said about the words of the Lord: Behold, you, King, "recollect first things";[22] say, I ask, what you have brought [into the world], or if you blush to speak, hear the Apostle: "For, I say, we brought nothing into this world" (1 Timothy 6:7). Certainly, as was the case when we were born, but still less can we take anything away. Because of this, you, King, have

---

[21] Gratian, *Decretum*, 12, q. 2, c. 50.
[22] St. Augustine, *Sermo* 61, c. 8 (PL 38. 412).

brought nothing, and you will take away nothing; why do you inflame yourself against the poor? Certainly, when in a certain case old tombs are broken open, the bones of the rich are not distinguishable from the bones of the poor. And Ambrose said: we human beings are born naked, we die naked, there is no distinction among the bodies of the dead unless perhaps the bodies of the rich stink more because they are distended with luxuries.

13. O Lord, my King, listen and diligently attend to what pertains to a good king, as is said in XXVI, the last chapter: The duty of a good king is to restore worn out and broken down churches and to build new ones, and to honor and defend the priests of God.[23] But, however, in these days the matter is turned into its opposite. For now, those from your household arise against the servants of Christ; the religious and the priests, who serve the patrimony of Jesus Christ, are despoiled and subjects are destroyed, whether paupers, religious, or others, being afflicted miserably and wretchedly, so that your servants fill their illicit appetites and extraordinary pleasures through the sorrows of others. And you, Lord King, know and understand well that you protract your stay in the houses of religious, sometimes for one day, sometimes for many, and you make many and infinite payments from the goods of the religious, whether through gifts or in other ways. And thus, what ought to be the goods of the paupers and of the churches, you consume, and this is not to build and restore churches, but to destroy and annihilate them. And I say to you, King, that however many the presents and gifts from those religious, and however great the payments they made to you and yours, they gave these as if unwilling, and truly they were made unwillingly, since they know, or they ought to know, that the goods of churches and of the religious are the goods of the paupers, and not of the rich (XVI, q. 1, *Quoniam quicquid*).[24] And I say this to you, that whatever you receive from them is nothing but a kind of extortion, for they give to you and to yours so that they may save their other goods unharmed, just as if a robber enters my home and I were to give him half of my goods so that I might be able to retain the other half securely; and nevertheless through the robber, through the violence, therefore, what took place was robbery, etc.

14. O Lord, my King, because now God's blessing has miraculously freed you from the custody of these who have permitted such robbery, and who refuse to give any sort of remedy, nevertheless they still perpetuate and

---

[23] Gratian, *Decretum*, dist. 96, c.16.
[24] Gratian, *Decretum*, 16, q. 1, c. 67.

commit all the aforementioned evils, with this one exception, that those from your court do not commonly seize the goods of the church, as they were previously accustomed to do. But hear, Lord, if you please, the evils that are done most recently: some come from your household to market with one commission, not on behalf of God, but of the devil, and they seize the sheep and oxen, the cows and the fattened pigs, that they are able to find, against the will of the owners and they pay nothing, on account of which all those who come to the markets are disturbed and upset, and so is the whole country round about. See, therefore, Lord, my King, in what danger you are on account of such deeds. A poor man comes to the market with one ox at a price of one mark and he has to pay one mark on a certain day or lose his own land. His ox is seized by your ministers and nothing is paid to him, because of which he loses his land, because he does not pay his debt on the day appointed. Some men, then, whose sheep and oxen are taken do not pay their debts to their creditors on the appointed day, on account of which they incur perjury, excommunication, and a reputation as dishonest people, and many evils happen on account of these seizures. Indeed, you are held in the presence of God for all these losses, about the occurrence of which you certainly know well, because those making these extortions have your letters for doing this. Take note, Lord King, of the judgment given against King David for a similar deed, as is said in 2 Samuel 12:1-7: "And the Lord sent the Prophet Nathan to David: He came to him and said to him:" Respond to my judgment. " 'There were two men in a certain city, the one rich, and the other poor. The rich man had very many flocks and herds, but the poor man had nothing but one little ewe lamb. ... The rich man took the poor man's lamb.' Then David's anger was greatly kindled against the rich man, and he said to Nathan, 'The rich man who has done this deserves to die, and he shall restore the lamb four-fold.' And Nathan said to David: 'You are that man.' " Although therefore, you, Lord King, have sheep and oxen, cocks and hens, almost to an infinite number, you take sheep and oxen not only from one person, but from many, and given that a poor woman has nothing except one hen, still you take it away, at least through your servants. See, therefore, in what manner you will reply to the Lord, your God. Yet if in the markets one who is rich has fat sheep and oxen, and shows letters of your protection, he himself can in some way free his own sheep and oxen.

15. O Lord King, blush and tremble at how they ask of you those letters of protection. It is nothing else than to say, in effect: "Unless, Lord King, not by reigning, but by robbing, you concede to me your letters, that is, of protection, lest someone from your household seize my goods against

my will," although anyone in the world ought to have his [property] by common law. Again, those from your household have seized from the forest of Windsor, and places of the area, the persons, wagons, and horses of paupers, and they compelled them to return to their own homes, through ten miles and back, to carry firewood, not only for three or four days, but for many, and they promised to pay them for the labor, but they paid nothing. And on account of this diabolical deed, the lands of the paupers were not cultivated, not planted, nor did the paupers have any goods by which they were able to sustain burdens of this sort. And therefore, they cry out to God, and their cry ascends to God, just as the cry of the sons of Israel whom the Egyptians burdened with labor ascended to God, as is said in Exodus 2, at the end of the chapter; such hardship, it is said, had not occurred even in the time of your father.

16. O Lord, my King, you ought to know that there are four sins which cry out to God from the earth, such as homicide. In Genesis 4:10-11, the Lord said to Cain: "Cursed are you on the earth. The voice of your brother Abel's blood is crying to me from the ground"; and oppression of the innocent, as it says in Exodus 2:23, "The cry of the Israelites, who have been weighted down under burdens by the Egyptians, ascends to God." Again, defrauding workers of their wages, as is said at the end of James (5:4), "Behold the wages of workers, who were cheated by you, . . . they cry out and their cries enter the ears of the Lord." Again, concerning the sin against nature, Genesis 18:20 states, "The outcry before me against Sodom and Gomorrah is great." And I say to you, King, that all the aforementioned sins cry to God against you. The first is murder, as Ecclesiasticus 34:25-26 says: "A meager diet is the very life of the poor; he who defrauds them is a man of blood; and he who offers a sacrifice from the property of the poor is like one who kills his neighbor." But you through your ministers, through all sorts of commissions undertaken by them, take away from your subjects bread, beer, oats, hay, and innumerable other things, on account of which many die. The second sin is oppression of the innocent, and the third is holding back the pay of the workers. There is sufficient evidence in the accusations brought above, and the whole people cry out about them. The fourth sin is against nature, for in a certain manner it is against nature that brother arise against brother, as Matthew 23:9 says: "You have one Father, who is in heaven." And Augustine states: "We are the sons of God."[25] And 1 John 3:1 says, "See what love our Father has given us that we should be,

---

[25] St. Augustine, *Sermo* 107, c. 2 (PL 38. 628 [quoting Psalms 81:6]).

and should be called, His children." Again, the duty of the king is to subdue the evil and to elevate the good, so that the good may live quietly among the evil, and it is said in 2 Samuel 7 that David was made king to feed the flock of the people of God, not to despoil it. But you, by your commissions, oppress the good and elevate and defend the evil, and thus you act against the natural duty of the king, for the king is said to be one who rules the people wisely, the republic usefully, and himself blamelessly. Any king ought to rule the people wisely, as Ecclesiasticus 10:1, 3 says: "The wise judge judges his people." And it is said in the same place, "A foolish king will perish through his people." Second, he ought to rule the republic usefully: he rules usefully when he attends not to his own, but to the common, utility. It is read of the Romans that their rulers, when they fought to acquire glory and to pursue liberty and to preserve the republic, always conquered their adversaries. But when they turned to robbery and greed, then they were always conquered. Third, the king ought to rule himself blamelessly, so that he might be immune from all vices which he blames in others, lest it be said of him as in Romans 2:1: "In passing judgment on another, you condemn yourself." Wherefore Isidore in Book 3, concerning the highest good, says that he is called king from rightly acting, and therefore from doing rightly the name of king is held, but by sinning it is lost.[26] Rightly, therefore, are they called kings who know how to arrange things by ruling both themselves and their subjects well.

17. O Lord, my King, just as those of your household do many evils, so it has just recently happened again that those who are from the household of your son do similar things in the area of Windsor. They destroy crops and pastures with their herds and they pay nothing, and they do many evil things in these days. And they drive out horses, sheep, and oxen, and other animals of the poor from their homes, and they install your animals and the animals of your son there. They seize oats, hay, and beans, and sheaves, the owners of these things being unwilling [to surrender them], and they pay a small amount of money to some men and nothing to others, and they do many other evil things. And they even steal from widows, orphans, and poor little women, and also from others, the chickens from which they have their sustenance, and they promise to pay one penny per chicken, although each is worth two pennies, and also they even make them swear how many chickens they have, so that they might choose from among them the ones they wish to take away. These things are notorious in the

---

[26] Isidore of Seville, *Sententiae*, 3.48.7.

area around Windsor. And so far I haven't even treated the evils that occur in secret!

18. And for you, Lord King, unless you ordain otherwise, the loss of your kingdom must be feared. According to Ecclesiasticus 10:8, "Kingdoms are transferred from people to people, on account of injustices, injuries, contumacies, and diverse harms." And I promise to you, Lord King, as long as such things happen by your authority and with your defense, that unless you amend the aforesaid things reasonably, you will be punished eternally and your son also. Even though up to now he may be innocent, if it happens that he reigns after you he will be punished at least temporally, or perhaps beforehand, unless the things that have happened are amended quickly. For Augustine says, "If he is sent into the fire who has not given his own goods to the poor, where do you think he should be sent who invades and seizes what is not his own? If he who has not clothed the naked is to burn with the devil, where do you think he who has plundered should find safety? With justice far away, what are kingdoms except great robberies? Thus a certain man who had been apprehended replied to Alexander the Great when he was asked by him why he had robbed on the sea; and this man replied to him: 'You rob throughout the world. But because I do it with one ship or two, I am called a robber, but you do it everywhere, therefore you are called a great emperor.' "[27]

19. And a son is punished for the sins of the father, according to 1 Kings 21:28-29: "And the word of the Lord came, saying: 'Have you seen how Ahab has humbled himself before me? Because, therefore, he has humbled himself before me, I will not bring the evil in his days, but in his son's days I will bring the evil upon his house.' " Nor does ignorance excuse him from the sin of the father, most of all since utility is taken away from him who is ignorant; likewise, if anyone acquires riches from robbery or plunder with his son remaining ignorant, ignorance does not excuse the son, unless after the death of the father he is forced to return things acquired evilly. Likewise, by the sin of Ahaz, the Israelites were surrendered into the hands of enemies; and by the sin of the sons of Eli the people were given into the hands of the Philistines. Likewise, when Gehazi sinned his leprosy was transmitted to this descendents. Likewise, by the sins of Ahab, his descendants lost the throne of the kingdom, etc. And children are punished bodily for the sins of parents, and a son sometimes dies more quickly because of the sin of his father; in 2 Kings 12:13-15, it is said that David sinned, but he

---

[27] St. Augustine, *Sermo 77*, (PL, 39. 1896).

repented, saying, "I have sinned against the Lord." And therefore the Lord said through the prophet Nathan to him, "You shall not die, but the child who is born to you shall die ... And the Lord struck his child, and it died." (Also see I, q. 4, Extra, *De poenis*, c. *In quibusdem et de usura e. usurarum*.)[28]

20. O Lord, my King, now there is a new burden introduced by those who are of your household. A certain scout came to get provisions in a certain rural village, for the twenty or thirty horses and the same number of servants who were of your household, and he brought with him one signed paper with an unknown seal, at least unknown to those of that parish, nor was it said in that letter how many servants and horses they had to provision. The men of the parish, intimidated because they did not dare to resist, admitted them, and went to great expenses for them, as happened in the time of your father; and the men of the parish, on account of the burdens laid on them, came together with that scout and his allies, so that [the servants] would leave and would give to them half a mark or five solidi or forty pennies. But in no way did they remit to them all the expenses that they had incurred. On the following day, or the second day, another scout arrived, with a certain letter, signed like the first, which made provision for servants and horses which were of the household of the Lady Queen, or the sister of the Lord King. These servants with their horses were worse than the first group. The men of the parish made an agreement with them, for a certain sum of money, so that they would leave. Having handed over the money, some of them left and some of them nevertheless remained, and they seized oats, hay, and other things and paid nothing; and they did this since, being robbers, they did not act according to the agreement. Certainly, as is said, it sometimes happens that some such man has a commission to one village for servants and horses, another man to another village, a third man has a commission to a third village, and so on. And since, as usually happens, those servants are malicious and receive practically nothing from their own masters, and they wish to make a handsome profit, either legally or illegally, they all gather together and come first to one village and show one commission and by virtue of that commission they seize oats, beans, food and drink, and many other goods through violence, through fear, through some such passion, because the simple people of one rural village do not dare to resist them because of the multitude of these men; and after they do this in one village, they leave and come to another village, and they show that commission, and they do similar things there, and so on.

---

[28] *Decretales, De poenis, In quibusdam* (V, 37); *De Usuris, De usurarum*, in VI (V, 5).

21. Finally, someone else came with a commission to provide stabling, hay, oats, and other things of this sort, and behold what injury he did to the inhabitants of the village: he seized ten or twelve carts, and for each cart he said he would be willing to pay six pennies for the stable and cart, and this would be little enough for such a cart. Nevertheless, he paid nothing nor did he distinguish the good stable from the bad one, since he said that he was willing to pay an equal price for the bad stable just as for the good one, and this is not justice. Likewise with the hay. However, when he seized twenty quarters of oats, he gave a *tallia* for seventeen quarters, and then the people of the parish carried [the oats] four or five miles, and indeed, they gained nothing for their labor. What justice or equity is this? According to Isaiah 59:14-15, "Justice is far away, for truth has fallen in the public square, and equity cannot enter. And truth has been forgotten." Such commissions were either not made in the time of your father, or for only a brief time.

22. But it is said by some people that certain men come with false commissions, but because country folk are afraid and do not dare to incur your anger, they obey any commissions, and therefore, because of a great many commissions of this kind they lose stables, hay, and oats, and many other goods these days. And from this, there is a great clamor among the people in the area of Windsor where you have your origin, although because of your origin you should spare these people more than others who live elsewhere, because it ought to be better [there] by reason of your origin than in other places (C. *prescripcio*).[29]

23. O Lord, my King, now hear another new charge. In the time of your father, when your father remained in one place away from his estate, that is, more than twelve miles, those of his household did not burden people. But today those men of your household come beyond such boundaries, and thus the people are more burdened in many ways through you and your men than the burden that occurred in the time of your father. Wherefore you are able to say to the people what King Jeroboam said in 1 Kings 12:14, "My father made your yoke heavy, but I will add to your yoke; my father chastised you with whips, but I will chastise you with scorpions."

24. But see there what happened to that king. For when servants come to a rural village with the horses of their lords, the further they are from your court the more likely they are to perpetrate evils. And if four servants with four horses come to one rural village, and remain there for four or five

---

[29] *Decretales, De praescriptionibus* (II, 26).

days, they themselves acquire for their horses, in the said village from various people, eight or ten quarters of oats, some through gifts, some through violence, some on account of fear. They do not tell their lords that they break down doors for hay and oats; and what is worse, after they feed the horses of their lords, they sell some of the oats which fetches more money. And thus likewise, it is no wonder that they deceive their own lords, because commonly lords are unwilling to keep certain servants unless they know how to live from plunder. And afterwards the servants leave with the horses, nor do they wish to pay anything.

25. Scarcely is there one man in the whole of your court who wishes to pay what is just for his servants and horses. And behold an example of how a few men follow a better path. One servant of your court came with one horse of his lord to a rural village; he chose for himself the best house of the whole village, and he sought stabling for his horse. Stabling was freely given to him which was worth, in London, four or six pennies, and in that village was worth less than one penny. Similarly, hay was freely given to him for one day which was easily worth two pennies in the same village, as was half a bushel of oats at a price of two pennies. The servant wished to have a fire for himself (and for his horse) at a price of one or two pennies; he himself wished to have better food and drink, perhaps a chicken. And so the owner of the house, out of further custom and obligation, spent by reason of his stay an estimated eight or ten pennies in food and drink. On the next day, when [the servant] had to leave he paid nothing for stabling, nor for his bed, nor for the fire; for the hay, he paid only one penny; for the oats, one penny; for food and drink, one penny and a half, because he received no more from his own master. And so, having made the calculation, he did not pay half of his own expenses.

26. But if all the servants of your court do thus, then it would be somewhat good, because it is better to have something than nothing. The rest of the servants of your court are not so courteous. No wonder that I have given the example of a servant who is better and more honest. And thus perhaps it can be said of the men of your court what is said in Genesis 18 and 19, that, an enquiry having been made in five cities for just men, not one could be found, except one man, namely, Lot. And therefore, it is of the utmost necessity that your household be ordered otherwise, lest the ruin of you and your court be feared, etc., as is said in the aforesaid chapters of Genesis 18 and 19. O Lord, my King, to make so many commissions is nothing other than to maintain the thieves and robbers of your court in their own errors and to subdue widows and poor people maintaining households, as is said in the foregoing. For it pertains to the duty of a king to

contain theft, to oppress the evil, and to elevate the good, so that evils are thereby corrected and the good live quietly among the evil (XXIII, q. 5, *Non frustra* and c. *regum*).[30]

27. In order to do this, I will give you an easy method without which you will not be numbered among the saved: that without delay you will order, and then have proclaimed, that no one of your household nor anyone else should seize anything from the goods of anyone against his will. If anyone does this, he will be hanged. It is better that someone should be hanged for a crime than that he should be sunk into Hell. For God does not judge the same thing a second time (XIII, in the last chapter; XIII, q. 6, *Si res aliena*).[31] And sin is not forgiven unless what has been taken is restored; this is one of the precepts of God, as is stated in Exodus 20:17: "Do not covet your neighbor's ox or donkey or any other goods that are your neighbor's." And it is said in X, c. 1 and 2: "The law of emperors is not above the law of God, but below, and it is not fitting for emperors, nor for anyone else, to presume against the mandates of God."[32]

28. For example, it is said in Exodus 22:5, "When a man causes a field or vineyard to be grazed over, or lets his beast run loose and it feeds in a field, he shall make restitution for the loss out of the best in his own field or vineyard." Therefore, you, King, should be held to be accountable for the damage done by your herds in the fields and pastures of others. Likewise, do not harm the widow and the orphan and the poor, because if you do, they will cry out to God and He will hear them. Therefore, however many widows and orphans there are these days crying out against you to God, etc. (XIII, *Que contra mores*, at the end of the chapter).[33]

29. Are not you, King, required to obey the precepts of God as much as any peasant? Certainly, and much more so, in that you have received much more from God, according to Genesis 39:8. You should think about all the goods you have received from God. Therefore, God forbid that you do anything against His will, just as Joseph did when he recalled to memory the benefits conferred on him by his Lord, and therefore wished to do nothing prejudicial to Him. Wherefore it is said of King Saul in 1 Samuel 15:26, "You have rejected the word of the Lord, and Lord has rejected you as king."

30. For example, it is said in Luke 10:27, "You shall love the Lord your God with all your heart, ... and you shall love your neighbor as yourself."

---

[30] Gratian, *Decretum*, 23, q. 5, c. 18.
[31] Gratian, *Decretum*, 14, q. 6, c. 1.
[32] Gratian, *Decretum*, dist. 10, c.1, 2.
[33] Gratian, *Decretum*, dist. 7, c. 2.

But you do not love your neighbor, on account of the fact that you seize a person's possessions against his will, nor do you love God. According to 1 John 4:20, "If anyone says, 'I love God,' and he hates his brother, he is a liar; for whoever does not love his brother, whom he has seen, how can he love God, whom he has not seen?" And it is said in 1 John 3:10, "In this it may be seen who are the children of God, and who are the children of the devil; whoever is not just is not of God, and whoever does not love his brother does not love God." Again, take note, King, of what is said in Matthew 5:23-24: "If you are offering your gift at the altar, and there remember that your brother has something against you, leave your gift there before the altar and go; first be reconciled with your brother, and then come and offer your gift."

31. But what sort of men are these today in this land who bear a grudge against you before the highest God? Certainly, nearly an infinite number of men from whom their goods have been robbed against their will. And therefore, go first to reconcile yourself to your brothers, and then offer an acceptable gift to God, and not beforehand. For by what audacity, what temerity, are the bishops and other prelates able to approach the altar for preparing that holy sacrament, that is, the body of Christ, who through their own ministers have joined in such things or have permitted them to be done and not stopped them? For one who permits anything to take place that he is able to impede, even though he has not done it himself, has virtually done the act himself if he allows it (Extra, VI, title *De regulis juris regula*).[34] Indeed, such people can neither prepare nor consume that holy sacrament, that is, the body of Christ, except to their own damnation. According to I Corinthians 11:29, "For whoever eats and drinks the body of Christ and His blood unworthily eats and drinks judgment upon himself." It is certain that the authority of the king cannot excuse them (II, d. *Timorem*; IX, d. *Quicumque* and c. *Imperium*).[35]

32. For in these things that are against the precept of God, one must not obey, but rather resist, the king, and he who does this obtains reward for himself. But it is against the precept of God to seize anything against the will of the seller, as treated above. And therefore, your prelates, priests, counts, barons, soldiers and whomever else you similarly commission, or whom you knowingly permit to do this sort of thing, should restore to the seller in any way they can the full value of the things you have rashly taken

---

[34] *Decretales, De regulis juris*, in VI (R.72).
[35] Gratian, *Decretum*, dist. 2, c. 25; 12, q. 2, c. 4; dist. 10, c. 5.

from others through your ministers against the will of the sellers. And then, having done penance, you will be able to approach the altar.

33. It is a wonder that some prelates, sound in mind, consent to this sort of deed, since they also are bound to rebuke the king and anyone else doing such things, and especially their own servants. According to Ezekiel 3:18–19, "If you give the impious no warning to turn from his impious way and live, that impious man shall die in his impiety; but his blood I will require at your hand. But if you warn the impious man, and he does not turn from his impiety, or from his impious ways . . ." (Also Extra, *De officiis ordinarii*, last chapter.)[36] If he dies, you have saved his life. For the crimes of servants are imputed to the negligence of the prelates, when the prelates have been negligent about correcting them; and he commits a crime, who, when he is able to correct, neglects to amend, nor does he secretly escape guilty by association who does not prevent an open crime, and it is an error there is no stopping (LXXXVI, d. *Inferiorum* and cap.; *Facientis*, II, *Negligere*; LXXXIII, d. *Error approbatur*).[37] And therefore, a prelate ought to proceed against anyone who is depriving another of his goods. If he does not dare to do this, all the bishops ought to convene and through their letters ought to excommunicate that powerful one until he return the goods. For bishops are responsible to God alone, and for the salvation of the people, enjoying respect, without any lukewarmness, to keep the peace firmly, mutually advising and helping one another. They should never neglect this through hate or love of anyone (XXIV, q. iii, *Si quis de potentibus*; X, c. *Praecipimus*).[38]

34. O Lord, my King, that prerogative which you say that you have — that is, to buy some things for a lesser price than the seller wishes to sell them for — is introduced to your damnation and evil, since a prerogative of this sort expels charity, and "God is love," as 1 John 4:8 says. No one desires your coming on account of purchases of this sort, and there is no one in your kingdom who is more needy for love than you, King. If, therefore, you wish to keep your kingdom for yourself and your son, you must make yourself loved by the people, but you will never be loved by the people as long as you wish to seize the things of others at a lower price than the seller wishes to sell them for. And therefore no region desires your coming, except those who are in London, where you do not buy things for a lesser price than the seller wishes to sell them for. But if you wish to buy like

---

[36] *Decretales, De officiis ordinariis,* in VI (I, 16).
[37] Gratian, *Decretum*, dist. 83, c. 5; 24, q. 3, c. 21; dist. 86, c. 3; dist. 82, c. 3.
[38] Gratian, *Decretum*, 24, q. 3, c. 21; dist. 91, c. 11.

some foreigner and pay the fair price immediately, then you will acquire the love of the people, and then the people will ask God that you come back to them every single year. Now, you judge for yourself whether it is more advantageous, useful, and honest for you that the people entreat God on your behalf and rejoice at your coming and sorrow at your leaving, rather than the contrary.

35. And, Lord King, you ought to know that you are not an emperor who can decide such a law of purchase that you can buy a certain thing for a lesser price than another can. But you are King of England, holding the whole kingdom of England in fealty from the Roman church. You know, or ought to know, that the King of England initially did not recognize anyone to be superior to him in temporalities, and neither did the King of France. But later on, the whole kingdom of England was made subject to rent and was held in fealty from the Roman church, on account of John, who was formerly King of England, the son of Henry II, who was succeeded in the kingdom by his son, King Richard, and then by John, in the time of Pope Innocent III. For John received the whole kingdom of England from the Roman church in fealty, on account of which the Roman church rallied around to help him get control of the kingdom of England, and sent a certain special cardinal legate (Extra, *Qui filii sunt legati*).[39]

36. And even granted that you were emperor, still you would not desire to buy anything against the will of the owners of those things, since it is a saying worthy of the emperor that he is to affirm himself bound by the laws, since his authority depends on the authority of the laws; or else it is a worthy saying about the laws, and it is said elsewhere, that although the emperor is not subject to the laws, nevertheless it is fitting for him to live for his own part according to the laws. And even granted the impossibility that you would be able to buy anything for a lesser price than the seller wishes to sell it for without sin; still, you ought not to do this on account of the sorrow and sadness which the people would then experience as a result on account of your coming, wherever you might wish to arrive.

37. Who is that Christian of sound mind when he knows in truth that all the people sorrow at his coming, and rejoice at his going, since they have great sorrow on his account? Indeed, it is a wonder how he is able to eat happily, or to drink, or, for shame, to appear before the people. And hear, Lord King, what is said in 1 Kings 21:2-19. "King Ahab spoke to Naboth, saying: 'Give me your vineyard, . . . for it is near me, and near my house;

---

[39] *Decretales, De officio legati*, in VI (I, 13).

and I will give you a better vineyard for it, or I will give you its value in money.' But Naboth answered, 'I will not sell it to you.' And Ahab went into his house vexed ... and he told his wife that Naboth would not sell him his vineyard. And his wife said to him: ... 'You are a great authority, and you rule your kingdom of Israel well. Arise and eat ... and I will give you that vineyard.' And the wife sent his documents to the great men who dwelt with Naboth," so that he would be destroyed by false testimony. That was done. And the wife came to Ahab, saying: "'Arise, take possession of the vineyard of Naboth the Israelite, who refused to sell it to you. For Naboth is no longer alive, but dead.' When Ahab heard that Naboth was dead, he occupied his vineyard," which he had refused to sell to him. "Then the word of the Lord came to Elijah the Tishbite, saying: 'Arise, go down to meet Ahab, king of Israel. ... Behold, he has gone down to the vineyard of Naboth that he may possess it. And speak to him, saying: Thus says the Lord, ... In the place where dogs licked up the blood of Naboth shall dogs lick your own blood.'" Therefore, I say to you, Lord King, that on account of the many kinds of injuries that your ministers did to paupers, the paupers were compelled to sell their lands, and then they died in misery. And therefore, you should look out for yourself lest a similar thing happen to you.

38. And attend diligently, Lord King, that the perverse custom of buying a certain thing for a lesser price than the seller wishes to sell them, for introduced by your predecessors, can in no way benefit you: for an evil custom, unless it is quickly torn up by the roots, is taken up and even kept so as to become a law of privileges, as is said in VIII, *Si mala consuetudo*.[40] Hence, you cannot protect yourself under the pretext of such customs, because passage of time does not lessen the sin; rather, it augments it, just as much as the crimes are graver, so much the longer do they keep the unhappy soul bound (Extra, *De consuetudine*, c. *Cum tanto* and Extra, *De symonia*, c. *Non satis*).[41] And Gregory says, in a certain homily, that habitual guilt binds the mind so that nowhere is it able to rise to righteousness, since where it persists for a long time of its own free will, it is difficult to arise from its sin, and now when guilt becomes inured, the spirit resists sin more weakly, since as many times as it is implicated in evil practices, so many times is it bound to the mind.[42] For scarcely is any evil custom remitted,

---

[40] Gratian, *Decretum*, dist. 7, c. 3.
[41] *Decretales, De consuetudine, Cum tanto* (I, 4); *De simonia, Non satis* (V, 3).
[42] St. Gregory the Great, *Homiliae in Evangelia* (PL 76. 1231).

and concerning the introduction of evil customs, one may grasp what is read concerning Arius. For it is known how great was the penalty of Arius, who introduced an evil custom. Wherefore Wisdom 4:6 says, "All children who are born of iniquity will testify to the sin of their parents and act as witnesses against them." That is, the more seriously those who introduce evil customs are punished, the more supporters and defenders of their crookedness they have. Wherefore Wisdom 14:16 says, "The iniquitous custom became stronger, and is observed as law."

39. O Lord, my King, if the aforementioned is unable to move you, hear now what happened concerning the goods of those who were using that privilege. For in the time of the last King Henry, all sorts of food, hay, oats, and all necessities were brought to his gate, since he himself seized nothing against the will of the sellers, since he bought and paid as one of the people. Afterward, in the time of that noble King Edward, your grandfather, at the beginning of his reign, as it is said, he seized nothing against the will of the owners of the things, even up to the eighteenth year of his reign, and in all that time there was peace and joy in that kingdom. But in the eighteenth year of his reign he began to use that diabolic prerogative, that is, to seize sheep, oxen, hay, and oats, and many other things, for a lesser price than the seller wished to sell them, for, and then immediately war broke out against him in Gascony, Wales, and Scotland, and he used that cursed prerogative all the way up until his death, and from that time there was never good peace in the land. But what happened to all his goods after his death? Indeed, that person whom the king loved least took possession, that is, Piers Gaveston, who lived in exile through that reign. No wonder that many goods in this time were evilly acquired by that king. Afterward, your father used in the whole time of his life that cursed prerogative, that is, he seized things for a lesser price than the seller or owner of the things wished to sell them for. And so you have heard perhaps what sort of death your father had and who took possession of his goods. No wonder, since much evil happened in this land through his foolishness and negligence.

40. And I say to you, King, that if you could know what I know, you would refuse to use that prerogative even in order to acquire all of the kingdoms of France, Scotland, Aragon, and Spain, and it would be better that you renounce that illicit privilege than to acquire all those kingdoms, according to Luke 9:25 and Matthew 16:26: "What will profit a man if he shall gain the whole world, and lose his own soul?" And better you should lose the kingdom than to consent that such a prerogative be further kept or permitted to exist, on account of which you will lose your soul. For this reason, one ought better to suffer all evils than to consent to evil. And I say

to you, King, that I would prefer that you should take away from your land that diabolical prerogative than that you should acquire for me all the kingdoms of England, France, and Scotland. God knows that I do not lie, and such is the case, because the salvation of one soul is more worthy in the sight of God than all the kingdoms of the present world. And if you, King, use that privilege, many souls will be damned, on account of seizures of this kind, according to this: "For sin is not forgiven unless restitution is made" (XIV, q. 3, *Si res*).[43] And I advise you, King, for the health of your soul, that as much as it is possible for you, you should make restitution of all the goods of your subjects that have been taken away from them unjustly by your servants. For thus St. Edward did, not your father but St. Edward, King and Martyr, for it is read in the life of St. Edward the King that this same Edward did not conquer the Kingdom of Norway by plundering the poor, nor by treasures of money, but with the sword of sanctity and with the arms of justice. Therefore, after he ordered the return of the money which he had taken in his carts to England, he saw at Mass, on the altar, in the hands of the priest, in the Body of Christ, as if in a mirror, the King of Norway fallen and submerged in the sea, after he had prepared a fleet to sail in order to devastate the land of England.

41. So if you, King, do thus, that is to say, if you observe the knowledge of the law, namely, if you live honestly and if you injure no one, and if you distribute to everyone what is his own, then you will be noble and this land of yours will be happy and blessed because of your good deeds, greatly pleasing in the sight of God and man, and then you will obtain victory over your enemies. According to Ecclesiastes 10:17, "Blessed is the land whose king is noble"; and Isaiah 59:1 says, "Behold, the Lord's hand is not shortened that it cannot save." Thus, God also wishes to be courteous, if you are kind, just as you are courteous to others. This is the first sign of nobility, namely, gratitude or recognition of benefits; and on the contrary, ingratitude or forgetfulness of benefits is a sign of rudeness. Wherefore it is clear that they are ignoble who dishonor God (that is to say, by committing sin) who honors them above all else, namely, by conferring honor and nobility on them in the present life for mutual benefit. Wherefore it is said in Isaiah 1:2, "Sons I have reared and set on high, but they have revolted against me"; and they are most rude who oppress your subjects, by whose labors they live, just as you did through your ministers before this time. The second sign of nobility is liberality. Wherefore God, who is most noble and

---

[43] Gratian, *Decretum*, 14, q. 6, c. 1.

most liberal, gives not only to his own servants, but also to his enemy, as Matthew 5:45 says: "For he makes his sun to rise on the evil and on the good." And just as liberality is the sign of nobility, so robbery is the sign of rudeness. Wherefore those who are reputed noble are most rude, since they do not cease from robbing the poor, since the goods of life are conferred on them by God, or borrowed from Him, just as happened to you through your ancestors before this time and you have allowed to happen. The third sign of nobility is clemency and mercy. Wherefore Seneca says: "No one should be more forgiving than the king and prince. The bees are the most angry and aggressive creatures, and they leave their sting in the wound. The king of the bees, however, does not have a sting, he does not wish by nature to be savage nor to seek revenge."[44] As a sign of this kind of clemency, the king is anointed, wherefore it is said 1 Kings 20:31, "The kings of Israel are clement"; and there follows: "Let us go to the king of Israel, perhaps he will save our souls." And in the Psalms it is said, "He has pity on the poor and the weak, and he causes the souls of the poor to be saved" (Psalms 71:13). And Matthew 11:29 says, "Learn from me, because I am gentle and lowly in heart; and you will find rest for your souls."

42. And just as clemency to subjects is a sign of nobility, thus cruelty done to them, or permitted to be done, is a sign of rudeness. Of this sort were your predecessors before this time and the servants of your court, who committed evils of this kind, as is clear in the many serious things written above. O Lord, my King, hear and understand that "in the days of Noah, ... men ate and drank, they married, ... until the day when Noah entered the ark, and the flood came and destroyed them all. Likewise, as it was in the days of Lot — they ate, they drank, they bought, they sold, they planted, they built. But on the day when Lot went out from Sodom the Lord rained fire and brimstone from heaven and destroyed them all," as is said in Luke 17:26-29 and Genesis 19. Similarly, concerning Dathan and Abiram, "They descended with their assembly and all their subjects alive into Hell," as is said in Numbers 16:32-33. These are from the written law and from antiquity. But do we not see in these days that certain magnates of this land eat and drink, and make feasts and dances, and do marvelous things, and suddenly they are seized and killed? And so their feasting and joy is changed into sorrow, according to Amos 8:10: "I will turn your feasts into mourning, and all your songs into lamentations." And there follows: "And those with them, like a day of sorrow; and his end like a bitter day."

---

[44] Seneca, *De clementia*, 1.19.2-3.

And what is the cause of this? Certainly, sins. And I believe that, among other sins, this is the greatest, namely, to seize any goods against the will of the owners. No wonder, so many of those are crying to God, and it is impossible that the prayers of so many people injured unjustly should not be heard. And Ecclesiasticus 35:16, 18-19, 23 says, "God will hear the prayers of the injured. . . . Do not the widow's tears run down her cheeks and from her cheeks her cry runs all the way up to heaven?" And there follows: "God renders vengeance."

43. And behold the wonders of God that occur to the guides of the king. Was not Piers Gaveston, who guided King Edward wherever he wanted, seized and killed, without harm to others? Afterward came Hugh Despenser, father and son; but the Holy Spirit abandoned them; they were seized and killed, without harm to others. Also, now at last, that great lord Roger Mortimer was seized and killed in the same way, although formerly when a great lord had to be seized, many murders used to happen among the community of the people, and almost infinite robberies then used to take place. But this could be the cause: the people were greatly weighed down by them, nor could they induce the king to keep the common law, namely, to buy things for sale at a market price. Wherefore Augustine says: "It is just that he who wishes to be ruled by a more powerful man should help the inferior over whom he himself is more powerful."[45] And because the aforesaid did not do thus, therefore they had a bad end in this world; perhaps they nevertheless had a good end as to the salvation of their souls. And they left no estate, since they had lost all their goods. No wonder, because they had acquired many things evilly, as is said. And therefore, I warn you, guides of the king, on behalf of God, that you should lead him well and wisely; if, when he and those of his household are engaged in buying and selling, they keep the common law and do not take the goods of others against the will of the owners, you need not fear ruin and also revenge from others. Therefore you should guide him cautiously, not as fools but as wise men, thereby redeeming your souls, since these are evil days; on that account, refuse to become imprudent by understanding what the will of God is. "Let no one seduce you by inane words," as is said in Ephesians 5:6. Wherefore Hugh of St. Victor said: "Tell me, where are the lovers of the world who were with you for a short time? Nothing remains of them except ashes and worms.

44. "Diligently attend to what they are or what they were. Just like

---

[45] Cf. St. Augustine, *De civitate Dei* 19.14-16.

you, they eat, they drink, they laugh, and they pass their days with pleasant things, and in a moment they descend into Hell (Job 21:13). Their flesh is given over to worms, and their soul to infernal fires, until, at last gathered into an unhappy group, they are enveloped in eternal flames. Those who were their allies in vices were allies in punishments, for one punishment binds together those whom one love binds together in crime."[46] No wonder, because they loved the world more than God. Wherefore James 4:4 says, "Whoever wishes to be a friend of this world makes himself an enemy of God, because friendship with this world is inimical to God." What, therefore, did this empty glory profit them? Brief joy, pomp of the world, pleasures of the flesh, deceptive wealth, a great household, and great desires? Where now is this laughter, where the great boasting, where the arrogance? From such great joy, such great sadness; after such great pleasure, how great the unhappiness; from this exalted position they have fallen into great ruin and great torments. Revelation 18:7 says, "To the extent the sinner has glorified himself and been in pleasure, in that measure give him torment and mourning." Whatever happened to them can happen to you, because you are a man, an earthly man, clay from mire, you are of the earth, you live of the earth and you will return to the earth. When the last day comes, it comes suddenly, and perhaps it will be today. It is certain that you will die, but it is uncertain in what way or when or where, since death awaits you everywhere. You also, if you are wise, will expect it everywhere. And therefore, rich men and lovers of the world are able to say in Wisdom 5:7-14: "The way of God is one that we have never known. What advantage has pride brought us? What has wealth and boastfulness conferred on us? All those things have passed like a shadow, passed like a fleeting runner. A ship sails across the waves of the ocean, but when it is gone, it leaves no trace; or like a bird that flies through the air, no trace is found of it ... It is the same with us — we are born, then we cease to be. We could leave no sign of virtue behind us; we are destroyed by our wickedness. Such is said in Hell, by those who have sinned." And Isidore says that the glory of this world is small, is perishable, and temporal power is fragile: "Tell me, where are kings, where are princes, where are emperors, where are the materially wealthy, where are the powerful of this world, where are the world's rich people? They pass as if shadows and they evaporate like ashes."[47]

---

[46] Actually not Hugh of St. Victor, but pseudo-Bernard of Clairvaux, *Meditationes piissimae de cognitione humanae conditionis* 3 (PL 194. 491A).

[47] Pseudo-Isidore, *De lamentatione animae peccatricis* 2.91 (PL 83. 865C).

45. O Lord, my King, since you have heard and understood the foregoing, I warn you on behalf of Almighty God and the Holy Church, and I beg you on behalf of your English people, that you keep the common law in buying and selling, that is, that no one from your court, or anyone else, seize anything for a lesser price than the seller wishes to sell them, for, nor that anyone seize anything not his own against the will of its owner. According to Isaiah 61:8, "I, the Lord, love justice and hate robbery." And if you will hear the people on this and concede this to them, you will have peace on this earth with your subjects. Wherefore Cassiodorus said in a certain letter: "In this the grace of the king is extolled and preserved, if he directs the people in the fairness of peace and keeps them in the strength of justice, and it is right for the king to keep the peace because he is brought to the praise of the people, if peace is loved by all. For what is it that better befits the king or the prince, or proclaims him, than a tranquil people, concord preserved, and the whole republic attired in honorable manners?"[48] For if you will not hear your people in this, a great tribulation will come upon you and then you will be able to say as does Genesis 42:21: "This suffering is merited because I have sinned against my subjects, seeing their trouble when they begged for help, but I would not listen, and therefore I am in trouble now." And this happened to your father; wherefore it is said in Wisdom 6:2-4, 6, "Listen, King, and understand ... This authority has been given to you by the Lord God, who will examine your works and scrutinize your thoughts; ... and because you have not upheld the law, and you have not walked according to God's will, quickly you will be given a most harsh judgment." And therefore, again I advise and warn you that you should not use any more the aforementioned prerogative as your father did, according to what Leviticus 18:30 says, "Do not do what was done by those who were before you." For what is unjust is not to be done. "But love the Lord God with all your heart, and all your soul, and all your strength. ... And do not forget God, who rescued you from the land of Egypt, from slavery," that is, from the custody of your mother, as is said in Deuteronomy 6:5, 13. And provide for yourself wise and God-fearing men from among all the people, in whom there is truth — men who hate avarice and, most of all, who are old and prudent, since as the Philosopher says in the book *Ethics*, "One should believe in old men as authority,"[49] not because they know a great deal, but because they have seen a great deal, and govern

---

[48] Cassiodorus, *Epistola* 23 (PL 69. 524A).
[49] A paraphrase of Aristotle, *Nicomachean Ethics* 1143b12-14.

your kingdom and yourself according to their counsel. And thus you will acquire love of God and of your people, "and you can sustain the precepts of God," and maintain them, as is said in Exodus 18:21, 23. And then there will be peace on this earth, observance of the law, human happiness, and what is pleasing to the Creator, the Giver of all gifts. May he who lives and reigns through the infinite ages of ages concede this to us. Amen.

Here ends the letter composed for Lord Edward, King of England.

The *Mirror of King Edward III*
[Second Version]

CHAPTER 1

1. O Lord, my King: "If you were wise and would understand, and would discern your end" (Deuteronomy 32:29). You should be wise, that is, you should know with your intellect the benefits that have been conferred on you by God. And you should understand, namely, the errors of your court; and you should discern your end, namely, your approaching and uncertain death, of which you do not know the sort or time or place. Surely, you should correct the errors of your court, errors that are damnable before the highest God, with all possible speed. For although you be king today, you do not know whether you will remain king tomorrow. Job 7:7 says, "Wind is the life of man." Proverbs 27:1 says, "Do not boast about tomorrow; you do not know what a day may bring forth." Ecclesiasticus 10:12 suggests that you may be a king today, perhaps tomorrow you will die; although nothing is more certain than death, nothing is more uncertain than the hour of death. For as a star glittering in the sky burns quickly and then suddenly goes out, and the spark of a fire is quickly extinguished and is reduced to ashes, thus quickly the life of a king and anyone else is ended and is changed to dust. Wisdom 7:5-6 says, "No king has known any other beginning of existence; for all, there is one way only into life, just like out of it." Lord King, see and diligently heed the benefits conferred on you by God; namely, that God created you not for the sake of your own advantage, since He did not need you; likewise, without any merit on your part, since you merited nothing before, and since you were absolutely nothing before. Likewise, know how He made you, as to your body, namely, an outstanding creature, and your soul, still more outstanding, inasmuch as you are created in the image and likeness of God, participating in reason, capable of eternal blessedness. Likewise, consider diligently and ponder in your heart,

when first you came by ship from foreign parts into this land, how humbly, how graciously, how devoutly, how joyously the English people admitted you, and stood by and aided you in everything you did against your rebels. Moreover, consider the gift of power, how the count of Lancaster humbled and, as is said, effaced himself on his knees before you near Bedford. And the cause of such humiliation was the goodness and holiness of that count, and your innocence along with the prayers of holy men. And do not forget how graciously, how miraculously, you were freed from the custody of your mother and others. Moreover, diligently heed how much honor the archbishops, bishops, abbots, priors, and other prelates of this land gave to you. And consider how much honor was granted to you by counts, barons, knights, burghers, and from each and every man of this land. Among all these, diligently heed how much you should thank God for all these things. When you have carefully considered these and the many other benefits granted to you by God, you will cause the errors of your court, or customs hateful to God and the English people, to be emended. And see what these errors are in a certain modest treatise, which begins thus: "O Lord, my King."

Chapter 2

2. O Lord, my King, how I wish that you were wise and would understand, and would discern your end. You should be wise, namely, you should consider whence you came, and you should understand, namely, in what state and danger you are, and you should discern your end, namely, what sort of death you will have. Consider this salvific warning, not in haste, but rather with zeal and deliberation. Since as incense does not smell except in the flame, so no sentence of sacred scripture releases its savor unless it is cooked in the heart. Therefore, how I wish you would be wise and understand, and discern your end. Behold, lord, three things are proposed to you in this mirror, namely, knowledge, understanding, and foresight. Therefore, the Lord wishes that you should know your present fleeting life, subject to many miseries and vanity, polluted by the filth of sins, corrupted by desire, and shortly to come to an end. Therefore, the Lord wishes that you should understand your fragile condition, since "naked you came from your mother's womb, and naked you will return to the earth"; "for out of the earth you were taken and into the earth you will return" (Job 1:21; Genesis 3:19). Attend carefully, because you have entered the misery of such life, you have lived your days in sorrow and trouble, and you will leave this

world in grief and sorrow, and you know neither the day nor the hour (Matthew 25:13). And distinguish then how the eyes are turned in the head, the veins are torn in the body, and the heart is rent by sorrow, and with this, you know how the dead are treated and buried; how then they are turned forwards and backwards; how the arms fall and the legs are rigid; how the bones lie; how they are dressed; how they are treated; how they are put into the ground; how they are brought to be buried; how they are covered with dirt. As Gregory says: "Whoever considers how he will be in death, he will always be fearful in prayer."[1] And therefore, "keep in mind final matters" (Ecclesiasticus 7:40) and the horror of judgment, and do not allow the fear of the burning fire of Hell to be far from the eyes of your heart. Therefore, you should understand your entrance into this pitiful world, your feeble progress, and horrible exit. Therefore, God wishes that you would diligently consider your end; and to provide for your end is the sum of all wisdom. And what are these last things? At least that hour [. . .][2] terrible, that pitiful hour, that terrible hour, at which your wretched soul is going to be taken, fearing and trembling, from your corruptible little body.

3. Lord King, believe me now, for the sake of considering this fearful matter you should prefer to possess foreknowledge rather than to have domination of all the world. For in the last very fearful hour, which of your friends, which of your parents, coming with swords and arms and war horses, can now offer aid to you? Out of all your dearest ones there will be none to console you. "They came at me from all sides and there was none to help; I was looking for my aid and there was none."[3] Therefore you ought often to consider with what fear one should fear, with what love one should love, with what honor one should venerate our Lord God Himself, who alone can offer you assistance after death. Recall often to mind the frightening day of your death, and how your wretched soul should leave its prison of flesh. You should provide for yourself, through your good works, whither you go, and do what is expedient for that fearful journey, and take care not to do what might stand in the way. In such a way, remembrance conceives contrition, contrition produces compunction, compunction devotion, devotion generates pious and humble affection toward God — pious on account of faith in the help of divine goodness and mercy, humble from the consideration of one's own fragility and wretchedness. For nothing in

---

[1] St. Gregory the Great, *Moralia in Job* 13.29 (PL 75. 1032).
[2] Lacuna in text.
[3] Pseudo-Augustine, *Speculum peccatoris* 5 (PL 40. 987). Much of the present passage is adapted from this medieval work.

this world inclines you more easily toward humility and care of yourself, expelling all injustice and perfecting sanctity and fear of God, than the consideration of your corrupt condition, the certain knowledge of your mortality, and finally, the remembrance of the terrible day of your death. According to Ecclesiasticus 7:40, "Remember your end and you will never sin."

CHAPTER 3

4. O Lord, my King, how I wish that you were wise and would understand and discern your end. You should understand, that is, you should hear and consider in your mind, the cries and sighs of men and women when rumors are heard regarding your arrival; and you should understand, namely, the joy which they have at your departure, and you should discern your end, namely, your lamentable death; surely with all the attention of your mind you should ordain some good way by which all the people would rejoice at your arrival and grieve at your departure. And this will be more honorable and useful for the king. And I will explain to you the way to do this simply below.

5. For all the English people can blush to have a king at whose arrival the people commonly are sorrowful, and whose departure makes them rejoice. Who does not engage in sighs and tears at his arrival, and most of all when the king himself ought to be affable, humble, gentle, and blameless? The cause of the people's sorrow at your arrival is the fact that your ministers seize many goods against the will of the owners for a smaller price than they wish to sell it for, since the goods are thus seized from them, although they are unwilling, at a fixed price. If they want to get the money owed to them by your ministers, it is necessary for them to go five or six leagues, or even more, looking for their money. And perhaps they are kept waiting for an entire day, and often it happens that they are not able to depart unless they give something [i.e., a bribe] in order to acquire the said money. And this is one cause of the people's sorrow. Another cause is that the scouts for your court, servants, and others seize men and horses working around the fields, and animals that plough the earth and carry seed to the field, so that the men and animals work two or three days in your service, receiving nothing for the work. Yet even in wartime this is not to be done, since in time of war, there ought to be security for priests, monks, monastic servants, and peasants who are coming and going, and working in the fields, as well as the animals which plough and carry seed to the field. And so much the more ought they to have security in time of peace such as now, except

in those places in which you come with your household, where there is no peace. And therefore, be warned. Likewise, note what happens when some members of your household want to have the men, horses, and carts in one parish. Those of the parish make an agreement with them for one-half mark or thereabout, so that they may remain at home and not work in your service. On the following day, or whatever particular day, others of your household come and seize horses and carts in the same parish, irrespective of those who, having given half a mark, believed that they had security. And therefore be warned. There are many other causes which are treated in this little summary that is entitled, "O Lord, my King."

Chapter 4

6. And behold, my Lord King, what the poor do when they get lodgings — [the poor] to whom things should rather be given on account of charity than things taken from them. When people hear something about your arrival they are sad, and at once, on account of fear, they hide geese, hens, and other goods, or they get rid of them, or they consume them by eating and drinking, lest they lose them upon your arrival. They act as if they think thieves and plunderers or such sorts of men are coming to their village. O woe! O shame! O disgrace! O infamy! O affliction! O ambition! O struggle! O compassion! O outcry! O damnation! O sadness! O error! O falsehood! O fraud! O theft! O plunder! O infidelity! O ingratitude! O instability! O labor! O tears! O lamentation! O martyrdom! O lying! O perjury! O danger! O fear! O scandal to you, King, and to all the English people, that such things should happen upon your arrival. Fie, fie, fie! Woe, woe, woe! that this sort of thing should be allowed to happen, when such things are preached about you through almost the whole world. And why do I say woe three times? You will see why in what follows. And therefore, Lord King, if you want what you ought to want — namely, that these kinds of disgraces be soon abolished from this land — in order that the people may rejoice in your joyous arrival and have sorrow when you leave, I counsel you, I ask you, on behalf of Almighty God and the Holy Church, and on behalf of the English people, and for the health and salvation of your soul, that you should cause to be legislated and ordained that no one, under severe penalty, should take anyone's goods against his will. But one should buy things only if one is able to agree with the seller, and one should immediately pay the money to the seller himself, in no way delaying payment against the will of the seller. And one should hire carts, horses, and the

labor of men in a manner in which one can contract for them more honestly, more easily, and better. And if this is so ordered and legislated, then men will come from everywhere and bring everything you need, even to your door. For thus men of this land did in the time of King Henry your great-grandfather, and on his arrival the people rejoiced greatly. And the people will do likewise on your arrival if you choose to do as he did.

7. For if you would act thus, you will have the blessing of God, and all the English, with the aid of God, will be at your pleasure and command; and because of the love which they will have for you, you will rule them peacefully, with triumph. But if you do not choose to order this, it must be feared that God will arouse war against you in which you will suffer great tribulation. And then if you would cry to God, perhaps God would not hear you. Proverbs 21:13 says, "He who shuts his ears to the poor man's cry, when he himself cries shall not be heard"; and in Proverbs 1:24-25 it is said, "I called and you refused ... and you have despised good counsel." And there follows in 27-30: "When tribulation and difficulty strike you, you will cry to God, and God will not hear you, because you have despised the teachings of your Lord and you would have none of my good counsel." And therefore you would heap shame and disgrace upon yourself, not to mention scandal which will never be blotted out in this world. Woe, woe, woe, my Lord King, that there are so many lamentations and sorrows surrounding your arrival, where there should be much rejoicing. And it is no wonder that there are sighs and lamentations upon your arrival, since in truth, which is God, I say that for my own person, whenever I hear rumors of your arrival and I hear your horn, I tremble all over, whether I am at home, or in the field, in church, or in the study, or even at mass. For when someone of your household beats on the gate, then I tremble even more. But when he beats on the door, then I tremble most of all. And thus, the closer he approaches, the more I tremble and am very fearful. And this fear remains in me as long as you tarry in these parts where I am, and thus, on account of many and diverse evils which come to the poor, through those who say they are from your court. Thus, according to Jeremiah 4:22, "They are wise in doing evil, but doing good they do not know." And Proverbs 2:14 says, "They rejoice when they do evil; and they exult in the very worst things." And such are chosen from your court in order to make provision for you. And from this it seems to me that your scouts, who come to make provision for you, would not come on behalf of God but of the devil. For indeed, there are good angels and evil ones. The good angel consoles terrified people by his appearance, as the Archangel Gabriel was sent to the Virgin Mary and said: "Hail Mary, full of grace, the Lord is

with you." When she heard this, she was troubled in her mind. And then the angel, comforting her, said: "Fear not, Mary, for you have found favor with God" (Luke 1:26-30). On the other hand, the evil angel, cloaking himself as an angel of light, strikes all the more terror into those who experience fright in his presence.

8. The same thing is rightly said about your scouts. Whenever rumors are heard about your arrival, and one horn is heard, almost anyone who is in the village trembles. Presently your scout comes to the village and, seeing him, all are sorrowful and are filled with dread. He does not say to them: "Fear not." But he says that he wants to have oats, hay, and stabling for the horses of the Lord King. And then these village paupers are greatly saddened and tremble, and do so more and more, etc. Presently, another comes in the same way, and he says that he wants to have geese, hens, and many other things. Then comes a third, and he wants to have grain, etc., and thus the sadness grows. 2 Corinthians 11:14-15 says: "Even Satan disguises himself as an angel of light. It is not so strange if even his servants disguise themselves as servants of justice. Their end will correspond with their deeds." And concerning this it seems to me that such scouts come not on God's behalf, but on the devil's. And do not take it wrong that I may say such things to you, according to Galatians 1:10: "If I pleased men, I would not be the servant of Christ." My Lord King, now believe me that, if you knew the danger in which you now exist, because of the myriad damnations which befall the poor on your arrival, you would not delay until tomorrow the appropriate remedy, which you can apply at once. And I hand over an easy remedy to you because any man should be able to be owner of his things. Namely, nothing should be seized against the will of their owners whose goods they are.

9. Perhaps some of your counselors, enemies of Jesus Christ and enemies of your soul, applauding you, would say what is said in Psalms 52:6: "God has dispersed the bones of those who please humanity." Therefore, you will not be king in your land, nor will you find food and drink and other things necessary for you. And I say to you, before God, that if the people were to be sure that none of their goods would be seized against their will, they would bring you everything you need, even to your gate, nor would the king have to beg in his country as recently. It does not hurt to try. And I warn you, so that you take healthful thought about the health of your soul, not to repeat anything your father did. Would that you took as much thought about the health of your soul as I do! For that evil prerogative of your court, namely, to seize things for a smaller price than the seller would want to receive, is damnable before God. But it has been much used and

inured in your court, from the time of your father and grandfather, which already lasted for forty years. And thus that evil prerogative seems prescribed. Truly, such a prescription does not hold at law, nor is it of any value, since it is against divine and human law, and moreover against good customs. Because of that, I tell you, my Lord King, that on account of such a prerogative infinite souls are in Hell. And therefore be warned, and order that cursed prerogative not to be observed by anyone for any reason. But this will be difficult. Ecclesiastes 1:15 says, "The crooked are difficult to correct." Ecclesiasticus 23:20 says, "A man in the habit of using words of reproach will never break himself of it, however long he lives." Proverbs 18:3 says, "When the wicked man comes to the depth of sins, he condemns it: but dishonor and disgrace follow him." Jeremiah 13:23 says, "If the Ethiopian can change his skin, or the leopard his spots, then you also can do good though you have taught evil."

10. I believe that, by the grace of God — on account of the prayers of many, because of scandal, because of the disapproval of the people, because of the infamy of this land, and because of your innocence, since, as is commonly said, you are guided toward good — through you the accursed prerogative will be abolished, especially by the grace of God. It is said in 1 Timothy 1:14: "The grace of our Lord overflowed for me with the faith and love that are in Jesus Christ." And I tell you, before God, that if you do this, greater merit will accrue to you than if you were to acquire all the kingdoms of the world. God knows that I do not lie, and that this is what you should do if you want to please Almighty God. According to 1 Thessalonians 4:3, 6: "This, your sanctification, is the will of God." And it follows: "Let no man transgress," namely, through violence, "not cheat his brother in business," as many provisors of your court do. And there follows in 1 Thessalonians 4:10, 12: "We exhort you, brothers, ... that you walk with those who are in public, and that you desire nothing of someone else," namely, through cupidity. But the provisors of your court have desired many things against the will of their owners, and therefore, if you want to please God, such things should be corrected. O Lord, my King, if only you were wise and would understand this, and discern what your end will be. You should be wise, that is, you should keep the life of St. Edward and his end in mind, and you should understand, that is, you should know very well the life of your father and his end; and you should discern what your end will be, namely, your coming death. But you know not what kind. Certainly, you should choose to imitate the life of St. Edward, on whose arrival all the people rejoiced (John 16:20), whenever he came to their land; and you should forsake the life of your father, on whose arrival

all the people commonly were sad. And this sadness has lasted until your arrival. But this sadness, with God's grace, will be abolished through you. And thus sadness will be turned into rejoicing. And then in the people of England great will be the joy, great the continuance of peace, great the wealth of possessions, as it was in the time of St. Edward, who was affable to all, praiseworthy for his chastity, with cheerful and decorous face, and most proven in prudence, as you are.

CHAPTER 5

11. O Lord, my King, if only you were wise and would understand this, and discern what your end will be. You would be wise, that is, you would know your debts and the debts of your father, and you would understand the danger to your soul and the danger to your father's, on account of the numerous debts, since your creditors are not paid; and you would discern what your end will be, namely, your lamentable death, God knows how it will happen. And surely if you would lower your expenses of your house and other extra expenses, your debts and the debts of your father would be quickly paid. Heed, Lord King, that such riches are not ours, but belong to us by accommodation, and therefore we should spend them not at our will but at the need of our brothers. If we should spend our goods for the need of our brothers, therefore we should not steal from them. Wherefore Augustine says the fact that riches are not ours is known in death, since they remain in the world and do not follow a man after his death. "When you take another person's goods when the owner is unwilling, you will be taken by the devil; and when you keep them, you will be kept by the devil."[4] Jerome says: "Those goods do not belong to a man which cannot follow after him."[5] Job 27:19 says, "When the rich man goes to sleep, he takes nothing with him; he opens his eyes, and finds nothing." Wherefore the Psalmist says, "They sleep their sleep, and they discover nothing, all those men with wealth in their hands" (Psalms 75:6). And elsewhere it is said: "Do not fear when a man becomes rich, when the glory of his house increases. For when he dies he will carry away nothing; his glory will not go down after him" (Psalms 48:17–18). Now think, Lord, about your father, what he recently possessed of the riches he had here, and the state in which his soul resides, because of his unpaid debts. I do not want to say anything about extortions

---

[4] St. Augustine, *Sermo* 77 (PL 38. 301).
[5] I have been unable to locate the source of this quote.

that happened in his time, but God will be appeased of his soul. And among other things, think about your various debts, and your many creditors, with all of their damages, because your debts were not paid in the appropriate time. Moreover, if you do not pay your debts, perhaps your son will not pay for you; about which Ecclesiastes 9:5 says, "The dead have no more reward; but the memory of them is lost."

Chapter 6

12. O Lord, my King, if only you were wise and would understand, and discern what your end will be. You should be wise, that is, you should think deeply about the lands and tenements of the dead that have devolved to you and your father. And you should understand, that is, you should know through inquiry or in some other way, what sort of lands or tenements were acquired unjustly through those dead ones; and you should discern what your end will be, namely, your terrible and lamentable death, and the danger to your soul, because you have detained such goods for so long. Certainly, you could cause all those goods to be restored without delay, along with all the fruits received from them, to all of those from whom said goods had been extorted or in some other way illicitly acquired. Or at least, if they be dead, restitution should be made to their heirs, since the sin is not forgiven unless what has been stolen is restored. It is said in Ecclesiasticus 40:13-14: "The wealth of wrongdoers will dry up like a torrent, and will resound like a clap of thunder in a downpour." And as the just man "when he opens his hands rejoices" by giving at least that which is held, "by the same token defaulters will come to utter ruin." Habakkuk 2:6-8 says, "Woe to him who multiplies what is not his — for how long? — and loads himself down with pledges. Will not your debtors suddenly arise, and those awake who will tear you up," your ambushers will keep watch, "Then you will have booty for them. Because you have plundered many nations, all the remnants (*sic*) of the peoples shall plunder you." See what happened to your father and so, woe to you.

Chapter 7

13. O Lord, my King, if only you were wise and would understand this, and discern what your end will be. You should be wise, that is, you should consider the conditions of those to whom you want to give some great gift, and you should understand, that is, you should keep in mind your infinite

debts, and the debts of your father, and the danger you are in because of the unpaid debts; and you should discern what your end will be, namely, your uncertain and inevitable death. Certainly, you should not make some great donation to someone before your debts and those of your father are completely paid. And therefore, Lord King, when you propose some donation for someone, first think about your debts, and the debts of your father, and place that as a sign above your heart (Song of Songs 8:6). And thus in your donations you should consider your power, the times, need, and the merits of the men to whom you are going to give anything. You ought therefore to bestow gifts according to your power, in measure, to needy and worthy men, since he who gives his gifts to those not in need or unworthy acquires no praise for himself. And whatever is given to the unworthy is lost. And he who showers his riches beyond his means surely will come to the bitter shores of poverty. For he who gives the goods of his kingdom to the unworthy and non-needy, such a king is a depopulator of the republic and destroyer of the kingdom and the regime. And wherefore, he is called prodigal, since he stands at a distance from providence. But he who gives in time of necessity from his goods to needy men, such a king is noble in himself and for his subjects, and his kingdom will prosper, and all his subjects will be at his pleasure and order. But, Lord King, if you would consider your power well, you cannot make huge donations. For, as is commonly said, all your movable goods do not suffice to pay your debts and those of your father, for which payment you are bound. And therefore, you have need to avoid foolish and excessive donations, and to avoid excessive expenses. And therefore, Lord King, when someone asks for some great gift, if you want to excuse yourself courteously, and to know if he is your friend, say to him: "Friend, I would very gladly give you that which you seek and much more, but it is commonly said in this land that all of my movable goods do not suffice to pay my debts; but when my debts are paid, I will happily do what you ask." If afterwards he seeks some large gift from you, you would know that he is not your friend, he does not love you truly, except as a dog loves and cherishes a meaty bone, and keeps it as long as he finds something in it to gnaw, but when it is bare, without meat, he leaves it. And you are like a tree that is loved and frequently visited as long as it has fruit, but when the fruits are gone little is cared about it. Wherefore Lord King, I want you to know that many men follow you as flies follow honey, wolves corpses, mice and rats grain; thus, because of your honors and riches they may follow you, but when your riches leave you, quickly such men will leave you, since they never loved you properly. Wherefore Gregory says, "The loss of joy puts the strength of love to the test: since one who abandons his neighbor in adversity is clearly guilty, because he did not love him in prosperity."[6] For when someone is loved in prosperity, it is uncertain whether the prosperity or the person is loved. Wherefore Ambrose said, "That is not a true friendship which exists toward rich people for the sake of their goods, but it is false adulation."[7] Proverbs 19:4 says, "Wealth multiplies friends, but a poor man is deserted by his friend." Ecclesiasticus 6:8, 10 says, "For one kind of friend is only so when it suits, but will not stand by you in your day of trouble ... And the friend will share your table, but not stand by you in a day of necessity." Ecclesiasticus 12:8 says, "In good times you may not always recognize a friend, but in bad times you will never mistake an enemy." And therefore, Lord King, I say to you that those who induce you to give them large gifts are not your true friends, although they seem to be friends, nor do they really love you. For if they love you according to God, they would seek the health of your soul, so that you would pay your own debts and those of your father rather than make such donations.

Chapter 8

14. O Lord, my King, if only you were wise and would understand this, and discern what your end will be. You should be wise, that is, you should keep in mind how much and how many are the expenses of your great warhorses; and you should understand how many good works of piety could be done in this land from these frivolous expenses; and you should discern what your end will be, namely, your tearful death. You should get rid of a large number of those horses, and you should pay your debts and the debts of your father; and instead of this kind of inordinate expense for horses, you should do works of piety. For Deuteronomy 17:16 says: "[The wise king] does not multiply his horses." But perhaps something should be said on the part of the king: it is proper for a king to have a multitude of great horses for the defense of his land. And I say to you surely, and before God, that it is not for defense of the land, but more for vanity and the destruction of the earth. Jeremiah 2:5 says, "Vanity they pursued, and vain they became." Wherefore, see and diligently heed, how and in what way these great and warlike horses benefit those great lords of this land. I do not want to name them, since they were seized very easily, defeated, and some of

---

[6] St. Gregory the Great, *Moralia in Job* 7. 24 (PL 75. 781).
[7] St. Ambrose, *De officiis ministrorum* 3. 22, sec. 134 (PL 16. 182).

them killed, and they lost all the horses along with all of their goods. Nor is it any wonder, since wherever they stayed, they caused many sorts of losses, both varied and diverse, through their custodians, especially to paupers. And in truth, which is God, the prayer of one good man is of more value to the peasant than all those war-horses. And likewise I say this to you, Lord King, that the prayer of one good peasant, religious or other person, is more beneficial to you even in war than all your war-horses. Exodus 17:11 says, "Moses raised his hands to heaven," praying, and through his prayer he conquered the enemy people. Judith 4:13 says: "You will remember Moses, the servant of God, who conquered Amalek who trusted in his strength and power," and his great horses, "and his great army and his chariots, not by making war, but by speaking holy prayers." For one holy man does more by praying than an infinite number of horses and sinners by fighting. Ecclesiasticus 16:3 says, "Better is one man fearing God than a thousand impious men." And prayers benefit more in war than physical provisions.

15. And now, Lord King, consider the expenses which you have in a year for one great horse. One great horse will have at least one custodial servant, who will receive a denarius each day for his expenses. For the horse again he will take one half bushel of oats, at one denarius, and hay at one denarius. Thus, the costs for one week are two solidi, seven denarii, out of which four or five paupers could be maintained. When you count the cost of one servant and one horse per year, the expenses run to six pounds, sixteen denarii. And it is commonly remarked how great the excess is because of the size and measure of the expenses for a year for servants and your horses. I do not want to say anything against them, about the robbery, extortions, and other evils they have done. Is it not, therefore, going to be good for you and wise counsel, that you should decrease the number of your horses for the sake of paying your debts and those of your father, or, if the debts will have been paid, to give as much to paupers, religious, and pilgrims, or to convert them into other pious uses? Surely it is, since whatever you do for your soul, it is yours; but whatever you have wasted, you have lost. Wherefore Ambrose says, "Men's goods are not theirs; they cannot take them with them. Only mercy accompanies the dead."[8] Therefore, consider what you have bequeathed to the poor to be yours; but whatever you have done for the sake of the world, consider it all lost. For the world

---

[8] Actually, this is Walafrid Strabo, quoting St. Ambrose, *Commenatrius in Lucam* 12. 19 (PL 114. 296).

is a pouch with a hole in it, and whatever is put in it will fall out. And I advise that you should not have any faith in your great horses, but only in the Lord your God, as Isaiah 31:1 says, "Woe to those who go down to Egypt for help, and rely on horses, who trust in chariots because they are many, and in horsemen because they are very strong." Judith 9:16 says, "The strength of God does not lie in the multitude of people, nor ... the strength of horses; but the prayers of the humble and mild always please you."

CHAPTER 9

16. O Lord, my King, if only you were wise and would understand this, and discern what your end will be. You should be wise, that is, you should carefully consider the honor granted to you by the men of this land, and you should understand, namely, the damage caused to them by your servants whenever you travel around your land; and you should discern what your end will be, namely, your wretched death, unless such things are changed. Surely you should apply a good remedy for the people of this land, so that they are not oppressed by your servants. And this is to be decreed: that each person is to be the owner of his things, so that thus nothing is seized from his goods against his will. And whoever would do something against this decree should be seriously punished, and besides that, he should incur the curse of God. Wherefore, Lord King, understand and you will not forget how the English people made you king. Therefore, be like one of them. As Ecclesiasticus 32:1 says, "If they have made you a leader, do not be exalted; be like one among them." Therefore, I advise that you should procure food and drink and other things necessary to you as one of the people, since perhaps you still do not understand how and in what way the English people can aid you against your adversaries, etc. Be well warned what is said.

CHAPTER 10

17. O Lord, my King, now heed carefully and write in your heart and never forget what I will say to you now. My Lord King, if only you were wise and would understand this, and discern what your end will be. You should be wise, that is, you should know the customs, statutes, and privileges of this kingdom that are ruinous to the poor or the Holy Church; and you should understand, namely, the prize coming to you if through you all these things are removed; and you should discern what your end will be,

namely, your future death, the kind, timing and occurrence of which you do not know. Surely you should cause to be removed all the customs of this kingdom and all the privileges and all the statutes, whether in the forests or other parts of this kingdom, that are damaging to the holy churches or the paupers or even to the community of this kingdom, with all your strength and with all the haste you can, when you have taken counsel. And from such an act, greater merit will accrue to you than if you would acquire for your son all the kingdoms of the world. Wherefore Seneca says: "What folly it is to procure much for your heir and to deny everything to yourself. For a great inheritance makes an enemy out of a friend. For he will rejoice more from your death by which he will gain more for himself."[9] And therefore I advise that, as much as you can, you should do all good works of charity. Job 14:10 says, "When a man dies, he is stripped bare and consumed." Likewise, 1 Corinthians 3:8 says, "Each shall receive his wages according to his labor." Galatians 6:9–10 says, "So let us not become tired of doing good; for if we do not give up, the time will come when we will reap the harvest. Therefore, as often as we have the chance, we should do good to everyone."

A Story

18. See, Lord King, and heed, and understand a popular story. It happened that in a certain kingdom, the king could not remain in the kingdom more than a year. But during that year he could to do whatever he wanted right up to the end of the year. Those from that kingdom to whom the election pertained chose a certain person as king. As soon as he had been elected, he acquired a great household and a large number of horses, and many goods, some of which he had acquired rightfully, some through wickedness, for the kingdom, but he had acquired nothing for himself. At the end of the year he was suddenly seized and was sent to a certain island, and, without hope of reprieve, he lived in wretched poverty and with many miseries. According to Jeremiah 16:13, "I will throw you out of this land into a land that you have never known, and you will serve other gods day and night, and they will give you no rest." Afterwards, someone else was chosen king, and he, heeding what had befallen his predecessor, took away everything he could get from the kingdom, and sent it to the island to which he would be

---

[9] Seneca, *Epistula moralis* 123.11.

sent after a year. At the end of the year he was sent to that island, in which he lived in the abundance of all those goods, since he had provided for himself beforehand. It is quite properly the same with regard to the kings of this kingdom and others after death. They are sent to a poor island, that is, their bodies are enclosed in a tomb. And see how they are cherished. Approaching their tombs, men say: "This was a good king, there was great peace in his time and there was always rejoicing on his arrival. He built many monasteries, he destroyed the evil customs of the land, and he carried out many works of charity. He did not seize any goods for a lesser price than the owner of them wanted to receive." And they report similar good things about him concerning what he did in his time. And especially, they beseech God for the sake of his soul and the souls of all the faithful departed. Behold how well he is cherished and abounds in delights. Proverbs 22:1 says, "Better is a good reputation than great wealth, and good grace than gold and silver." Ecclesiastes 7:2 says, "Better is a good name than precious perfume." One king who builds a monastery of religious or one religious house of the poor acquires much more for himself than if he had built a thousand castles in his kingdom. As is commonly said, where there is one castle, the entire country all around is worsened because of it, but where there is one monastery of religious, the whole country around is improved. On the contrary, passing the tomb of another king, they say about him: "He was a tyrant, there was no peace in his time, he did not pay his debts; he stole goods from the poor, geese and hens, hay and oats; he stole, and he did many other evil things, and whenever he came the whole country became worse. There was always sorrow and sadness on his arrival, whenever he came." Moreover, at the end, when they have recounted all his evils, then they say: "God spare his soul." Behold how badly his soul fares after his death, when so many evil things are told about him. But about the souls of other kings, who knows? I say to you that he who does good acts will have eternal life, and he who conducts himself badly, unless he repents worthily before death, will be in the eternal flames. And then they can say what is said in Wisdom 5:6–16, "We are the ones who wandered off the right road. We never lived in the light of righteousness; we never caught the first glimmer of its light. All our lives we wandered across unmarked deserts, instead of following the road which the Lord wanted us to travel. . . . We bragged about how rich we were. And now, what good has it done us? All those things are gone now; they have disappeared like a shadow, like something you hear and then forget. A ship sails across the waves of the ocean, but when it is gone, it leaves no trace. You cannot tell it was ever there. A bird flies through the air but leaves no sign that it has been there, save only the sound of its wings as it beats through the thin air. It speeds along, riding through the thin air by the force of its wings, leaving behind no trace of its passing. An arrow splits the air when it is shot to a target, but at once the air closes up behind it, and no one can tell where it passed. It is the same with us. We are born, and then we cease to be. We left no sign of virtue behind us; we were destroyed by our wickedness. Such things do sinners say. For what hope do wicked people have? Only ... the hope of smoke in the breeze. Their hope lasts no longer than our memory of a guest who stays one day and leaves the next." But about good kings, thus is it said in Wisdom 5:16-17: "The just will live forever. The Lord will reward them; the Most High will protect them. They will receive royal splendor and a magnificent crown from the Lord's hand." And therefore, Lord King, be warned, and do all the good works that you can do. Whatever you can do, do well, work urgently while you live (Ecclesiastes 9:10), since the dead can do nothing more than what they have done, and their memory is forgotten (Ecclesiastes 9:5). And therefore, do all the works you believe will please God. Men do not know their end, but like fishes they are seized with a net, and like birds they are captured in a trap; thus many men are seized at a bad time (Ecclesiastes 9:12). Thus you should provide well for yourself while you live, and whatever foolish things you do, remember [...][10] Know, too, that you do not occupy the enduring city here, but we seek the future one (Hebrews 13:14). For it was thus with the kings and princes in antiquity, and ought to be in all, that they had foresight and considered their future death. For as it is said in the life of John the Almoner, in ancient times, as soon as the emperor was crowned, the builders of monuments immediately approached him, saying: "Lord, from what metal do you order your monument to be built?" This insinuates to him, at least, that corruptible and transitory man should have care for his soul, and should dispose of the kingdom piously.[11] As the divine Wisdom [Ecclesiasticus 7:40] says, "In everything you do, remember your end and you will never sin." For meditation of death is like the bridle restraining man lest he exercise cupidity or lust. Thus it is told that many philosophers came to the dead Alexander the Great, when he was put in his golden tomb. About him one said: "Yesterday, Alexander made his treasure of gold; now, on the contrary, today gold made a treasure of him." Another philosopher said: "Yes-

---

[10] Lacuna in text.

[11] Leontius of Neapolis, "Life of St. John the Almsgiver," in *Three Byzantine Saints*, ed. E. Dawes and N. H. Baynes (Crestwood, NY: St. Vladimir's Seminary Press, 1977), 228–229.

terday, all the world did not suffice for Alexander; today two or three ells of cloth in which he can be wrapped suffice." A third said: "Alexander ruled the people; today the people rule him." A fourth said: "Alexander could free many from death; today he cannot avoid the darts of his death." A fifth said: "Yesterday, Alexander led an army; today he is led by them to the tomb." A sixth said: "Yesterday, Alexander pressed upon the earth; today he is pressed upon by it." A seventh said: "Yesterday, the peoples feared Alexander; today they call him vile." An eighth said: "Yesterday, Alexander had no equals; today he has all equals." If you would consider these things well, you would provide for yourself. Therefore, Ecclesiasticus 7:40 warns, "Remember your end." And Ecclesiastes 7:3 says, "Better it is to go to the house of mourning than to the house of feasting; for to this end all men come; let the living consider what their future will be." And you should know that nothing profits you as much as temperance in all things, and frequent consideration of the uncertain brevity of life; and whatever you do, consider your death always, since no one is so ignorant that he does not know that sometime he is going to die. But when death approaches nearby, one trembles and cries. But why tears, why trepidation, when all are led by this necessity? You go whither all things go, and in accord with this law you were born. This happened to your father and your ancestors; this will happen to all after you. And remember this, when you doubt that you will die: many thousands of men have already died. Wherefore Seneca said: "You should fear death because of the necessity of dying: for death spares no one."[12] Likewise, [fear death] on account of its speed, as Job 7:7 says, "My life is like the wind." Likewise, [fear death] on account of the uncertainty of the place, time, and method. Likewise, one should fear death because of the confrontation with evils: for sins and demons present themselves to you in the final hour. And death should be feared because it is bitterness to sinners. Ecclesiasticus 41:1 says, "O death, how bitter is your memory to the unjust man." But one is unjust who seizes the goods of others, when they are unwilling. When you have understood these things well, Lord King, I forewarn you that you should remove that evil prerogative, namely, to seize the things of others for a lower price than the seller wishes to sell it for. If you do not do this, you will see the time in which you would rather have banished from your land that evil prerogative and the evil customs of this land than to have acquired all the kingdoms of the world. And therefore, be warned for the future.

---

[12] I have been unable to locate the source of this quote.

Chapter 11

19. O Lord, my King, if all the aforesaid things cannot move you to banish that evil prerogative, namely, to seize the things of another for a lesser price than the owner of those things wants to receive, hear how Louis, formerly King of France, gave these holy teachings to his son Philip about how to live, so they may induce you to abolish that evil prerogative from your land. And it is my counsel that you should hold to that mode of living. Proverbs 3:21-26 says, "Keep the law and counsel, and they will be the life of your soul, and adornment for your neck. Then you will walk on your way securely, and your foot will not stumble. If you rest you will not be afraid; when you lie down, your sleep will be sweet. Do not be afraid of sudden panic ... The Lord will be with you and keep you." And now hear diligently and understand well those holy teachings.

20. In A.D. 1270, Louis, that most Christian king of the Franks, died. And these are the warnings which the king made on the spot to his son Philip and, as is said, wrote them with his own hand: "I especially warn you, son, that you should, above everything else, love God with all your heart and all your strength, for without that, you will have no salvation."[13] From this warning it follows that you should not seize nor permit to be seized from anyone through your servants those things for a lower price than the seller wishes to receive. For you will not seem to love your brother from whom you seize his things against his will. But as 1 John 4:20-21 says, "He who does not love his brother, whom he has seen, cannot love God, whom he has not seen. And we have this commandment from Him: that he who loves God should also love his brother." But you do not love your brother when you seize his things against his will, given that you should pay him the true price. Since Christ says in the Gospel [Matthew 7:12; Luke 6:31], "Whatever you would wish men to do to you, so do to them." What you would not want to be done to you, you should not do to others. But you would not permit that someone should take your things from you, with you unwilling, unless you were given the true price you wish to receive from him. Again, according to 1 John 2:4, "He who says that he loves God but does not keep His commandments is a liar." But

---

[13] The quotations throughout Chapter 11 are from Jean de Joinville's "Les enseignements de Saint Louis à son fils," which forms part of his *Histoire de Saint Louis*, a French-language "mirror" of the thirteenth century. William seems to have translated this text into Latin himself, as I am unaware of any earlier Latin version. An English-language edition of the text may be found in René Hague, trans., *The Life of St. Louis* (New York: Sheed and Ward, 1955), 213-216.

this is one of the commandments (Exodus 20:17): "Do not covet the things of your neighbor." Besides, it is said in 1 John 3:17: "He who has the goods of the world, and sees his brother in need, yet closes his heart against him, how does God's love abide in him?" Surely, in no way. I say that much less is the charity of God in one who steals geese, hens, etc. against their owners' will, since as it has commonly been said, your household seizes things, as if from beggars, to whom it would be better to give than to take from.

21. "Again, you ought to keep yourself from all which you know displeases God, namely, from all sin, so that you would rather permit yourself to suffer more than all the martyrs rather than to commit some mortal sin." From this warning, it follows that one ought not seize anything against the will of the owner, since the will of God is that you should not covet the goods of another, their owner being unwilling. In 1 Thessalonians 4:12, it says, "Desire nothing of someone else." Exodus 20:17 says, "Do not desire the oxen or donkeys of your neighbor," against his will, "nor other goods that are his." All the more, they should not seize things against their will, since it is worse to take than to covet. If, moreover, you knew in another case that your servants were taking the goods of another, against his will, it is feared that what is said will come back to you, as Isaiah 47:11 says, "Evil shall come upon you, . . . and you do not know whence it comes. And misery shall come on you suddenly, of which you know nothing."

22. "Likewise, if God would send some adversity to you, you should endure it calmly and with thanksgiving, knowing that it is for your good and that you have deserved it." Job 5:17 says, "Happy is the man who is corrected by God." In Hebrews 12:6 it is written, "God disciplines him whom He loves." "But if God brings some prosperity to you, you should humbly give thanks to Him, and be warned lest hence you become worse either through vainglory or in some other way, since you should not offend God on account of His gifts." From this warning, it follows that you should not take anything against the will of the owners of those things. If you were to do that, you offend God, since it is the commandment of God, "Do not covet things of your neighbor"; "Do not desire oxen," as was noted above. Do not wonder if God should send you persecution and tribulation, if you would seize goods from another, against his will. As Isaiah 33:1 says, "Woe to you who destroy, will you yourself not be destroyed?" See what happened to your father.

23. "Likewise, I warn you to confess often, and that you should choose honest and discreet confessors who know how to teach you what you ought to look out for and what you should do. And you should be so modest that your confessors and your friends could securely correct you if it

were necessary." From this warning, it follows that you should not take anything against the will of the seller. For your confessor will tell you that this is against the commandment of the Lord, to take something against the will of the owner of the thing, as is said in Exodus 20; see Ecclesiasticus 19.5: "He who hates correction shortens his life." And a good confessor should enjoin you that in no way should you permit such things to happen in your days, if you want to save your soul. And your confessor should be expected to tell you this. Wherefore Seneca in his letters says: "If you would bear with the defects of a friend, do the same with yours as well, therefore you should take away his as well as yours, as much as you can."[14]

24. "Likewise, if you have some desolation of heart, tell that to your confessor or some other worthy man, and then you will bear it more lightly and joyfully." Heed, Lord King, what your confessor or some other good man will, among other things, say to you: "My Lord King, you should deservedly have desolation of heart, since numberless men and women have desolation of heart when you arrive because your household seizes the goods of others against their will." And therefore you should order that in future such things should not occur, lest you incur great desolation of heart, sadness, and sorrow.

25. "Likewise, gladly hear the office of the Church, and when you have been in church a long time, be warned lest you divert your attention or speak vainly. Instead, you should observe everything devoutly either through prayer or heartfelt meditation, and more especially you should pay devout attention during the secret of the mass, at the hour of the consecration of the body of Christ." But heed, Lord King, if you want the office of the Church and your prayers and good works to help you, first be reconciled to your brothers from whom you have received many goods and to whom you have not paid debts, and finally you should order in your heart that the goods of another should not be taken from him against his will. As Matthew 5:23–24 says, "If you are offering your gift at the altar, and there remember that your brother has something against you, leave your gift there before the altar and go; first be reconciled to your brother; and then come and offer your gift."

26. "Likewise, you should have a pious heart toward paupers, the wretched, and the afflicted, and use power and counsel to aid them." But pay heed, Lord King, that you do not attend to this warning, since you know or you should know that your household takes the goods of many

---

[14] Not the *Epistolae*, but Seneca, *De beneficiis* 6.39.1.

paupers, when they are unwilling; but one should give to them rather than take from them. Take and freely hear these words of God, both in the open and in secret. But heed, Lord King, what the preacher will among other things say: that you should not permit anyone from your household, nor anyone whomsoever, to take the things of others, when the owners are unwilling.

27. "Likewise, freely obtain for yourself indulgence from many and various prelates of the Church." But understand, Lord King, that such indulgences profit you nothing as long as you use that evil prerogative to seize the goods of another for a lesser price than the seller wishes to sell it for, since he who is not charitable profits nothing from indulgences. Accordingly, in 1 Corinthians 13:3, it says, "If I give away all that I have to feed paupers, and I deliver my body so that it may be burned, but have not love, I gain nothing." For the treasures of the Church are not given as indulgences to its enemies, and I think that such are those who are outside charity.

28. "Likewise, you should love the company of good men, whether religious or seculars, and shun the society of the depraved." But heed, Lord King, that all of those who take the goods of others against their will are depraved men, and you should banish all such men from your court, by virtue of the aforesaid warning.

29. "Likewise, you should always love the good in your neighbor, and hate the evil. And do not allow any word conducive to sin to be said before you, or a word of detraction about another, or any word of blasphemy about the saints is said, without taking steps to see that it is avenged." And from this warning, it follows that you should take nothing from the goods of others against their will, because if you did, it would be evil, and you should hate this, by virtue of the aforesaid warning. The Psalmist says, "Whoever loves God, hates evil," etc. (Psalms 96:10).

30. "Likewise, as a result of all the benefits granted to you by God, thus you should thank God, so that you might be worthy to receive even greater things." But heed, Lord King, because your ingratitude is very great, since God has conferred so many benefits on you, as you know, yet you through your ministers seize infinite goods from others, although they are unwilling, just like a thief. You ought to know that as liberality is a sign of nobility, so robbery is a sign of barbarism. Wherefore many nobles, who are counted nobles by the opinion of men, are barbarians, since they do not stop seizing the goods of paupers, although unwilling, from whose labors they live.

31. "Likewise, you are to conduct yourself justly toward your subjects, so that you hold to the line of justice, leaning neither to the right nor to the left. And you should always prefer more the part of the poor, rather

than the rich, until you are sure of the truth." Deuteronomy 17:20 says, "The king may not turn aside to the right or the left, so that he and his sons may continue long in his kingdom." Ecclesiasticus 4:33 says, "Fight to the death for justice and God will eliminate your enemies for you." From this warning, it follows that you should not allow anyone to seize the goods of others against their will. If you allow that, you do not hold to the line of justice, since it would be justice to return to someone what is his. For nothing should be stolen, as your servants do.

32. "If someone has a quarrel with you, you should be more concerned for their case until there is agreement between you concerning the truth, and thus your counselors should stand up immediately for justice." But understand, Lord King, that thousands and thousands of people have cases against you for the debts you have not paid. You should, therefore, ordain some good method through which your debts can be paid and, since you have delayed payment, you are bound for all the damages of creditors.

33. "Likewise, know for certain that if you hold something from someone else, either from your ancestors or from your own time, you ought to restore it immediately. Moreover, if it be something hidden, you should diligently inquire through discreet and faithful men." And from this warning it follows that all the goods of the dead which have devolved to you which you have unjustly acquired through those dead people, you should restore to those to whom by right they belong. But, as is commonly said, you do not do this.

34. "Likewise, love peace, since all your subjects are preserved in peace and justice, and in particular, religious and ecclesiastical persons. For it is said of King Philip ... that certain of his counselors said the same thing to him — that many clerics had brought damages upon him, by usurping his rights, and it was a wonder that it was tolerated. To them, the king wisely and humbly answered: 'I well believe that you speak the truth, but when I think of the benefits which God has conferred upon me, better that I want to be patient rather than to arouse scandal between myself and the Church.'" From this warning, it follows that your servants should not seize anything for a lower price than the seller wants to receive, and if they were to do that, peace and justice would not be served. Romans 13:8, 9 says, "He who loves his neighbor has fulfilled the law." And there follows, "You shall not covet" the goods of your neighbor. Now, praise God, there is peace in all this land, except for those parts into which you come. And as a result of this you should blush, since you should keep peace and lead others with all your efforts firmly to keep the peace.

35. "Likewise, love churchmen and keep their peace as much as you

can." 2 Corinthians 13:11 says, "Keep the peace and the God of love and peace will be with you." "Likewise, assist them in necessities and especially in those through which God is greatly honored in the world." From this warning, it follows that you should not seize the goods of another when he is unwilling, because if you do there is no peace.

36. "Likewise, honor your parents; obey them reverently." From this warning, it follows that you should not take the goods of another when he is unwilling, since it violates the commandment of God, who ought to be your father. Exodus 20:17 says that you ought not to covet the goods of others. Therefore, all the more you should not take the things of others when the owner is unwilling. Matthew 7:12 says, "Whatever you wish that men would do to you, do so to others." But you do not wish for anyone to take your goods when you are unwilling, unless he wants to pay the true price to you. Therefore, you should not do that to others nor should you permit it when your servants do that, if you want to please God. "Likewise, the goods of the Church should go to suitable persons, by the counsel of spiritual men and to those who hold no benefice." In the same way, Lord King, I advise that you order matters concerning hospitality and your household according to the counsel of spiritual men. You should diligently attend to your debts, and the debts of your father and grandfather, which are, as it is said, infinite. Be warned that you will be bound to payment of them all.

37. "Likewise, be warned lest without great counsel you would begin a war with some Christians. And if it happens, take care, lest innocents or churches or the property of churches be punished without cause, and as quickly as you can, end the war and your struggles, and moreover those of your subjects," as blessed Mauricius did. But take heed, Lord King, because without good counsel, you make war every day, taking the goods of various men when they are unwilling. And therefore, I advise for your comfort and honor that you end such wars without delay, if you want to save your kingdom for yourself and your son, and this is to order that everyone can be owner of his things, namely, that no one take another's goods when he is unwilling.

38. "Likewise, you should be solicitous so that you would have faithful bailiffs and provosts, and inquire diligently how they act. Likewise, [inquire] about your hospitality." But, Lord King, I tell you for certain that they deceive you and yours about food and drink and other necessities, at least in that they take many goods of others against their will. For from this they incur the indignation of God and the English people, as was noted above. And I want you to know, Lord King, that it is not wise to keep such

a multitude of men and horses at your expense, as you do, from which arises not peace in this land, praise God, but great foolishness. For is he not foolish who spends more than he has in goods? Certainly he is. But it is commonly said that all of the moveable goods which you have in the world, multiplied threefold, would not suffice to pay your debts and the debts of your father and grandfather, for whose payment you are bound; with what audacity would you dare to cause such great expenditures? You should not believe that your son would want to pay your debts, any more than you want to pay your father's debts. And therefore I suggest that you cut the expenditures of your house, so that you can satisfy your creditors, and those of your father and grandfather, if you want to save your soul. Therefore, it is necessary for you to beware of excessive and abundant expenditures, and foolish and excessive gifts, so that in future you may wage war for our God. Excess expenditures are the destruction of the kingdom, because when excess expenditures exceed the returns of the cities, and thus when there are insufficient returns and growing expenses, kings have extended their hand towards the things and incomes of others. Truly, their subjects, because of the injury, have cried out to the Lord God on high and glorious, who, sending a strong wind, afflicted them vehemently, and the people rose up against them and almost wiped their names from the earth. And therefore be warned, and heed, lest you forget what happened to your father.

39. "Likewise, be always obedient and devoted to the Roman church and to the lord pope, as your spiritual father."[15] And I say to you, Lord King, that it is not at the pope's will that your ministers take people's goods against the will of the owners of the goods, since the pope himself, from whom you hold all the English land, does not do this, nor is he permitted to do it in places in which he resides. Therefore, you cannot do this, and most of all since it is against the will of God. Exodus 20:17 says that you should "not covet the things of your neighbor."

40. "Likewise, work so that all sin may be banished from your land, especially blasphemy and heresies." Heed, Lord King, so that they do not rule in your court; and first remove it, namely, that your ministers take much, although those whose goods they are be unwilling. And regarding that sin, enough was noted above.

41. "Likewise, remember to recognize and give thanks to God about his benefits, and heed that the expenditures of your house be kept moderate." But understand, Lord King, that you are not thankful for the benefits of

---

[15] This sentence is not found in Joinville's *Histoire*.

God, from whom so many benefits were given to you, so long as you permit your ministers to take many goods from the poor who have to provide lodging, [when it is the poor] to whom rather things should be given by way of charity. Concerning the expenditures of your house, moreover, ensure that they occur with moderation. I say to you, Lord King, that there is no man in this land who is more in need than you that the expenditures of your house occur with moderation, since there is no one who owes so much, and therefore in future you should provide well for yourself, so that the expenditures of your house occur with moderation, on account of your debts that have to be paid to many and diverse creditors. Consider the Lord King of France, with how much moderation, how wisely and sagaciously, he meets the expenses of his house. And just as he himself acts wisely, I suggest that you should do likewise. And this is best for the health of your soul, so that you can be quickly freed from diverse and numerous debts.

42. "Likewise, if I pass away before you, I wish that you cause my soul to be aided faithfully in masses, prayers, and alms, and that you would ask the holy congregations of the kingdom to devote themselves to intercessory prayers." And I counsel that you do this same thing for your father; and along with this you should cause to be ordered and ordained for the soul of your father, since he is greatly in need, and for the salvation of your own soul, that in future no one of your court nor anyone else will take anyone's goods against his will. If you do not want to do this, I do not know how you will come to be numbered among the saved, nor enter the kingdom of God, as is evident above in the first warning of Saint Louis. And, Lord King, you ought to know what is said in Romans 14:17: "The kingdom of God is not food and drink, but justice, peace, and joy." But where you come in this land, you cause injustice to many men, from whom goods are seized against their will, and in this there is neither peace nor joy. And it is said in 2 Corinthians 13:11: "Keep the peace and the God of love and peace will be with you." But when you come with your great household, and your ministers take many goods against the will of the owners, there is not peace there. And therefore it should be greatly feared that the God of peace and love is neither with you nor with your household; and therefore be warned about this for the future.

Chapter 12

43. O Lord, my King, I beseech you not to be annoyed if I still speak to you in this way once again. When someone of your household comes to a

village to provide for your arrival with geese and hens, among other geese and hens he takes from one poor woman a hen from which she could have four or five eggs to maintain herself and her children; he gives her one denarius, or at most one and a half denarii, and sometimes nothing. This poor woman did not want that hen to be sold for three denarii. This hen, since she is fat, is prepared for your mouth. You are happy from eating that hen, the poor woman is sad; you laugh, she cries; you fill your stomach with the hen which you have unjustly acquired, she is hungry and begs her bread; you feast splendidly on many ill-gotten foods, she has virtually nothing to eat. You are in the fullness of riches, she in dire poverty; you are in golden clothes, she in shabby garments; you have much, she has need; you display hospitality with knights and others by enjoying delicacies, she displays hospitality tearfully with her children crying for lack of bread. I ask you: by what audacity, what boldness, what impulse, do you dare to eat such a hen? Out of such hens and geese, along with other things you have extorted, you make your feast with joy and singing, but I promise you that all such things will be changed into mourning and sadness unless a remedy is quickly applied to this; according to Amos 8:10, "I will turn your feasts into mourning, and all your songs into lamentation." Such joy winds up as eternal punishment just as delight becomes mangy and sorrowful. Job 21:12-14 says, "They sing to the tambourine and the lyre, and rejoice to the sound of the pipe. They spend their days in prosperity, and in a moment descend into Hell. They say to God, 'Depart from us, we do not wish the knowledge of your ways.'" Isaiah 33:1 says, "Woe to you, destroyer, will you yourself not be destroyed? Woe to you who despise, will you yourself not be despised? When you have eaten your prey, you will become prey." See what happened to your father.

44. But so far God has spared you, and this, I am certain, is because of your innocence and the mercy of God. But in short, you should fear that unless you cause those aforementioned things to be amended, trials and anguish will come to you. And if then you cry to God you should fear that God will not hear you, since so often I have cried out to you about the poor in order that you would banish the evil prerogative from this land, that prerogative which is contrary to divine and human law, namely, to take another's goods for a lesser price than the seller wishes to receive, and you do not listen to me. In Proverbs 21:13, it says: "He who does not wish to hear the cry of the poor will himself cry out to God and he will not be heard." Proverbs 1:24, 25, 27, 29 says: "I have called," namely, through sane doctrine, "and you refused; I have extended my hand," namely, by giving many goods to you, "and you have not heeded." And it follows:

"When distress and anguish come upon you, then you will call me and I will not hear you, ... because you had contempt for my discipline and did not choose fear of God and would have none of good counsel." Isaiah 63:4, 5 says, "For the day of vengeance came, ... and I looked, and there was no one to aid; I sought, and there was no one to help." And heed carefully, Lord King, what is said in Luke 16:19-31. For a rich man did not want to give anything to a certain beggar who was lying at his door, covered with sores. That beggar died and he was carried to heaven by angels. The rich man died and he descended to Hell. This rich man, as Gregory said, was punished not because he stole another's goods, but because he did not give from his own goods to the needy.[16] Therefore, by what punishment is one who takes goods from the needy to be punished? If the one who did not help the needy with his own goods was stricken with infernal damnation, it is sure that it will be by a much greater punishment, since in Hell there are many diverse punishments, as in heaven there are many different mansions (John 14:2).

45. Therefore, I warn you, King, again and again, for the health of your soul, that you should not permit the things of others to be taken from anyone for a lower price than the seller wants to receive for them. And he who does not agree to this ordinance will not be counted among the saved; according to the Psalmist: "Let them be erased from the book of life, and let them not be written down" (Psalms 68:29) Such people are not just, and therefore they will remain with the unjust, namely, in Hell where there is no redemption. But it is a wonder — and grieved over, and marveled at in no small way — and it should also be sorrowed over, by what boldness, what temerity, led whither by diabolical spirits the men of very great learning are. When dwelling with the Lord King, they dare to eat such hens and geese, and other things which were unjustly acquired, although they cannot pretend ignorance of such a thing, because this is notorious, even if the Lord King might pretend not to know. Would that they would heed and understand every day, before dinner, that which is said here; according to 1 John 4:16, "God is love, and he who abides in love abides in God, and God in him." But it is sure that those who consent to such seizures are not charitable, since consenting and doing are to be punished equally. And that they are not charitable is evident from what is said according to 1 John 3.17: "He who possesses the goods of the world, and sees his brother in need, yet closes his heart against him, how does the love of God abide in

---

[16] St. Gregory the Great, *Homiliae in Evangelia* 40.3 (PL 76. 1304D).

him?" And how much less abides the charity of God in heaven when one consents that the goods of the poor be seized although they are unwilling, since such geese and hens, and many other goods, are seized for the use of the king and his household.

46. But perhaps the clerks of the court, worldly-wise men, excuse themselves and say that they do not consent to such deeds, but that such things happen, although they are unwilling. Nay, rather, surely they consent, and the participants are offenders before the supreme God. From such roosters and hens and other goods they knowingly eat, since more credence is placed in deed than in word, and more is done by fact than is shown by word. Thus it is said in Titus 1:16: "They profess to know God, yet they deny him by their deeds." Just as 2 Thessalonians 3:5, 6 says, "May the Lord direct your hearts in love." And there follows: "Keep away from any brother who walks out of the way." And if one does not resist an error, one approves of it. Besides, according to Augustine, "Charity is an act of rectitude, keeping one's eyes always on God; and charity feeds the hungry."[17] But, my Lord King, your ministers rob the hungry when they take roosters and hens from the poor. Likewise Bernard says, "Proper charity is to nourish concord."[18] Wherefore Ecclesiasticus 25:1-2 says: "There are three things ... that are delightful to God and men: concord between brothers, friendship between neighbors, and husbands and wives living together happily." Therefore, when those of your household take the goods of others for a lesser price than the seller wishes to sell it for, there is no concord, but discord, no love of brothers, but rather hatred and evil work. James 3:16 says, "Where jealousy and contention exist, there will be disorder and every vile practice." Therefore, learned men, and others having the spirit of God, dwelling with the Lord King, ought with one mind to approach him, or else someone discreet in their name, who will say that he should not permit such seizures to be made in the future against the will of the owner; because, since the awareness is present, it is not permitted (either for one's self or for others) to eat, possess, or seize such things, and thus the king might be honorably induced to forsake that evil prerogative.

47. But it should be feared that it might be said of many learned men and others dwelling with the Lord King: "His watchmen are blind, ... they are all dumb dogs, they cannot bark, dreaming, lying down, loving to slumber." And there follows: "They have all turned to their own way, each to

---

[17] I am unable to locate a source for this quotation.
[18] St. Bernard of Clairvaux, *Epistola* 11, sec. 4 (PL 182. 111C).

his own gain, from the highest to the lowest," as is said in Isaiah 56:10–11. Nor is it any wonder, as is said in Isaiah 1:23: "Everyone loves money and runs after gifts." And Jeremiah 8:10 says, "From the least to the greatest, everyone is greedy." And therefore they can fear what is said in Job 15:34: "Fire consumes the tents of those who openly accept payments." But they will change themselves from these, and then they will induce the Lord King to banish the evil prerogative, according to 2 Timothy 2:21: "If one purifies himself from these things, then he will be a vessel sanctified in honor, and useful to God for every ready good work." Proverbs 25:5 says, "From the king's presence remove wickedness, and on justice his throne will be founded."

Chapter 13

48. O Lord, my King, if only you were wise and would understand this, and discern what your end will be. You would understand, that is, you would closely consider how it benefits, and how it can benefit, you to have the love of God and the love of your English people; and you should understand what the harm is and how it can harm you to have the hatred of God and the hatred of your English people; and you should discern what your end will be, namely, your death, the timing, nature, and location of which God knows. Surely you should order yourself and your household in such a manner that you should have the love of God and of your English people. And I say to you, before God, that you will never have the love of God and of your English people as long as your servants, with your consent, seize the goods of others for a lower price than the seller wishes to receive. Psalms 96:10 says, "Whoever loves God hates evil." But it is evil and unjust to take another's goods when their owner is unwilling; since certainly you would not do this to a friend whom you love. And this is a commandment of God, that you should love your neighbor as yourself. Matthew 22:37–38 and Luke 10:27 say, "Love God with all your heart and all your soul, and with all your mind, and your neighbor as yourself." For I want you to know that you do not have the love of the English people as a good king should have; with a good king the people rejoice at his arrival, and the people greatly desire the arrival of a good king; but with your arrival, as is commonly said, the English people sorrow, and they do this because of the seizures that your servants make.

49. And therefore I tell you, Lord King, if such seizures and depredations continue with your consent in your court until your death, you will say: Woe, woe, woe. And why do I say that you will say "woe" three

times? The first woe is that you were ever born. And why? Since there was always woe, whenever you came into your land. But the greater woe for you will be when your soul leaves your body and is free for the devil. But the greatest woe of all for you will be when your soul is carried off to Hell, and there it will be in woe and will suffer without end. And this will be by the correct judgment of God: since just as from your arrival there was woe in whatever place you stayed, because of the extortions which your servants committed, with your permission, namely, to seize the goods of others for a lesser price than they wanted to sell them for, so your soul, after death, will remain in woe until, on judgment day, the body will reunite with the soul and the body along with the soul will be condemned together to eternal flames, for those who were allies in vices will be allies in punishments. For one punishment ties together those whom one love bound together in crime.[19] And therefore take heed. And because of such dangers, you should not hesitate to banish that evil prerogative, namely, to take things for a lesser price than the seller wants to receive. According to Ecclesiasticus 5:8-9, "Do not delay your return to the Lord, do not put it off another day; for suddenly the Lord's wrath will come, and at the time of vengeance, it will utterly destroy you." Moreover, heed diligently and never forget what is said in Deuteronomy 11:26-28: "I set before you today a blessing and a curse; a blessing, if you obey the commandments of the Lord your God; a curse, if you do not obey." Therefore, this is one of God's commandments, as Exodus 20:17 says that you should not covet the things of others when their owner is unwilling. Therefore, even more, you should not take the things of others through your servants, with the owner unwilling, especially when there is peace in this land, as there is now, praise God.

50. If, moreover, you do not want to banish that evil prerogative, you can fear what is said in Psalms 118:21, "Evil are those who wander from your command." In Exodus 2:23-24 it says: "The people of Israel groaned under their bondage, and cried out for help, and their cry under their tasks came up to God. And God heard their groaning." And in Exodus 3:7-8, the Lord said to Moses: "I have seen the affliction of my people who are in Egypt, and have heard their cry because of their taskmasters; I know their sufferings and I have come down to deliver them out of the hand of the Egyptians." Thus it will be for you. Unless you banish that aforesaid evil prerogative from your land, the Lord will free the English people from

---

[19] Pseudo-Bernard of Clairvaux, *Meditationes piissimae de cognitione humanae conditionis* 3 (PL 184. 491B).

your hands more quickly than you think. Moreover, you can fear the great evils and dangers that are named in Deuteronomy 28. Think about your predecessors, what now they possess out of all the goods of the world that they had, and how they were taken away from this world. However, if you would banish that evil prerogative from this land and "walk in the precepts of God, ... God will give you your rains in their season, and the land shall yield its increase, and the trees of the field shall yield their good fruit." And there follows: "And you shall dwell in your land securely, and have peace in your land," as is said in Leviticus 26:3-6. Deuteronomy 4:39-40 says, "Know, therefore, this day and consider it in your heart that the Lord is God in heaven above and on earth beneath; there is no other God. Therefore, you shall keep His statutes and His commandments, ... that it may go well with you, and with your children after you, and that you may prolong your days in the land which the Lord your God gives you." Ecclesiasticus 3:22 says, "What God commands you, always think that." In the same (Ecclesiasticus 29:14), it is written, "Place your heart in the precepts of the Most High, and you will find it more profitable than gold." And if you would do this, you could go securely to war with your enemies, as Deuteronomy 20:1, 3-4 says, "When you go forth against your enemies, and see ... an army larger than your own, do not fear them the Lord your God is with you." And have someone proclaim to the people thus: "Do not fear, do not retreat, or be in dread of your enemies, because the Lord your God is in your midst, and He will fight for you against your enemies, and He will save you from danger," etc.

51. And you may know for certain that if you keep the commandments of God, infinite good things will come to you, about which is said in Deuteronomy 28:1-8,10-11: "If you keep the commandments of the Lord your God, ... He will set you high above all the nations that dwell on the earth. And all these blessings shall come upon you: ... Blessed shall you be in the city, and blessed shall you be in the field. Blessed shall be the fruit of your land and the fruit of your beasts, ... and the young of your flock. Blessed shall be your storehouse, ... and blessed shall be your coming in and your going out. The Lord shall cause your enemies who arise against you to perish in your sight; they shall come out against you one way, and flee before you seven ways. The Lord will command the blessing upon your barns, and all the works of your hands." And there follows: "And all the peoples of the earth shall see that you are called by the name of the Lord, and they shall be afraid of you. And the Lord will make you abound in all prosperity," etc. Wherefore, Lord King, you should know, according to many wise men who speak with inspiration, that it is right that the royal majesty obey

the laws it instituted itself, not in appearance of falsehood, but in evidence of fact, so that all may know that the king himself fears the highest God and is subject to divine power. Then men who are accustomed to revere and fear the king when they see him will both fear and revere God. But if only in appearance he shows that he obeys the laws, and in his works, if he be an evildoer, since it is difficult to keep evil deeds hidden and unknown to the people, he will be reproved by God and condemned by men, his deeds will be shown to be foolish, his empire will be lessened, the diadem of his glory will lack honor. And therefore, Lord King, be warned and take care, lest someone should seize the goods of others against their will, since it is against the established laws.

Chapter 14

52. O Lord, my King, heed carefully that forty years have already passed, namely, from that time in which the noble King Edward your grandfather began to use the aforesaid prerogative, namely, to take the things of others for a lesser price than the seller wishes to receive. During these years, there was not so much peace in this land as now, and already a year has passed; [there is presently peace] except in those parts in which you make your journey. For in those places there should be peace and joy; but there is neither peace nor joy. Nor is it any wonder, since, as is said in Isaiah 48:22 and 57:21, "There is no peace for the wicked, says the Lord." Ezekiel 13:10 says, "They have misled the people, saying, 'Peace,' and there is no peace." And therefore, you should fear danger to you, as it says in 1 Thessalonians 5:3: "When the people say there is peace and security, then suddenly destruction will come upon them." And thus the people are greatly burdened upon your arrival, since your ministers seize their goods against their will. But I hope, by the grace of God, that the peace and joy of this land, which have already lasted this year, are the first days of peace and joy that will occur upon your arrival in the future. And this is to order and ordain that no one is to seize the goods of another against his will. And unless you do this, there will never be joy on your arrival and you should fear greatly that the people of this land will rise up against you. Be well warned. And therefore this is my counsel, so that the people will rejoice at your arrival and be sad and sorrowful on your departure. And then it will be said about you, as in 3 Ezra 8:28, "Blessed be the Lord God of our fathers, who placed this in the heart of the king, that he might glorify the Lord God in Jerusalem," and in all the English lands, and thus the greatest honor will accrue to you,

and there will be peace and joy whenever you travel around your kingdom. And then you can say, according to Isaiah 39:8, "There will be peace and truth in my days." Hebrews 12:14 says, "Strive for peace among all, ... without which no one will see God." 1 Peter 3:10–12 says, "He who would love life, and see good days, ... let him divert from evil and do right; let him seek peace and pursue it; for the eyes of the Lord are upon the just, and His ears are open to their prayers." How much of it is from you, when all people have peace? And thus you will begin to be counted among the number of the saved.

Chapter 15

53. O Lord, my King, heed carefully and write on your gates, in the courtyards of your chamber, and on each and every door and window — and every day consider in your heart, and read at table, and never forget — that salvific and oft-repeated divine counsel that the omnipotent Lord counseled through the blessed Moses in Deuteronomy 32:29: "If you were wise and would understand, and would discern your end." O wondrous and useful sentence! Not once, but often, day and night, it should be repeated. If only you were wise and would understand this, and discern what your end will be. If you were wise, that is, you should know the way to heaven, in which there are riches, delights, and honors. There [you will find] the highest security, the highest happiness, happy freedom, happy blessedness. And you should understand, namely, the way that leads to Hell, in which is found intolerable sadness, incredible stench, horrible fear, horrid visions of demons, a confusion of sinners, the despair of all the good.[20] And you should discern what your end will be, namely, the day of your death, which will come suddenly, and will perhaps be today. For it is certain that you will die, but uncertain when or how or where. Surely, if you would know, you would choose and keep that way which leads to heaven, and leave off that one which leads to Hell. But the right way to heaven is to obey the commandments of God, and the way to Hell is not to keep them. Wherefore, among the commandments of God, as is said in Exodus 20:17 and in Romans 13:9, one of them is: "Do not covet the things of your neighbor." Therefore, you should not take the things of another for a lesser price than the seller wishes to receive. If you do so, or if any one of your men does so

---

[20] This passage contains echoes of Pseudo-Bernard, *Meditationes piissimae de cognitione humanae conditionis* 3 (PL 184. 492A).

with your knowledge, then you are on the way to Hell. When you offend in one matter, you are guilty in all, since every virtue suffers defect from one vice. For while you continue in one sin, you lose all goodness; as Ecclesiastes 9:18 says, "He who sins in one thing loses much good." And therefore, for the salvation of your soul, you should choose for yourself the way that leads to heaven, namely, you should in no way permit that the goods of another be taken against his will, especially in time of peace, as there is now, praise God. And thus you can keep yourself on the way that leads to eternal life (Matthew 17:19). May Christ, the Son of God, who lives and reigns without end, bring you there. Amen.

When you have corrected the errors previously mentioned, and begun on the warnings of the Saint King Louis, then I will teach you how to please God and the people, and thus you will walk along the right path to the joy of heaven. To that end may our Lord Jesus Christ bring you. Amen.

Introduction to
Whether a Prince Can Receive the Goods of the Church for His Own Needs, Namely, in Case of War, Even Against the Wishes of the Pope
by William of Ockham

TAXING THE CHURCH

Among the most contentious issues confronted by the theorists of medieval political life was the demarcation of the so-called "liberties" of the church, that is, the rights over persons and property enjoyed by ecclesiastical government independent of the oversight or control of secular rulers. In England, the conflict about the nature and extent of these liberties was almost as old as the Norman invasion itself: successive archbishops of Canterbury and their clerical colleagues clashed repeatedly and deeply with the Anglo-Norman and Plantagenet monarchs, sometimes with tragic results. A prime source of conflict between clerical and temporal spheres, in England and throughout Europe, was the right of kings to impose forms of direct taxation upon the estate of the church. The developing monarchies of Western Europe were desperate to generate as much revenue from their subjects as possible, and the church, long a major beneficiary of earthly largesse, was ripe for harvest. As a consequence, political authors of the age devoted a considerable amount of attention and reflection to the relative privileges enjoyed by ecclesiastical and secular authorities over the property of the church. The preceding treatises by Walter of Milemete and William of Pagula illustrate — albeit from opposite perspectives — that the threat of royal exactions was never far from the mind of fourteenth-century English thinkers.

Those clerics and their defenders in England who objected to royal taxation generally proceeded by raising two points. First, they maintained that no ecclesiastical goods whatsoever may be granted to laymen without the express permission of the pope. Second, they held that the property of the church does not in any case pertain to the clergy to concede, since it has been given to churches for the performance of good works and righteous causes only. These claims were sometimes asserted separately and sometimes together. But each appears in a wide variety of documents dating from the early decades of the fourteenth century.

The appeal to a papal prerogative of prior approval constituted a means of resisting the taxes of lay rulers throughout Europe during the late Middle Ages, reflecting the decree of the Fourth Lateran Council of 1215 that clergy must consult with the pope before acquiescing in the fiscal demands of secular governments. The basis for this papal authority was, however, articulated differently according to local intellectual and historical variations. In France, where the papacy's interference with taxation of the church had stirred a major conflict with King Philip IV in the 1290s, we find pointed justifications of the papal right to confirm exactions couched in terms of the extreme position that the See of St. Peter commanded lordship (*dominium*) over all earthly possessions, lay as well as clerical. When Giles of Rome proclaimed in his *De ecclesiastica potestate* of 1302 that "the church is more *dominus* of your property than you yourself are,"[1] he expressed succinctly the intellectual framework within which the dispute about the powers of the pope was to occur in France. In England, however, the pope was viewed by clergymen less as a protector than as an excuse to temporize and evade the king's levies. Between 1301 and 1324, the pope allowed successive English monarchs to tax the churches of the realm to the sum of £230,000.[2] It was not the pope, but the lesser clergy of England, occasionally with the support of their bishops,[3] who invoked the declarations of the Fourth Lat-

---

[1] Giles of Rome, *De ecclesiastica potestate*, ed. Richard Scholz (Weimar: Böhlau, 1929), II.7.

[2] W. E. Lunt, *Financial Relations of the Papacy with England to 1327* (Cambridge, MA: Harvard University Press, 1939), chap. 7.

[3] W. A. Pantin, *The English Church in the Fourteenth Century* (Cambridge: Cambridge University Press, 1955), 128.

eran Council and of Pope Boniface VIII in order to avoid granting assent to royal aids.

The suspicion that appeals to the papacy by the English church were a ruse to delay or circumvent subsidies was recorded in fourteenth-century texts. For instance, in the poetic chronicle attributed to Peter Langtoft, which is dated early in Edward II's reign, Robert Winchelsey, archbishop of Canterbury in Edward I's time, refused to accede to that king's financial demands without prior papal approval. Langtoft has Winchelsey respond to Edward that "under God there is no soul alive in the whole world who has over holy church power or mastery, except the pope of Rome. ... The pope is our head, he keeps and rules us, and he has made a statute which binds us closely, on privation of rent and prelacy, that neither tenth, or twentieth, nor half, nor part none of us give to thee or any other, without his commandment and allowance."[4] While refusing to accept papal authority,[5] Edward postponed the exaction some weeks to another clerical convocation. At that assembly, Langtoft's Winchelsey reaffirms his vow that "no one of this church should be any more taxed ... without command of the pope, who ought to govern them."[6] Edward then resorted to arbitrary confiscation of ecclesiastical goods, but ultimately relented entirely and made restitution.[7] Interestingly, when the same events are described some two decades after Langtoft by the anonymous author of the *Vita Edwardi Secundi*, papal approval has ceased to be the central issue at hand. In the interim, the pope comes to be viewed as a collaborator with the king in oppressing the church. "Amongst all the provinces in the world," the *Vita Edwardi Secundi* complains, "England alone feels the pope a burden."[8] Consequently, the chronicle reports, the "decree of 'Caesar Edward'" that "the fruits of the church should be taken" is resisted by Archbishop Winchelsey on the grounds of a general exemption. According to the author of the *Vita Edwardi Secundi*, Winchelsey "said that it would be contrary to all law for the king to have authority over the goods of clerics, whom the imperial law marked out with many privileges, and made free from every exaction. This, too, is intended by canon law."[9] The claim of a papal prerogative to review

---

[4] Thomas Wright, ed., *The Political Songs of England* (London: Camden Society, 1839), 311–312.
[5] Wright, *Political Songs*, 313.
[6] Wright, *Political Songs*, 316–317.
[7] Wright, *Political Songs*, 317.
[8] Denholm-Young, ed., *Vita Edwardi Secundi*, 46–47.
[9] Denholm-Young, ed., *Vita Edwardi Secundi*, 41.

clerical taxes is replaced in this version by a broader principle of legal exemption.

Nevertheless, the use of papal authority to resist the king's financial grasp remained a vital and viable means of resistance to royal levies on the part of the English clergy. The *Vita Edwardi Secundi* recounts another incident during Edward II's reign when the archbishop of Canterbury and his episcopal colleagues supported a royal subsidy, whereupon the "community of the clergy urged ... that they should be quit of this kind of payment." It was reasoned that "without special papal authority, no portion of ecclesiastical goods ought to be granted to laymen."[10] While the bishops in this case succeeded in imposing the king's tax, Edward was still compelled to send a mission directly to Rome during the following year, the purpose of which was to beseech "the pope to deign to help the king for a time, as he had expended all his treasure for the defense of the realm and the church." When "the pope refused to put the church or the tithes of the church into the hands of laymen," Edward unhappily accepted his decision.[11] The pope's wishes were to be respected, for they could impose a far more concrete barrier to royal taxation of the clergy than the bare assertion of legal exemption. In particular, the pope could enforce the liberties of the church by sentence of excommunication against laymen exacting levies without his authorization.[12]

The line of defense provided by the papacy against royal intrusions into ecclesiastical freedom was matched by an alternative justification derived from the terms under which the church possessed its property. A customary canon law precept stated that ecclesiastical goods were bestowed upon clerics in trust for the needy, to whom they in some sense actually belonged.[13] The canonist Hostiensis wrote that "pope and churches hold the goods they have not as their own, but as common possessions, that thence they may help all men suffering want," since "what belongs to the church ... is given for the common welfare."[14] The precedent for such a view extends back to St. Jerome and St. Augustine, both of whom held that the poor are entitled to whatever goods the church and its servants possess.[15]

---

[10] Denholm-Young, ed., *Vita Edwardi Secundi*, 76–77.

[11] Denholm-Young, ed., *Vita Edwardi Secundi*, 79.

[12] This specter is raised by Langtoft's Winchelsey in *Political Songs*, 312.

[13] Brian Tierney, *Medieval Poor Law: A Sketch of Canonical Theory and Its Application in England* (Berkeley: University of California Press, 1959), 34–44.

[14] Quoted in Tierney, *Medieval Poor Law*, 42–43.

[15] Boniface Ramsey, "Wealth," in *Augustine through the Ages*, ed. Allan D. Fitzgerald (Grand Rapids, MI: Eerdmans, 1999), 876–881.

Essentially the same position is regularly espoused by authors in early fourteenth-century England as an explanation for clerical refusal to grant royal taxes. We have already observed how William of Pagula expresses concern about the impact of royal taxation of the church upon its capacity to serve the poor, citing precisely the canon law dictum that ecclesiastical property in fact is reserved for the poverty-stricken. The *Vita Edwardi Secundi* also complains that the payment of tithes to rulers has "despoiled churches of the poor,"[16] a position echoed by the English clergy who objected to royal exactions "because by reason of the price of grain and the failure of the harvest, when the king's portion and other necessaries had been put aside, rectors would not have the wherewithal to give to the poor."[17] The author of the chronicle insists, in particular, that the king ought not to "wage war upon his enemies from the wealth of the church, which belongs to the poor, but from the royal treasury."[18] The *Vita Edwardi Secundi* goes so far as to predicate the eventual disasters of Edward II's reign on royal efforts to tax church goods: "This kind of contribution, which burdens the church, may bring about the Lord King's ruin. For the goods of the church are the goods of the poor. Never has it augured well to despoil the goods of the poor or the church."[19] Whether this observation is prescient or merely opinion informed by knowledge of later events is unclear, but it reflects the widely held view (found also in William of Pagula) that rulers who oppress the least and lowest of their subjects will soon be punished for their abuses.

WILLIAM OF OCKHAM AND ENGLAND

In the summer of 1337, representatives of the English King Edward III and the German King Ludwig of Bavaria concluded negotiations leading to the formation of an alliance driven by mutual political interest.[20] Edward, who was in the midst of preparations to pursue by force his dynastic claim to

---

[16] Denholm-Young, ed., *Vita Edwardi Secundi*, 46.

[17] Denholm-Young, ed., *Vita Edwardi Secundi*, 76–77. The accuracy of this protest may be judged by consideration of the evidence provided by Ian Kershaw, "The Great Famine and Agrarian Crisis in England, 1315–1322," in *Peasants, Knights, and Heretics*, ed. Rodney H. Hilton (Cambridge: Cambridge University Press, 1975), 85–132.

[18] Denholm-Young, ed., *Vita Edwardi Secundi*, 78.

[19] Denholm-Young, ed., *Vita Edwardi Secundi*, 77.

[20] H. S. Offler, "England and Germany at the Beginning of the Hundred Years War," *English Historical Review* 54 (1939): 608–631.

the French crown, received from Ludwig the title of imperial vicar-general *per Alemanniam et Galliam*, an act that conferred upon him sovereign rights over subjects and lands west of the Rhine. In turn, Edward promised to provide Ludwig with the money that he required to stabilize his own position within Germany and to compel the papacy to recognize formally his claim to be Emperor. This treaty, the greatest achievement of Edward's early diplomatic program, was solemnized in a ceremonial meeting between the two rulers during September of 1338.

One figure who no doubt witnessed these events was William of Ockham, the Franciscan philosopher and theologian living in exile in Munich, under the protection of Ludwig, as a result of a dispute with Pope John XXII. Ludwig had sheltered Ockham and numerous other intellectuals who had run afoul of the papal court at Avignon, assembling as a result a powerful group of polemical advocates for his cause. The sealing of the agreement between Edward and Ludwig is usually thought to have occasioned William's composition of *Whether a Prince Can Receive the Goods of the Church for His Own Needs, Namely, in Case of War, Even Against the Wishes of the Pope* (to which I shall refer by the abbreviated name *Whether a Prince . . .*),[21] an analysis of the rights of the English monarchy in relation to the church. The tract can be read both as a polemical favor to Ludwig, whose access to Edward's largesse depended upon the English king's ability to raise funds, and as a tribute to the deeds of the sovereign of his native land — a land to which circumstances would never permit him to return.

William was born about 1285 in the village of Ockham (Occam) in Surrey, and seems to have been educated at Oxford in the standard curricula of theology and liberal arts, although his familiarity with canon law suggests some training in that subject as well.[22] He was ordained at St. Mary's, Southwark, in 1306, and joined the Franciscan order at an unknown date. Following his education, he taught in the Franciscan schools, including at Oxford. His fame in the history of Western thought has largely derived from his reputation as a founder of the philosophical school of metaphysics and logic commonly known as "nominalism." Whether this attribution is properly deserved by William or not, he was certainly a commanding pres-

---

[21] The title was not Ockham's own, but was inserted into the best manuscript of the treatise by a much later hand than that of the original scribe.

[22] The following biographical sketch relies primarily on Leon Baudry, *Guillaume d'Occam: Sa vie, ses oeuvres, ses idées sociales et politiques* (Paris: J. Vrin, 1949) and Jürgen Miethke, *Ockhams Weg zur Sozialphilosophie* (Berlin: Walter de Gruyter, 1969).

ence on the intellectual terrain of late medieval Europe — perhaps the greatest philosopher that England produced during the Middle Ages.[23]

William's acclaim as a philosopher did not produce universal respect from his colleagues. A fellow Oxford master, John Lutterell, who was quite possibly envious of his colleague's growing notoriety, arranged for William to be called away from England in 1324 to the papal court at Avignon in order to respond to questions about the orthodoxy of some of his positions.[24] While awaiting the disposition of his case, William came into contact with Michael of Cesena, the Franciscan vicar-general, and other leaders of the so-called Spiritual wing of his order, who had been summoned to Avignon to defend their refusal to submit to John XXII's condemnation of their principles. William, who seems to have taken no part in the controversy prior to this encounter with the Spirituals, soon became convinced that Michael was right to object to the pope's attempted suppression of their vision of Franciscan ideals. Of even greater concern, William arrived at the conclusion that John XXII himself had lapsed into notorious and dangerous heresy. Accompanied by several prominent figures in the Spiritual movement, William fled Avignon in 1328 and met Ludwig's party, retreating from a disastrous excursion into Northern Italy, in Pisa. According to a certainly apocryphal story, William asked for the German ruler's protection with the plea, "Protect me with your sword, O Emperor, and I shall protect you with my pen."[25]

Such tales aside, it is clear that William was led away from his philosophical and theological pursuits and toward a program of polemical writing on behalf of the Spiritual Franciscan cause and of his protector, Ludwig. Initially, he took up the issues associated with the criticism of the Spirituals both within and without the Order, composing several apologias during the 1330s and beginning to formulate his withering attack on the foundations of papal rule. These include *The Work of Ninety Days*, *A Letter to the Friars Minor*, *Against Benedict*, and Part One of the *Dialogue*.

Commencing with *Whether the Prince . . .* , however, William initiated an examination of the relationship between the church and the authority of secular government. The tract is most reliably dated on internal and exter-

---

[23] On William's philosophical and theological doctrines, see Marilyn McCord Adams, *William Ockham* (Notre Dame: University of Notre Dame Press, 1987).

[24] C. K. Brampton, "Personalities in the Process against Ockham at Avignon, 1324-1326," *Franciscan Studies* 25 (1966): 4–25.

[25] C. K. Brampton, "Ockham, Bonagratia, and the Emperor Lewis IV," *Medium Aevum* 31 (1962): 81–87.

nal evidence to the period between late 1337 and early 1340 at the extremes, and probably to 1338 or 1339.[26] The text breaks off abruptly (in both extant manuscripts) in the middle of its thirteenth chapter; whether pages are lost, or William failed to complete the work, is unknown. The thirteen chapters of *Whether the Prince*... can be divided into roughly two coherent segments. The first six chapters provide a general sketch of William's attack on the principle of the papal plenitude of power, marshalling evidence from scriptural, canon law, patristic, and theological sources. The second half of the treatise turns to the immediate political purposes at hand, which are announced in the prologue: justifying the obligation of English clerics to aid the king with the property of the Church, and undermining any claim that the pope may licitly prohibit them from doing so. Here it is legal sources that form the overwhelming share of the references, although Aristotle and Cicero both receive a single mention each.

Whether the Prince... signals a watershed in the development of William's political and ecclesio-political thought. Thereafter, all of his writings move away from strictly ecclesiastical concerns and toward wider issues of the relationship between the papacy and temporal government, especially the Empire. Among these works were *Eight Questions on the Power of the Pope, A Short Discourse on Tyrannical Government, On the Power of Emperors and Pontiffs*, and the second and third parts of his uncompleted masterpiece, the *Dialogue*. Several of these works were to exercise a considerable influence upon later medieval and early modern political thought; the *Dialogue* is sometimes acclaimed a "classic" of the late Middle Ages, on par with Marsiglio of Padua's *Defensor pacis*. William died in 1348 or 1349, in exile and unreconciled with the papacy.

WHETHER THE PRINCE...: DOCTRINES

Given the primary goal of *Whether the Prince*... to defend the taxation policies of Edward III in support of his efforts to claim the French crown, it is evident that William shapes the heart of the treatise in response to the major arguments that had been adduced to deny the English king's right to impose levies upon the property of the church. His reference point, consequently, is the prevalent mode of justifying clerical resistance to such sub-

---

[26] H. S. Offler, "Introduction" to *An princeps*, in idem, ed., *Guillelmi de Ockham: Opera Politica*, 2nd ed. (Manchester: Manchester University Press, 1974), 1: 221–222.

sidies in England, as he had experienced it.[27] William begins this project with a reminder, posed in Augustinian terms, that all property-holding is a function not of natural or divine right, but of human law, particularly the law of kings. The "law of kings" signifies to him the legal conditions that accompany the transfer of temporal goods, given the essentially feudal arrangement of property and power (suggested by the term *dominium*) that obtained in fourteenth-century England. In the typical medieval understanding, the alienation of goods, including their assignment to the church, is never unconditional. A "burden" is always attached to such a transfer requiring that ecclesiastical possessions be used only for "holy purposes," a phrase that comes to have considerable significance for William. The main issues posed by royal taxation of the church are legal ones, then, and *Whether the Prince* ... reads in some ways like a judicial brief or opinion.

With these guiding precepts in mind, William attempts to refute the arguments favoring papal interference with lay taxation of the English Church. If the pope has the right or power to affirm or deny royal levies, he reasons, then he must have acquired such a right or power from a definite source. Specifically, since all jurisdiction and lordship in England pertain ultimately to the king and his law, the pope may rightfully possess such a prerogative only on the basis of royal concession. William invokes a doctrine embedded deep in the English system of government and property-holding, namely, that inasmuch as "all titles were based on grants or confirmations by the king," it fell to the crown alone to determine the correct or incorrect usage of property and related rights.[28] This principle becomes in *Whether the Prince* ... the indispensable foundation for all power wielded in the realm, ecclesiastical as well as lay.

William's task, then, is to determine whether the papacy had at any time acquired a demonstrable privilege on the basis of which it might exercise authority over the property of English churches. He reports, not surprisingly, that he can find no evidence that the pope had been conceded such a privilege of prior approval to royal taxation. Just in case such a record is located, however, he still insists that it could never be judged valid. William appeals to the medieval commonplace that the legitimacy of positive human enactments rests upon a "higher" standard of justice. According

---

[27] Although some have adopted the view that English experience was irrelevant to the tract; see A. S. McGrade, *The Political Thought of William of Ockham* (Cambridge: Cambridge University Press, 1974), 22.

[28] Joseph R. Strayer, *On the Medieval Foundations of the Modern State* (Princeton: Princeton University Press, 1970), 38.

to him, the measure of justice is the public welfare: any privilege that impedes the good of the community as a whole and the established rights of its members lacks a grounding in justice. Since papal authority over ecclesiastical goods diminishes the rights of both king and clergy, it must be condemned as "contemptible." Moreover, an instance of papal refusal to approve a subsidy would produce the manifestly unjust and inequitable situation in which the costs of defending the realm and the common benefit would be borne by laymen alone rather than the laity and clergy together. Consequently, no privilege conceded by the English crown, either past or present, may claim validity if it grants to the pope a right to veto or otherwise intercede in matters pertaining to the common good. The pope is to be treated no differently from any other lord who claims rights within England: when the exercise of a prerogative conflicts actually or potentially with the well-being of the kingdom or with the legitimate liberties of individuals, it is to be suppressed and erased.

William also rejects the assertion, derived from canon law, that church property enjoys a general immunity from lay taxation. The key questions for him concern the source of the immunity and the impact upon the common good. He insists that no just and reasonable subject would imperil the realm and its laws by refusing to assist his ruler. Clerics are not, simply by virtue of their status, to be exempted from the preservation of the collective welfare of the kingdom. Citing the widely employed Roman law maxim *Quod omnes tangit ab omnibus approbetur*,[29] William infers that all English subjects — the clergy as well as the laity — have a duty to protect the public weal. Those who hide behind clerical exemption, and yet enjoy the benefits afforded by royal defense, are guilty of a great injustice against not merely the ruler, but also the whole community of which they are members. Moreover, the king who denies to the church any privileges or immunities concerning taxation is not susceptible to excommunication. If such a sentence is pronounced, indeed, it occurs on the basis of an unjust right and need not be feared; rather, it is rendered void by its own judgment. William's opinion reflects the commonplace legal principle that any judicial determination containing "manifest vice and intolerable error" is not binding on any person. The twelfth and thirteenth chapters of *Whether the Prince*..., in which this topic is addressed, defend this position primarily with reference to canon law.

---

[29] See Gaines Post, *Studies in Medieval Legal Thought: Public Law and the State, 1100–1322* (Princeton: Princeton University Press, 1964), 163–238, 451.

William also discusses in *Whether the Prince* ... the other main clerical argument against royal levies prevalent in fourteenth-century England, namely, that the poor and needy are the true owners of church goods. His rebuttal of this position involves two distinct strategies. First, he invokes the conditional basis on which property has been granted to the churches of England. When clerics receive temporal goods from laymen, they do so in order that "righteous causes" may be served. Williams suggests, in turn, that when the phrase "righteous causes" occurs in documents authorizing donation, it ought to be assigned a liberal interpretation: among such causes must be included defense of the realm and its laws. Why? He argues that submission to the common good constitutes one of the foremost of "righteous causes." This is the case even if the needs of the poor must be overlooked as a result. Reversing the customary view, William maintains that the righteous cause of the good of the whole is to be preferred to the welfare of any segment of the community. (No wonder scholars have encountered great difficulties in reconciling his political thought with his nominalist philosophy.[30]) He justifies depriving the poor — on the authority of Cicero and Aristotle — on the grounds that the benefit of the totality is bound to be more "righteous" than the advantage of any of its lesser component parts. Clerical duty thus lies in meeting the demands of the king when the public good requires it. While the poor ordinarily merit the assistance of the clergy, they may never be regarded as the true owners of ecclesiastical property. Rather, the goods of the church are held in common by the entire community, rich as well as poor, and must always be used in whatever manner is most congenial to the public welfare. And it ultimately pertains to the king, as the ultimate guardian of the common good, to determine the appropriate use of such goods in a given set of circumstances.

Whether the Prince ... additionally pursues a second line of argumentation in response to those who would prefer the poor to the country as an entirety. It is generally agreed, William admits, that the clergy must donate ecclesiastical temporalities to those who are in need. But who, he asks, could have a greater need than the king when he is safeguarding the realm and its inhabitants? Indeed, the king, who has generously and even lavishly

---

[30] Alan Gewirth, "Philosophy and Political Thought in the Fourteenth Century," in *The Forward Movement of the Fourteenth Century*, ed. Francis L. Utley (Columbus: Ohio State University Press, 1961), 124–164; A. S. McGrade, "Ockham and the Birth of Individual Rights," in *Authority and Power*, ed. Brian Tierney and Peter Linehan (Cambridge: Cambridge University Press, 1980), 149–165; and McGrade, *The Political Thought of William of Ockham*, 173–196.

endowed (along with his predecessors) many religious institutions, protects the possessions of the church. Lest the clergy seem ungrateful and arrogant, the debt owed to the king ought to be repaid by the church in the form of subsidies necessary for its own protection. The clerical obligation to provide for the king when circumstances require is, then, simply an extension and application of the principle that clergy must contribute for the purposes of alleviating the needs of others. The king's office is greater than that of anyone over whom he governs; therefore, when the king is in need, his need will be greater than that of any of his subjects. To someone in such great need, the property of the church cannot rightfully be denied. Acceding to royal exactions, far from depriving those (such as the poor) who are in need, should actually be lauded as the supreme form of Christian charity and binding upon the religious as a result of their divine calling. Indeed, William insists upon this principle not merely in times of dire need, such as war, but even when other common burdens, such as ransoming prisoners and maintaining infrastructure, must be met.

Although written by William some fifteen years into his exile from England, *Whether the Prince* ... nonetheless constitutes an interesting contribution to the emergence of distinctively English modes of political thought. It takes square aim at the arguments marshaled by defenders of the autonomy of the English church from financial obligations to the crown, challenging them by reinterpretation of the materials — especially scriptural, patristic, and canon law sources — that conventionally were employed to authorize ecclesiastical prerogatives and immunities. *Whether the Prince* ... thus deserves a place of importance not only in the *opera politica* of William of Ockham, but also in the history of political ideas formulated in fourteenth-century England.

Whether a Prince Can Receive the Goods of the Church for His Own Needs, Namely, in Case of War, Even Against the Wishes of the Pope

William of Ockham

PROLOGUE

When the truth is expressed in succinct terms, some questions are cut short and not dealt with carefully. At times such truth seems to be supported by obscure and invalid arguments; at other times, it appears vulnerable to sophistic attacks. Occasionally it takes on the appearance of falsity, to such a degree that it in no way restrains those who are resistant to the truth (especially those affected by or accustomed to false and erroneous teachings), but rather is judged laughable by less profound minds and provides the simple with an opportunity to err, as they undo one loop under the surface, they are visibly seen to tie up the knot [tighter].[1] Nevertheless, people today are sick of lengthy works and they rejoice in brevity. For this reason, I will try to illustrate in a brief discourse that our most serene and glorious prince and lord, lord Edward, by the grace of God King of England, legally, rightfully, and indeed, deservedly, must be helped, not only by laymen, but also by secular prelates, religious, and other clerics under his lordship from the goods of the church, in his battle against enemies attacking him and usurping his rights unjustly; that if his intent is pure, no human statute, judgment, or legal proceeding, even if it should come from the pope him-

---

[1] Cf. St. Gregory the Great, *Moralia in Job* 2.3 (PL 75. 556).

self, stands in his way; that any judgment brought against him because he pursued justice for himself, even if it comes from the pope himself, is null and is not to be either feared or obeyed; that the Roman emperor is permitted to call to his aid those who support and obey him; and that pious men (*viri religiosi*) who adhere to imperial justice and who pursue the causes of the faith are in no way bound by judgments brought against them.

If I say anything in contradiction to the truth, I will add a correction for whomever it concerns and, whether this error is noticed by myself or by someone else, I will not delay in retracting it at the proper time and place.

CHAPTER 1

No one doubts, I think, that Edward, the magnanimous and so far unconquered — and by the grace of God never to be conquered — king of England, who is flourishing in the splendor of his race, celebrated in story, beautiful in form, sublime in power, wealthy in moral riches, graceful and strong in probity, and fearless in dealing with difficulties, is waging a just war (the details of which are known to all). I so assume that this is agreed upon that I do not propose to discuss it or call it into question. But I do intend to demonstrate with obvious proofs that the prelates and clerics subject to him are bound to offer him help in his just war not only from their private property but also from the goods of the church, and that the pope himself can in no way prohibit them by virtue of his plenitude of power, and that, if in fact he does make this prohibition, *ipso facto* and by law it will be null and have no force.

Next, so that this and other matters appear more clearly, and in order to find a better way of answering the objections which can be brought on the other side, I think that above all a certain erroneous understanding of the papal plenitude of power should be dismissed.

Some think that the pope possesses from Christ such plenitude of power in temporal matters as he has in spiritual, so that he can do everything, and that everything which is not found contrary to human or divine law is subject to his power; that only those things which mankind as a whole prohibits as unchangeable and indispensable in the name of divine or human law, and which are either forbidden or disapproved of themselves and not through any human ordinance, injunction, or prohibition of any sort, are prohibited to his plenitude of power. Thus, according to some, although the pope can err by precipitating or forbidding or impeding certain such things which of themselves are neutral, whatever he does in this way is an accomplished fact, even though it should not have been. Many things should not be, yet are, accomplished facts; witness the canonical sanctions.

These people base themselves principally on the words of Christ, who said to Peter and through him to all his successors: "I give you the keys of the kingdom of heaven: And whatever you bind on earth shall be bound in heaven; and whatever you loose on earth will be loosed in heaven" (Matthew 16:19). These people gather from these words that Christ promised to Peter, and through him to his successors, the popes, without any exception, such plenitude of power that he could do anything, because everything should be understood by a comprehensive statement (*verbo generali*) (di. xix, *Si Romanorum*; i, q. i, c. *Sunt nonnulli*; xiv, q. iii, c. *Putant*).[2] They say that Innocent III clearly understands the papal plenitude of power in this way when he says in Extra, *de maioritate et obedentia*, c. *Solita*, "The Lord said to Peter, and in Peter he said to his successors: 'Whatever you bind on earth will be bound in heaven,' etc. and He made no exceptions, saying 'Whatever you bind,' etc."[3] In these words, so it seems, it is clearly stated that Christ made no exceptions to the power of Peter and his successors; therefore, we ought not to make any exceptions either. For if, as is held in xxxi, q. i, *Quod si dormierit*, ii, q. v, c. *Consuluisti*, and di. lv, c. *Si evangelica*,[4] we ought not to make exceptions, define, or determine whenever the canon does not do so, so much more surely must we not make exceptions, define, or determine when Christ does not do so. For Christ did not make exceptions, define, or determine when he promised Peter and his successors power over the rest of humanity, but said in an unspecific and general way, "Whatever you bind," etc. Therefore, we ought not to make any exceptions at all; the pope possesses such a plenitude of power from Christ, such that he can do anything, in the manner posited above.

Chapter Two

But granted that under a certain understanding, it ought to be conceded that the true pope has a plenitude of power in some way, since it says in *de auctoritate et usu pallii*, c. *Nisi* that when the pallium is handed to the archbishop, the "plenitude of the papal office is conferred" on him[5] — granted that

---

[2] Gratian, *Decretum*, dist. 19, c. 1; 1, q. 1, c. 114; 14, q. 3, c. 2.
[3] *Decretales Gregorii IX, De maioritate et obedientia, Solitae* (I, 33, 6).
[4] Gratian, *Decretum*, 31, q. 1, c. 13; 2, q. 5, c. 20; dist. 55, c.13.
[5] *Decretales Gregorii IX, De auctoritate et usu pallii, Nisi* (I, 8, 3).

this can be understood wrongly and with prejudice to the papal authority — nevertheless the pope does not have the fullest power in temporal and spiritual matters, nor does he have that plenitude of power which is attributed to him. Indeed, there are those who consider this opinion heretical and exceedingly dangerous to Christianity as a whole.

There are many different proofs that the pope does not have such plenitude of power in temporal and spiritual matters. The Christian law from Christ's institution is a law of freedom *(lex libertatis)*, so that by the edict of Christ it is not of greater or equal servitude as the old law. This is clearly evident from Scripture. James calls it the law of perfect freedom, saying: "For whoever looks forward in the law of perfect liberty and remains in it," etc. (James 1:25); and Paul says, "Nor was Titus, who was with me, since he was a Greek, compelled to be circumcised, although some wanted it done. Pretending to be fellow believers, these men slipped into our group to spy out our liberty which we have in Jesus Christ, that they might bring us into bondage; but in order to keep the truth of the Gospel safe for you, we did not give in for a minute" (Galatians 2:3–5). And in [Galatians] 5:12–13: "I would that they were even cut off which trouble you. For, brethren, you have been called into liberty, only do not use liberty for an occasion to the flesh." And in [Galatians] 4:31: "We are not children of the bondwoman but of the free, in which liberty Christ has freed us." And in 2 Corinthians 3:17 he says: "Where the spirit of the Lord is, there is freedom." And Peter, according to Acts 15:10, says: "Why do you tempt God to put a yoke on the necks of his disciples which neither our fathers nor we could bear?" And in the same place James says: "I judge that we do not alarm those who have turned to God from the Gentiles, but write to them that they abstain from contamination of idols and from fornication and from strangled beasts and from blood" (James 5:19–20). This opinion of James, and likewise of Peter, was approved of by the Holy Spirit in all the Apostles and by universal general assent and by the entire church congregated at that time when this was added ([Acts] 15:22–23): "Then it pleased the Apostles and the elders, with the entire church, to choose men from themselves and to send them to Antioch with Paul and Barnabas, Judas who was surnamed Barsabas, and Silas, the first men among their brothers, and they wrote a letter through them saying: 'Apostles and elder brethren.'" And later ([Acts] 15:28–29): "For it seemed good to the Holy Spirit and to us to impose nothing more on you than this: that you should abstain from sacrifices offered to idols and from blood and from strangulation of beasts and from fornication. And if you keep from these things, you will do well." It can gathered from these and many other examples that Christians have been freed from various servitudes by the law of the Gospels and the teachings of Christ, and that they are not as oppressed by the law of the Gospels as the Jews were by the old law. Augustine clearly hints at this in the examinations of Januarius, and it is said in the *Decretals* (xii, c. *Omnia*). Reprehending certain people for burdening Christians with observances which, although not illegal, were excessive, he says, "For although they cannot be found to be against the faith, they so oppress this religion which the mercy of God wished to be free, with only the fewest and most well chosen sacramental obligations, that the condition of the Jews would be more tolerable. Even if they did not know the era of freedom, at least they were subjected to legal sacramental obligations and not to human presumptions."[6] From these words it appears that God's mercy desires that the Christian religion be more free with respect to obligations, even those not in themselves illicit, than matters were under the old law. Consequently, the law of the Gospels is called the law of freedom, not only because it frees Christians from the servitude of sin and the law of Moses, but because through the law of the Gospels Christians are not oppressed by a servitude as severe as or more severe than the servitude of the old law.

This is clearly proven by the fact that Christians converted from Gentiles. This is dealt with in Acts 15:31. When they received the letter of the Apostles and elders, they were joyful because of its consolation, as it says there. But if they had been freed from the servitude of the Mosaic Law and another servitude as great or more severe was placed upon them, they would justifiably have grieved at such a disturbance. A person who is snatched from one servitude, especially a divine one, and is placed under another, greater one, especially a human one, is desolate and pained rather than consoled.

Therefore, in no way are Christians held in such servitude in spiritual or temporal matters by the law of the Gospels as by the old law. It may be granted that if they wanted to of their own will, they could subject themselves to more, and that some are subjected to more by human law, so that several authorities on the freedom of Christian law ought to be understood negatively. But if the pope had such plenitude of power in spiritual and temporal matters through the ordination of Christ, the scriptural authorities which say that the law of the Gospels is the law of freedom could not be understood either positively or negatively, because it would be a law of horrific servitude and of incomparably greater servitude, in temporal as in

---

[6] Gratian, *Decretum*, dist. 12, c. 12 (also St. Augustine, *Epistola* 55.19, [PL 33. 221]).

spiritual matters, than the servitude of the old law. For all Christian kings and princes and prelates and clerics and all laymen would, through the law of the Gospels, be slaves of the pontiff according to the strictest definition of the word "slave," according to the definition which is accepted legally or by the general run of people. For no temporal lord of any sort could have such power over a slave that he could impose anything on him, provided it was not contrary to divine law or natural law (*ius naturale*). For the power of no emperor, king, or individual could stretch to those things that are contrary to divine or indispensable natural law.

Therefore, the pope could, if he had such plenitude of power, take away the honors of kings and princes and other clerics and laymen, and deprive them of their possessions and rights without blame and without reason. He could even submit kings to the power of peasants and common people, and appoint the former as ploughers of fields and set them to any kind of common tasks. These ideas are absurd, and they clearly detract from the freedom of the law of the Gospels which is taken from divine scriptures. Wherefore not only is it untrue that the pope has a plenitude of power of this kind, but the concept is heretical, pernicious, and dangerous to people everywhere.

It is not valid to say that this opinion is not dangerous because *de facto* the pope does not exercise power of this sort, although if he began to exercise such power over kings and other Christians, there would be reason to fear the most frightful and dangerous rebellions and revolutions and wars which would spring up. But even if it is said, "The pope does not try such a thing," it is still, I say, invalid. For in these matters, we must consider what can by law happen as well as what in fact does happen. Therefore, it is not sufficient that the pope does not try such things; by law he must not be able to try them. For there would be grave dangers if he presumed to exercise power of this sort through greed, ambition, fear, hatred, or love, or through malice, simplicity, or ignorance. This opinion must be censored as pernicious, dangerous, and heretical.

So far, it is proved that the pope does not have a plenitude of power of this sort from Christ in temporal and spiritual matters. For if he had such a plenitude of power, he would have an equal power in all countries, kingdoms, regions, and provinces. For if he had more power in one place than in another, he could not do everything against divine and human law in all lands. But the pope does have a greater power in one country than he does in another; witness Innocent III, who (in *de haereticis*, c. *Vergentis*) clearly distinguishes the lands under the temporal jurisdiction of the pope from others, saying, "In the lands subjected to our temporal jurisdiction, we decree that the property of heretics be confiscated, and in others we leave this to be done by the secular powers and princes."[7] Therefore, the pope does not have such plenitude of power in every country.

Furthermore, when Christ made Peter head and leader of all the faithful, He did not intend to provide principally for the temporal use, convenience, and honor of Peter and his successors, but for that of His church, which He had acquired with His own blood. Consequently, He did not give him and his successors power and authority so that the entire church could be endangered. Paul is clearly hinting at this (2 Corinthians 13:8) when he says for himself and for the Apostles, that is, all prelates, "For we can do nothing against the truth, but for the truth." And later, "Therefore, I write these things being absent, lest being present I should use sharpness, according to the power which the Lord hath given me to edification, and not to [your] destruction" (2 Corinthians 13:10). It can be understood from these words that the Apostles received their power from the Lord for themselves and for their successors, not to endanger, but to help, the faithful. Wherefore the need of the church and not the honor, convenience, or need of the person who holds the office of pontiff is provided for through that office. Indeed, reason bears this out. Just laws, canonical and civil, are instituted for the same reason. Princes and prelates are given preference to those beneath them so that they might be closely tested by arguments and authorities. But, as it says in di. iv, c. *Erit autem lex*, laws ought to be instituted, "not for private convenience, but for the common good."[8] Those who are placed in authority over others, especially pontiffs, do not receive power from God for their own convenience or honor. Moreover, if a plenitude of power of this kind in both spiritual and temporal matters had been bestowed on Peter and his successors by Christ, it would provide principally for the temporal convenience or honor of Peter and his successors and not for the good of the church, since such a power could easily overflow at the risk of endangering the entire church. Therefore, the pope does not have such plenitude of power in temporal and spiritual matters.

Again, one who should not become involved in secular affairs, who ought rather to abstain from business of this sort, does not possess on a regular basis a plenitude of this kind of power, especially not in temporal affairs. For it is vain to give power for the general good to one who must not exercise it constantly and vigorously. But the bishops and successors of

---

[7] *Decretales Gregorii IX, De haereticis, Vergentis* (V, 7, 10).

[8] Gratian, *Decretum*, dist. 4, c. 2.

the Apostles, among whom the supreme pontiff has first place, are forbidden and are counseled by the Apostles and holy fathers not to involve themselves in secular affairs but to abstain from them as much as possible. Thus the Apostle, writing to Bishop Timothy, says, "Let no soldier of God be involved in secular business" (2 Timothy 2:4). And again, in the apostolic canons, at di. lxxxviii, c. *Episcopus*, we find: "A bishop or priest or deacon may in no way assume private cares, or otherwise he must lay down his office."[9] This opinion is found in innumerable sacred canons as xxi, q. iii, c. i; di. lxxxviii, c. *Episcopus nullam*; xvi, q. i, *Sunt nonnulli*; Extra, *Ne clerici vel monachi se immisceant saecularibus negotiis*, throughout; xxi, q. iii, c. *Placuit* and c. *Cyprianus* and c. *Mollitiis* and c. *Hii, qui* and c. *Sacerdotum*; and in very many other places as well.[10] Therefore, the pope does not in general possess such a plenitude of power, and especially not in temporal affairs.

Again, it is usually a function of royal power, and not papal, to judge secular causes and to carry out those functions which belong to temporal jurisdiction. This point can be demonstrated through innumerable sacred canons and the glosses on them, both of which are found in di. xcvi, c. *Duo sunt*, c. *Cum ad verum*, and c. *Si imperator*; and Extra, *de iudiciis, Novit*; and di. x, c. *Quoniam*; Extra, *Qui filii sint legitimi*, c. *Causam*; and xxiii, q. v, c. *Sunt quaedam*; Extra, *Qui filii sint legitimi, Per venerabilem*; Extra, *de foro competenti*, c. *Ex transmissa* and c. *Ex tenore*; and Extra, *de maioritate et obedientia*, c. *Solitae*; and in very many other places.[11]

Furthermore, Christian emperors, kings, and princes, and many other laymen and clerics, possess true temporal jurisdiction and true lordship (*dominium*) over temporal affairs, yet not from the pope; therefore, the pope does not possess a plenitude of such power in temporal affairs. In proof of this point: pagan and other non-believing emperors did not possess, either before the incarnation of Christ or after, a truer temporal jurisdiction nor a truer lordship over temporal affairs than believing emperors do now. Rather, a succession of holy scriptures and the testimony of the Fathers

---

[9] Gratian, *Decretum*, dist. 88, c. 3.

[10] Gratian, *Decretum*, 21, q. 3, c. 1; dist. 88, c. 1; 16, q. 1, c. 25; *Decretales Gregorii IX, Ne clerici vel monachi se immisceant saecularibus negotiis* (III, 50); Gratian, *Decretum*, 21, q. 3, c. 3, 4, 5, 6, 7.

[11] Gratian, *Decretum*, dist. 96, c. 10, 6, 11; *Decretales Gregorii IX, De iudicii, Novit* (II, 1, 13); Gratian, *Decretum*, dist. 8, c. 8; *Decretales, Qui filii sint legitimi, Causam* (IV, 17, 7); Gratian, *Decretum*, 23, q. 5, c.39; *Decretales, Qui filii sint legitimi, Per venerabilem* (IV, 17, 13); ibid., *De foro competenti, Ex transmissa, Ex tenore* (I, 2, 6 and 11); ibid., *De maioritate et obedientia, Solitae* (I, 33, 6).

openly hold that many infidels both before and after the incarnation of Christ possessed true temporal jurisdiction and true lordship over temporal affairs, and not from the pope nor from another believing priest, although these rulers often abused their jurisdiction and lordship. But an abuse of true power, either of jurisdiction or of lordship, in no way reduces that true power, as Augustine openly maintains and as is found in xiv, q. v, c. *Neque*.[12] Therefore, Christian emperors possess or can possess true temporal jurisdiction and true temporal lordship, yet not from the pope.

Moreover, one can expressly ascertain from sacred scripture that most pagans had true temporal jurisdiction and true lordship over temporal affairs, so that a contrary opinion must be considered heretical. This can be demonstrated and openly proved by authorities of the Old and New Testament, namely, Genesis 23:17-20, 31:32, 37-38, 39:5, and 41:35; Deuteronomy 2:4-6, 9, 18-19; 1 Kings 9:11 and 19:15; 2 Chronicles, in the last chapter [36:22-23]; 1 Ezra 1:1-2; Isaiah 45:1; Tobit 2:20-21; Daniel 2:37-38 and 5:18; Matthew 2:1 and 17:24-25; Luke 1:5, 2:1, and 3:12-14; John 19:11; Romans 13:1,7; 1 Corinthians 7:20-21; 1 Timothy 6:1-2; Acts 16:37, 22:25-28, 24:10, and 25:10-11; 1 Peter 2:13-14, 18.

Furthermore, the pope does not possess universal lordship and proprietorship in particular, nor the right of disposing as he pleases of temporal affairs. In proof of this: if the pope did possess such supreme lordship and right, no one else would have any rights whatsoever over any temporal matters beyond what had been given him by the pope, which the pope could revoke at any time he pleased. This is contrary to both divine and human laws. Since Christ, who was a passible and mortal man, and whose vicar the pope is, refused to possess such particular supreme lordship and such a right (as is plainly demonstrated in many authorities of divine scripture, and in as many, if not more, long works of the saints), how much the more does Christ's vicar, the pope, not possess such universal lordship and right of disposing of all temporal affairs?

Chapter 3

Of these many authorities, a few (which can be supported by more copious citation of divine scripture and the holy fathers) are presented here to prove that the pope does not possess such a plenitude of power in temporal and

---

[12] Gratian, *Decretum*, 14, q. 5, c. 9 (citing St. Augustine, *De bono coniugali* 14 [PL 40. 384]).

spiritual affairs. This will now be demonstrated by the assertions of our forefathers.

Thus, Peter says in his first canonical letter, "Neither should you be lord amongst the clerics" (1 Peter 5:3), and the same is found in the ordinance of Clement at xi, q. 1, c. *Te quidem*: "You should live a blameless life and shine in the greatest zeal, so that you abandon all other pursuits of this life; you should not give surety, nor be an advocate in legal actions, nor should you be found in any occupation which entangles you in worldly concerns. For Christ does not wish to reckon you today as a judge or as an advocate of secular affairs."[13]

Again, Ambrose on Luke [20:21-25]: "Christ does not possess the image of Caesar, for He is the image of God. Peter does not possess the image of Caesar, for he said, 'We have forsaken all things to follow you' [Matthew 19:27]. The image of Caesar is not to be found in James and John, because they are the sons of thunder. But it is found in the sea, in which there are dragons with broken heads above the waters [Psalms 73:13], and that greater dragon, his head broken, is given to the people of Ethiopia as food. If Christ, therefore, did not resemble Caesar, why did He pay the tax? He did not give from Himself, but returned to the world that which was the world's. And if you do not wish to be subject to Caesar, do not possess what belongs to the world. If you have riches, you are subject to Caesar. If you want to owe nothing to an earthly king, give up all your goods, and follow Christ."[14]

Again, Jerome says to Nepotianus: "Bishops know that they are priests, not lords."[15]

Gregory, discussing in his *Moralia* the words of the Apostle, "If therefore you have such secular disputes" (1 Corinthians 6:4), says, "Let those examine earthly concerns who perceive the wisdom of exterior things; those who are well provided for in spiritual matters should not become involved in earthly business, so that they may be strong to serve the greater good while not compelled to deal with the lesser."[16]

The Gloss on the same words of the Apostle says, "Set them to judge who are 'contemptible,' that is, some wise men who are nevertheless deserving of less esteem. For the Apostles in their travels did not have time for such business. Therefore, he wished to have as examiners of such business

---

[13] Gratian, *Decretum*, 11, q. 1, c. 29.
[14] St. Ambrose, *Expositio Evangelii secundum Lucam*, 9 (PL 15. 1802).
[15] St. Jerome, *Epistola* 52 (PL 22. 533).
[16] St. Gregory the Great, *Moralia in Job*, 19.25 (PL 76. 125).

wise men who remained in their places, faithful and holy, not those who hastened about here and there because of the Gospel."[17]

John Chrysostom, in his book of dialogues which is called *On the Dignity of the Priesthood*, Book 2, Chapter 3, says, "When secular judges convict wrongdoers under the law, they show that their authority is complete, and compel them, even unwillingly, to submit to their methods. But in the church it is necessary to make men better not by force but with their consent, because the law does not give us the authority to restrain men from sin."[18]

In the sixth book, he says, "For we are not discussing military command nor earthly rule, but that power which requires the virtue of angels."[19]

And about that passage in Matthew 20[:25], "The kings of the Gentiles," he says, "The princes of the world exercise dominion over those who are weaker, and subject them to slavery and plunder them and make use of them even to death for their own profit and glory. But princes of the church must serve those who are below them and give them whatever they have received from Christ, so that they neglect their own interest in gaining benefit for others."[20]

Origen says about the same passage, "'You know that the princes of the Gentiles exercise dominion over them,' that is, they are not content merely to rule those they have subdued, but they strive to rule them with violence. Amongst yourselves, however, who belong to Me, there will be no such thing. For just as all bodily things rest upon necessity, but spiritual things upon choice, so you who are spiritual princes, that is, prelates, must base your preeminence over them on love and not on fear."[21]

Bernard in the first book of *On Consideration* to Pope Eugenius says, "Your power is over sins and not possessions; because of the former, not the latter, have you accepted the keys of the kingdom of heaven, to keep out wrongdoers, not property owners."[22]

In the second book, he says, "What else has the blessed Apostle given to you? 'What I have,' he says, 'I give to you' [Acts 3:6]. What is that? One thing I know: it is not gold or silver, for he says, 'Gold and silver are not

---

[17] *Glossa Ordinaria ad I Corinthios 6:4*, s.v. "Saecularia igitur iudicia," "contemptibiles."
[18] John Chrysostom, *De sacerdotio*, 2.3 (PG 48. 634).
[19] John Chrysostom, *De sacerdotio*, 6.1 (PG 48. 678–679).
[20] Pseudo-Chrysostom, *Opus imperfectum in Mattheum*, hom. 35 (PG 35. 830).
[21] Origen, *Commentarium in Mattheum*, 16.8 (PG 13. 1391).
[22] St. Bernard of Clairvaux, *De consideratione*, 1.6 (in *Opera*, vol. 3, ed. Jean Leclercq and H. M. Rochais [Rome: Editiones Cistercienses, 1963]).

mine.' It may be that you can claim these for yourself for some other reason, but not by apostolic right. For he could not give you what he did not possess, but what he had he gave you: responsibility for the churches, as I have said. Why not lordship? Listen to him: 'Not as lords over the clergy but as examples to the flock' [1 Peter 5:3]. And lest you think this is said from humility alone and not as truth, here is the voice of the Lord in the Gospel: 'The kings of the Gentiles exercise lordship over them, and they who have authority over them are called benefactors' [Luke 22:25], and he concludes, 'You are not such.' It is plain: lordship is forbidden to the Apostles. Therefore, do you who are a lord dare to usurp for yourself apostolic power? And do you who possess apostolic power dare to usurp lordship? Clearly you are forbidden to have both. If you desire to possess one and the other at the same time, you will lose both. Otherwise, do not think you are excluded from the number of those of whom God complains, 'They ruled, and not through Me; they have set up princes, and I did not know them' [Hosea 8:4]. But if we have the prohibition, let us also have the rule: 'He who is greater amongst you, let him be as one who is lesser, and let him who rules be as one who serves' [Luke 22:26]. This is the form of the apostleship: mastery is forbidden, service is enjoined."[23]

In the third book he says, "You err if you think your apostolic power to be not only the supreme but also the only power that is instituted by God. If you believe this, you disagree with him who said, 'There is no power but from God' [Romans 13:1]. Consequently, the words which follow, 'Who resists the power, resists the ordinance of God' [Romans 13:2], although principally they are said on your behalf, are not said only for you. For he then says, 'Let all souls be subject to higher powers' [Romans 13:1]. He does not say 'to a higher power' as if there were only one, but 'higher powers' to show there are many."[24]

In the same book to Eugenius he says, "I do not think that those who say this can show where any one of the Apostles acted as a judge between men," and a little later, "I read that the Apostles were brought to judgment, I do not read that they sat in judgment. They will be judges in the future; they have not been in the past."[25]

And again to Pope Eugenius, "Who will grant me to see the church of God as in former days, when the Apostles cast their nets to capture not

---

[23] St. Bernard of Clairvaux, *De consideratione*, 2.6.
[24] St. Bernard of Clairvaux, *De consideratione*, 3.4.
[25] St. Bernard of Clairvaux, *De consideratione*, 1.6.

gold but souls? Who will grant me to hear your voice, that strong voice: 'Your money perish with you' [Acts 8:20]."[26]

And again to Eugenius, "Say to yourself, 'I was an abject in the house of God' [Psalms 83:11]. How then am I 'lifted over peoples and kingdoms' from poverty and abjectness?" And further on, "When the prophet was similarly elevated, he heard, 'Root up and pull down, and lay waste and destroy, and build and plant' [Jeremiah 1:10]. What is there of haughtiness in this? Rather, spiritual labor is here expressed in the figure of rustic toil. Let us likewise, highly as we regard ourselves, feel that a service has been imposed on us, not that we have been granted a power." And further on, "Learn that you need a hoe, not a scepter, to carry out the work of a prophet."[27]

And again to Eugenius, "It is not of you that the prophet said, 'And the whole earth will be his dominion' [Psalms 2:8]. That is Christ, who claims this possession by right of creation, by the merit of redemption, and by the gift of the Father. For of whom else has it been said, 'Ask of me, and I will give you the peoples' [Psalms 2:8], etc. Leave to Him possession and lordship, and receive for yourself the care. This is your part; do not extend your hand further. You are set in power in order to watch over and manage and serve and provide for. You are set in power in order to be of use, as 'a faithful and prudent servant whom the lord has set over his household' [Matthew 24:25]. To what purpose? 'To give them food in season' [Psalms 103:27], that is, to minister, not to command. Do this, and being a man, do not wish to dominate over men, so that no iniquity may dominate over you. Therefore, if you know that you are the debtor, not the lord, of both wise men and foolish, your greatest duty is to care for them," etc.[28]

Chapter 4

It is apparent from the foregoing and innumerable other places not only that the pope does not possess that plenitude of power which the previously mentioned advocates assign to him, but also that many other noteworthy points have been raised about this power, which it is useful for Christians to know; and that from these points a further proof may be drawn for the argument that the pope does not possess such a plenitude of power.

---

[26] St. Bernard of Clairvaux, *Epistola* 238.6 (PL 182. 430).
[27] St. Bernard of Clairvaux, *De consideratione*, 2.5–6.
[28] St. Bernard of Clairvaux, *De consideratione*, 3.1.

From scripture it is clear that the pope does not have in particular a universal lordship over and control or possession of all temporal matters, since in the last-quoted authority, namely, St. Bernard's, it is expressly stated that Christ, not the pope, has the universal lordship over and possession of all temporal matters; that this is true of Christ as much with regard to His divinity as with regard to His humanity after the resurrection and glorification; and that this is by no means true of the pope, since Christ did not give to Peter (who abandoned all things because of Christ) lordship in general of all things; and that this can also be deduced from the twelfth and the fifteenth authorities.

Secondly, from the foregoing it follows that the pope not only does not possess universal lordship over all things through the institution and ordination of Christ, but also that he is not the lord of other men; this is affirmed both in substance and in statement by the first authority, from St. Peter; and the fourth, from St. Jerome; and the twelfth, from St. Bernard; and the sixteenth and seventeenth, also from Bernard. Accordingly, the pope is by no means to be called "lord" because he has received from Christ any temporal lordship over the bodies of men or of their possessions. He may rightly be called "lord" by the prerogative of his order and office which distinguishes him from other men, just as rich and powerful prelates or poor religious are sometimes called "lord" by virtue of their sanctity or religiosity or rank, although it is clear that they have no temporal power even over themselves.

The third point, which follows from the foregoing, is that not only was the papal power instituted by God, but also many other powers, namely, secular ones, have been instituted by Him as well, as is positively stated in the thirteenth authority, that of St. Bernard. For although most powers of the church are established by God through the medium of the papal authority, secular powers, such as those of the Emperor or kings or other preeminent men, are established by God not through the authority of the pope but through the authority of human beings; and they receive their power not from the pope but from God. Therefore, royal power comes not from the pope, but from God through the medium of the people, who receive from God the power of setting over themselves a king for the sake of the common good.

The fourth point is that the pope does not receive from Christ, through St. Peter, the power of directing temporal affairs on a regular basis, nor of involving himself in secular matters, nor of passing judgment on such matters. This is clearly deduced from the second authority (St. Peter), the fifth (St. Gregory), the sixth (St. John Chrysostom), and the eleventh and fourteenth (both of St. Bernard). For Christ only instituted rectors of His faithful in spiritual matters, to be employed regarding spiritual affairs for the sake of gaining eternal life, as long as temporal and secular business was by custom dispersed among the laity. He gave the clergy no regular authority over temporal affairs except the power and the right of asking the laity for those temporal things that are required for their maintenance and for the necessary execution of their spiritual offices. However, by this injunction, He did not forbid them the power of acquiring temporal things in another way, of possessing them lawfully, and even of sitting in judgment upon them. He also wished them to have the occasional power of directing temporal affairs and of becoming involved in them, during times of need caused by the excessive wickedness of the laity or something similar, lest the company of the faithful or the ministers of the church, like a flock that lacks a shepherd and is not strong enough to set up a suitable ruler for itself, be exposed to intolerable danger, or to spiritual or bodily death, because there was a lack of this kind of power.

The fifth point is that the pope does not possess as much power as Christ possessed, which we are given to understand from the last-quoted authority (of St. Bernard). And no wonder. For since the pope is only the vicar of Christ in that he is the successor of Peter, and since the vicar of someone who is a vicar himself is not equal in power, it follows that the pope does not possess as much power as Christ possessed. Therefore, although Christ held in particular the possession and universal lordship of all temporal things, notwithstanding that He was a passible and mortal human being, still it cannot be inferred from this that the pope has acquired a similar power and lordship.

The sixth point is that the power which the pope receives from the ordination of Christ extends on a regular basis only over those things which are useful and necessary to the Christian people, and which do not involve any damage or notably great loss either to the faithful or to non-believers. Such things may rightly be seen to be provided for the governing of the church and not for the use, glory, convenience, or honor of the person who is raised to the supreme pontificate; as is clearly stated in the ninth authority, which is from St. John Chrysostom, and the tenth from Origen, and the sixteenth from St. Bernard.

The seventh point is that the keys of the kingdom of heaven, which are given to the pope, extend on a regular basis to sins and crimes, and not to possessions, as the eleventh authority of St. Bernard states openly. Since, by the reasoning of this authority, the keys do not extend to possessions, by the same argument they do not affect the temporal laws of the laity.

The eighth point is that the power of the keys of the kingdom of heaven, which is given to the pope by Christ and which extends to sins and crimes, is not binding on a regular basis, as is stated in the seventh and eighth authorities, from Chrysostom, and the tenth, from Origen. For when St. Peter received the keys of the kingdom of heaven from Christ, he received a general authority over all sins without exception. But over purely secular sins and crimes, for which secular judges were provided to mete out just and sufficient punishment, St. Peter received no binding power in contentious jurisdiction (*in foro contentioso*), lest the power of secular judges be wholly absorbed by the power of Peter, against that saying of the Apostle when he speaks of secular power in Romans 13:4, "If, therefore, you are an evildoer, beware: for not without cause does he bear a sword"; and that saying of St. Peter, "Be subject to every human creature because of God; whether to the king, as supreme, or to the lords as being sent by him for the punishment of evildoers" (1 Peter 2:13–14). Therefore, the power of the keys given to St. Peter was not generally binding in contentious jurisdiction. However, in penitential jurisdiction, Peter received authority over all sins and crimes, because he received from Christ as well the power, by sound instruction and healthful exhortation even in public, unhindered by the objection or prohibition of anyone whatsoever, at whatever time may be expedient, of bringing sinners and criminals to the worthy fruits of penance, even those who have been sufficiently and justly punished by the secular judges; and he also received binding authority over purely spiritual crimes. St. Peter possessed, and his successors possess, such a binding power over secular crimes on occasion; in what cases they possess this binding power, I will not say just at present.

From any of the foregoing points, as from other catholic assertions raised along with them, it can be concluded by necessary argument that the pope does not possess that plenitude of power which the previously mentioned defenders claim for him, to the detriment not only of the laity but of the clergy as well. But for the sake of brevity, I omitted to introduce this point into the foregoing notes.

Chapter 5

Having looked into these matters, we must now respond to those arguments that purport that the pope does possess such a plenitude of power. To the first argument, that Christ promised such a plenitude of power to Peter and his successors when He said, "I give you the keys," etc., because everything must be understood by that comprehensive phrasing (*verbo generali*), we answer that although the words of Christ are phrased comprehensively, they must not be taken in the widest possible sense and as admitting of no exception. For from this interpretation heretical absurdities obviously follow. The first is that Christ promised to St. Peter and his successors power equal to the power of Christ, because Christ neither had nor could have any power greater than that of being able to do all things without exception.

The second absurdity is that the pope, from his plenitude of power, could act contrary to divine and natural law, particularly in cases in which God can act against such laws. Thus, just as God commanded Abraham to kill his innocent son — nor did He command wrongfully, because He is the lord of life and death (for divine law and the law of nature do forbid the killing of the innocent) — so the pope, in the plenitude of his power, could command the faithful to kill innocent people, and the faithful of Christ would obey; this is a manifest heresy.

The third absurdity, as we deduced earlier, is that the pope, from his plenitude of power, without blame and without cause, could deprive kings of their kingdoms and give them to peasants to be despoiled.

The fourth is that the pope, from his plenitude of power, also without blame and without cause, could separate a man unwillingly from his wife after the marriage had been consummated, and the man would have to obey him in this.

Innumerable foolish, dangerous, and heretical absurdities follow if the words of Christ quoted above are to be understood as admitting no exceptions whatsoever. These words must by no means be taken in the widest possible sense, but with exceptions, even though they are phrased in a general way. Thus a comprehensive word often is not to be given a wide meaning (Extra, *de iureiurando*, c. *Ad nostram noveris audientiam*, and i, q. i, c. *Iudices*);[29] further as the Gloss notes about Extra, *de appellationibus*, c. *Sua nobis*, "A general word often has a restricted sense."[30] Numerous examples of this are to be found in divine scripture. I will cite but a few that treat of power and subjection.

Therefore, St. Peter in his first canonical letter says, "All human creatures are subject because of God" (1 Peter 2:13), and afterwards, "Servants, be subject in all fear to your masters" (1 Peter 2:18). The Apostle says at

---

[29] *Decretales Gregorii IX, De iureiurando, Ad nostram noveris audientiam* (II, 24, 21); Gratian, *Decretum*, 1, q. 1, c. 23.

[30] *Glossa ordinaria ad Decretalis II, 28, 65, s.v.* "tertio appellare."

Romans 13:1, "Every soul must be submissive to its lawful superiors"; in Colossians 3:20, "Children, obey your parents in all things"; in Ephesians 6:5, "You who are slaves, obey your human masters with fear and trembling"; in Colossians 3:22, "Slaves, obey your human masters in all things"; in 1 Timothy 6:1, "Those who are bound to slavery must think their masters to be worthy of all respect"; in Ephesians 5:24, "As the church is subject to Christ, so should wives be subject to their husbands in all things." All these texts are phrased as general statements, but must be understood as admitting of exceptions, so that silly, dangerous, or irrational heresies may not be inferred from the apostolic doctrine. So also must the aforementioned promise of Christ be understood rightly and in the light of appropriate exposition, and with its exceptions which can be gathered from other places in divine scripture and by manifest reason, even though this promise was phrased in general words.

In the same way, we must exclude from that earlier mentioned general statement, "Whatever you shall bind," etc., all interpretations which in the opinion of everyone universally are contrary to divine law and the law of nature; and in the same way we must except those interpretations which would involve great and notable damage and loss to the liberties and rights of temporal emperors, kings, princes, and other laymen, and of clerics as well, which belong to them by natural law, the law of peoples, or civil law, either before or after the institution of the law of the Gospels. To these the papal power scarcely extends on a regular basis, since one must not disturb the rights of others without cause and without guilt (Extra, *de iudiciis*, c. *Novit*).[31] However, it is reasonable that the papal power should extend this far on occasion, as in a case of the greatest immediate benefit or need, in order that the community of the faithful be provided with all necessities through Christ, lest it be exposed to extreme danger because of ignorance, laziness, powerlessness, cowardice, through any unlawful desire or malice of anyone. For Christ does not wish to subjugate all men in slavery to the supreme pontiff, nor does He wish the pope to be preeminent over others for his own benefit, but for the common good. And therefore the supreme pontiff does not receive from Christ the power of depriving others of their freedoms, rights, and property at his own pleasure; nor has Christ given the supreme pontiff other authority whereby the faithful may easily be exposed to temporal or spiritual danger; but He has preferred him to all so he might be useful, giving him no power by which he can disturb as he pleases the

---

[31] *Decretales Gregorii IX, De iudiciis, Novit* (II, 1, 13).

rights of others, which they possessed amongst themselves or amongst their ancestors and predecessors before the promulgation of the law of the Gospels, or which they acquired later by such law and legitimate method as their ancestors employed before.

The keys of the kingdom of heaven and the power of binding and loosing which were given to the supreme pontiff extend firstly and principally to sins in penitential jurisdiction *(in foro poenitentiali)*. When they are committed, the doors of heaven are shut fast as if with bolts, but are opened to the faithful by the power of love. As St. Augustine testifies in his sermon on the dedication of the Temple: "Just as the gates of life are closed to us by evil deeds, as if by late hours and bolts, so beyond doubt are they opened by good deeds."[32] The Savior extended the power of binding and loosing to this extent, as is expounded and stated in John 20:22-23, where He makes express mention of sins, saying to all the Apostles: "Receive the Holy Spirit; whose sins you will forgive, let them be forgiven, and whose sins you will retain, let them be retained." Therefore, the power of binding and loosing has respect to a penitential jurisdiction over sins, and the power of temporal judges to punish the guilty is not affected by the power of the supreme pontiff.

Moreover, the power of the supreme pontiff, which Christ promised to him through the person of St. Peter, as is told in Matthew 16:18, "Thou art Peter, and upon this rock," etc., regularly extends not only to penitential jurisdiction over sins, but to all spiritual matters as well, although not those which are supererogatory, but those which are to be done by necessity — a distinction made both in speech and by the Gloss on Extra, *de constitutionibus*, c. *Cum omnes*[33] — and those which it is expedient for the head of the Christians to have authority over. Nonetheless, on occasion this power extends to a contentious jurisdiction over sin and to temporal affairs; as in a case of the greatest immediate benefit or necessity, where there is no one else who is more nearly affected by these circumstances, who desires [to use] this power, and who can act beneficially in a case of this sort. And the regular power over spiritual matters done by necessity, which it is expedient for the head of Christianity to possess, and this occasional power in contentious or public jurisdiction over temporal affairs, were promised to St. Peter more by these words of Christ, "Thou art Peter, and upon this rock I will build my church," than by those others, "Whatever you bind on earth," etc.

---

[32] St. Augustine, *Sermo* 229 (PL 39. 2166).
[33] *Glossa ordinaria ad Decretalis* I, 2, 6, s.v. "constitutum."

As we find in the decrees (di. xxii, c. *Sacrosancta*; and di. xxi, c. *Quamvis*; and xxiv, q. i, c. *Rogamus* and c. *Loquitur*), the holy fathers apparently arrived at the conclusion that these words of Christ ("Thou art Peter," etc.) either gave or promised to St. Peter primacy over all churches.[34] Therefore, those other words, "Whatever you shall bind," etc., either promised St. Peter only authority in penitential jurisdiction over sin; or else, along with this authority, he was promised authority of a second kind: regular over spiritual matters and occasional over sin in penitential jurisdiction and over even temporal matters. Both of these have been discussed above. In no way was he promised that plenitude of power in both spiritual and temporal matters which that earlier, disproved opinion ascribed to him, because he was given authority by Christ on a regular basis only over those things which are of benefit to the common good. The authority of others over temporal matters is untouched, since it is more expedient for the laity to arrange and manage these matters than the pope, who ought to concentrate on spiritual matters and separate himself in the usual course from secular business.

Consequently, to the opinion of Innocent III cited above, we answer that Innocent believed that Christ excepted from the regular and occasional power of the supreme pontiff nothing which it was beneficial to the common good for him to have control of. He did not mean that Christ excepted and wished to have excepted from the regular power of Peter and his successors anything which not only was opposed to catholic truth, but he was indeed convinced of the contrary, as Innocent says in these words (Extra, *Qui filii sint legitimi*, c. *Per venerabilem*): "Not only in the patrimony of the church, over which we exercise full power in temporal matters, but in other areas as well, which we have investigated for good reasons, do we exercise occasional power."[35] From this it follows that, according to Innocent III, the pope does not receive a regular temporal jurisdiction from Christ in all areas; therefore, he does not receive from Christ full power over temporal affairs, since the patrimony of the church does not exist immediately from Christ but through the generosity of the Emperor. Therefore, again, according to Innocent III, Christ does not mean that nothing at all should be excepted from the power of the supreme pontiff; therefore all the words of Christ about the power of the supreme pontiff, no matter how obscurely and loosely worded, are definitely to be understood in the light of suitable exposition and as admitting of exceptions.

---

[34] Gratian, *Decretum*, dist. 22, c. 2; dist. 21, c. 3; 24, q. 1, c. 15, 18.
[35] *Decretales Gregorii IX, Qui filii sint legitimi, Per venerabilem* (IV, 17, 13).

With regard to the argument that, if we must not except what the canon does not except, how much the less are we to except what God does not except; and that God makes no exception when He says, "Whatever you bind," etc., we answer that when the canon makes an exception in one place and does not make an exception in another, it is clear either from divine scripture or from inviolable reason what is to be excepted and what we must except. In the same way, when Our Lord does not explicitly and openly except something in one place and in another does explicitly except it, it is perfectly clear, either from His acts or words or from other places in divine scripture, that He wishes something to be excepted and that we must make that exception. For at Mark 10:9, He made no explicit exception in His words when He speaks of the union of man and woman, saying, "What God has joined together, let no man put asunder." But in another place He made an exception, when He said at Matthew 5:32, "Any man who dismisses his wife, except it be for adultery, makes her a prostitute"; and we must also make this exception. Many other examples of this can be given, but I pass over them for the sake of brevity. Therefore, although Christ made no explicit exceptions when He said, "Whatever you bind," etc., nonetheless we may conclude from other places in scripture and from necessary reason that He wished many things to be excepted from the regular power of Peter and his successors, as if this were established by precedent, and we must make this exception.

Chapter 6

At this point we should respond briefly to certain allegations by which some seek to prove that the pope has a plenitude of power of this sort.

Whoever has both swords, namely, the material and spiritual swords, seems to have a plenitude of power of this sort. Now, the pope has both swords, material and spiritual, as evidenced by Bernard, who, speaking about the material sword in the fourth book to Pope Eugenius, says, "If the material sword pertained to you in no way, the Lord would not have said, 'It is enough,' but 'It is too much,' when the Apostles said, 'Behold these two swords' [Luke 22:38]."[36] Therefore, the church possesses both, spiritual and temporal; therefore, the pope has a plenitude of power not only in spiritual matters, but also in temporal ones.

---

[36] St. Bernard of Clairvaux, *De consideratione*, 4.7.

We answer this by saying that both swords do belong in some way to the pope without, however, a plenitude of power of this sort, especially in temporal matters. For the material sword belongs to the pope in two ways. In one way, in that by his suggestion and encouragement (indeed, if necessary, by his order), it is drawn out and justice is duly done by the possessor of the secular power, or by another if he to whom it belongs and who is rightfully responsible for its use neglects to do so, either by ignorance or laziness or some other cause, when he could and should have. Bernard seems to imply this when he says, "It [the material sword] is to be unsheathed by you; if not by your hand, then by your nod of assent." And again, "Therefore, both the spiritual and the material sword belong to the church; but the former is used by the church whereas the latter is used on behalf of the church. The former befits the priest, the latter the soldier, but certainly they are used with the assent of the priest and at the order of the emperor."[37] For a soldier in countries which are not subjected to the temporal jurisdiction of the pope ought not draw his sword regularly at the nod, that is, the suggestion, encouragement, or prescription, of the pope, unless the emperor, king, or other secular power, to whom it is subject, orders it. In this way, the material sword belongs to the regular power of the pope in some fashion. From this it can be inferred clearly that, by the very fact that the material sword is found in the church in this way, the pope does not have that plenitude of power which oft-recited opinion asserts that he has.

The material sword pertains to the casual power of the pope in another way. If in circumstances, say, of the greatest usefulness or the direst and most pressing need, the emperor or whoever possesses the material sword cannot or will not draw it out at the behest or order of the pope, the pope should be able to commit its use to another and to order someone whom he knows to unsheathe it justly, bravely, and powerfully. So it clearly appears that, although the material sword belongs in some way to the pope, nevertheless he does not have, especially in temporal matters, such a plenitude of power.

Clearly this is what was meant when Christ ordered Peter, saying, "Put your sword back in the scabbard" [Matthew 26:52; John 18:11]. It is as if he said, "The material sword is rightfully yours, not because you own it (*non dominio*) but because you have the authority to encourage and, if necessary, order its use when the opportunity arises. However, you will keep it con-

---

[37] St. Bernard of Clairvaux, *De consideratione*, 4.7.

cealed in its sheath so that you will not draw it out by yourself; nor shall you let it be drawn out by anyone else to the detriment and harm of the secular power, to whom it belongs, with respect to lordship, use, and control over it when it is used. In this way, you will know that by my authority alone you ought not usurp for yourself this particular sword." Bernard says this as well when he is writing to Pope Eugenius, "Why do you try to usurp the sword a second time, when you have been told to put it back in its sheath?"[38] From these things it can clearly be concluded that the pope does not have a plenitude of power of this sort in temporal matters. For if it were so, he would be able to unsheathe it by his hand, and not just by his nod, by divine law. Not only would he have the sword concealed in its sheath, but he would have a greater and fuller power than any secular power of unsheathing it by himself. Not only would he be able to commit its use to the emperor, he would even be able rightfully to take away the use of the sword from every mortal and reserve it for himself alone.

Even if no one possessed the use of the material sword except with the permission of the pope, it still would not be possible to infer from this that the pope has a plenitude of power of this sort. Natural freedom, by which men are naturally free and not enslaved, is not taken from all men by the power of the material sword, which was granted to those placed on high for the use of subjects, "for the praise of good ones and the punishment of evildoers" (1 Peter 2:14). Therefore, the power of the material sword in no way extends itself to anything that detracts from the freedom and benefit of good men. For this reason no emperor has ever had such a plenitude of power in temporal affairs, either before the papacy or after it. For never have all men been slaves of a single man who was nothing but human; though granted that all men are slaves of Christ, even if many do not recognize themselves as such.

Another argument is brought forth to prove that the pope has such a plenitude of power, namely, that the pontificate that Christ gave to Peter was much more powerful than the pontificate of the Old Testament. But God said when he was establishing the priesthood in the old law, "Behold, I have set you above the nations and kingdoms, that you might root out and pull down and destroy and ruin and build and plant" (Jeremiah 1:10). Therefore, the pope also has in the law of grace such a plenitude of power.

But this allegation is lacking in many ways. First, many more earthly matters (*carnalia*) were deputed by divine ordination alone to the pontifi-

---

[38] St. Bernard of Clairvaux, *De consideratione*, 4.7.

cate of the old law than to the pontificate of the new law. So the pontificate of the new law does not regularly have more power in earthly matters, although it does in spiritual ones (granted that on occasion it does have equal power in earthly or temporal matters). Secondly, in those words spoken to Jeremiah, as Bernard testifies, guardianship (*ministerium*) and farm labor, not lordship, are imposed on the supreme pontiff. As Bernard says, "There is need of a hoe, not a scepter."[39] For Jeremiah was not established as a prophet above the nations and kingdoms that he might rule over them in temporal matters and of his own free will take away people's things and temporal laws and bestow them on whomever he pleased. Rather, he was set up above the nations and kingdoms so that, by the hoe of preaching and exhortation, he might root out and pull down and destroy and ruin vices and wrongdoing, and plant and build virtues. Thirdly, these words were not spoken by one exercising a pontificate, even if they were said to a priest. Granted that Jeremiah was a priest, I do not remember reading that he was the high priest or pontiff; wherefore it cannot be concluded from these words that the pope has such plenitude of power. Fourthly, these words were spoken to Jeremiah not as a priest, but as a prophet, inasmuch as he had a special responsibility. From these arguments, it is obvious that we cannot conclude from these words that the pope has such a plenitude of power, especially in temporal matters, even though we cannot deny that he regularly has great power in spiritual matters and occasionally in temporal ones.

Another allegation is brought up to support the above opinion, namely, that minor matters ought to be under the control of whoever controls major ones. According to the Apostle, "Shall we not judge angels? How much more, then, things that pertain to this life?" (1 Corinthians 6:3). Here the Apostle proves that, from the fact that angels, who are greater, are subject to our judgment, things of this life ought to be judged by us also. But the pope has a plenitude of power in spiritual matters; therefore, he must have a much greater plenitude of power of this sort in temporal matters, which are lesser.

To this, we answer that minor matters ought not always to be subjected to him to whom greater matters are subjected. It often is expedient that greater matters are committed to greater people, and lesser ones to lesser people, so that their offices are not confused. Nevertheless, the minor matters that are necessary for the running of a community or congregation ought to be subjected, like the major matters, to that congregation or com-

---

[39] St. Bernard of Clairvaux, *De consideratione*, 2.6.

munity, if it is not under the control of someone else. The Apostle speaks to this situation. He is not speaking in the person of the pope, but in the person of the entire community or congregation of the faithful, wishing that, if the truthful can judge angels, so much more those material things which are necessary to the faithful and in which matters they [the faithful] are in no way subjected to princes not of the faith. Even in the time of the Apostle, the faithful were not servants of the emperors or any other princes not of the faith. Indeed, many secular things could be used in accordance with natural liberty. And with respect to many secular things, they were able to raise these in court amongst themselves, since they were not allowed to have recourse to judges not of the faith. So that "the name and doctrine of the Lord be not blasphemed" (1 Timothy 6:1), they did not seek the judgment of the temporal laws of emperors or those not of the faith, but solved their disagreements by a pact or judgment. And such was their power in judging temporal matters that he who was over them in spiritual matters did not have such power regularly. Wherefore it may be that, though the pope regularly has a certain plenitude of power — though not the one that the aforementioned opinion ascribes to him — he still does not have it regularly in temporal matters, which are lesser. Because, as has been mentioned, it is expedient that the one responsible for greater matters hardly concerns himself with minor ones and that he does not have regular power over them. Nevertheless, the secular things necessary to the community of the faithful, and which are minor, are subjected to that community in the person of its minor members, namely, the laity — in the same way that spiritual matters, which are major, are entrusted to it in the person of the pope — so that the community does not lack anything it needs. Nevertheless, the community does not have such a plenitude of power in temporal matters, since many faithful are in no way to be considered in a servile condition with respect to any purely human power, but rejoice and excel in natural liberty. And so in no way can it be said that the pope has such plenitude of power in temporal matters, since he does not even have it in spiritual matters, unless his power in spiritual matters is equal to the divine power or the power of Christ, whose vicar he is, and by this fact inferior in power.

But perhaps someone says that the pope exercises on earth the comprehensive mandate (*generali legatione*) of Christ and that therefore everything without exception is understood to have been yielded to him. To this it is easy to answer that many things are understood to be excepted under a general mandate, unless they are specially expressed. The pope exercises a general mandate not for his own honor and good, nor that he might upset, diminish, and confound the legitimate temporal rights of others, but for the good of the entire community of the faithful without violating significantly the rights of others. For this reason, all power that takes away from the common good (which Christ set before and preferred to the private good of the pope), or from others' freedoms and rights to any great degree, is understood to be excepted under the general mandate which the papacy exercises. A diligent reading of the entire scriptures will show that no such power is specially expressed in them. This mandate, then, is general and meets the needs of the entire community of the faithful, being necessary and salvific. Because it is general, every necessary power which it befits the head of the Christians to possess with respect to those things that must be done is yielded to the pope, excepting the temporal laws and freedoms of subjects. It is expedient, necessary, and salvific that all power of which no special and explicit mention is made, whether in spiritual or temporal matters, is understood to be excepted, if this power causes conflict to a great degree with the temporal laws and the liberties granted by God and nature to the faithful. (However, any such power ought not to be considered forbidden.) In this way, the pope does not have, through his comprehensive mandate, the power of restricting or removing the freedoms granted to the faithful by God and nature, unless there is a special mention made of them in the mandate and when reason correctly based in genuine scriptures judges them to be restricted in case of need or emergency. And if he does otherwise, his deed will not hold in law unless it acquires strength by the negligence or criminality of the one whose freedom is restricted, or through some other cause. Let the pope know that it has in no way been yielded to him by the general mandate that he might rule with strictness and power. Let him know that he has been given ministry, not lordship. Let him know that he has been set above all not for himself, but for the good of others, because he is to provide not for himself principally but for others. Let him know that he has received his power from the Lord in order to build, not to spoil, disturb, and lessen the rights of others.

But someone might ask: who is to explain and decide when the pope has power and when he does not? For if it is not clearly and specifically expressed when he has the power, and if he was given only a general mandate, one to which there are many exceptions that are nevertheless not specifically mentioned, and moreover many things are understood in vows, oaths, pacts, promises, and orders that are nevertheless not set down at all explicitly, who decides? To this we answer that the first and infallible rule in this matter is sacred scripture and correct reasoning. Therefore, it is for the man who understands sacred scripture sensibly and correctly, and who leans on unerring reasoning, to explain and determine cases of this sort by a truthful declaration. It is the responsibility of the general council, and even of the pope, if he understands the truth in this sort of case, to explain and determine it in an authoritative statement which would be strong enough to oblige all the faithful not to teach otherwise. If, however, the pope presumes to determine the issue against the cause of truth, he must in no way be believed. Those who through a knowledge of sacred scriptures and their own judgment know that he erred are obliged to reprimand him at the right time, place, and circumstance, lest they be guilty of consenting to his errors to their own damnation, "because an error which is not opposed is approved" (di. lxxxiii, *Error*).[40]

Now another allegation is brought forward to prove that the pope has such a plenitude of power in spiritual and temporal matters. It says in Genesis 1:16 that "God made two great lights," by which the two powers, spiritual and temporal, are understood. The ecclesiastical power is understood by the larger light, namely, the sun, and the secular power by the lesser one, namely, the moon. Therefore, just as the sun is more noble and worthier than the moon, which gets its light from the sun, so the secular power is inferior to the ecclesiastical and receives its merit from it. Consequently, the ecclesiastical power, which is found most fully in the pope, has a plenitude of power over the secular power.

To this we answer that this allegation can be shown to be more against the proposition than for it. Even if the sun has some influence over the moon, the moon does not depend on the sun in terms of its substance, movement, and many other things. So, although the power of the pope, which has to do with spiritual matters, is nobler and worthier than the secular power (spiritual matters being more worthy than temporal ones), and although the pope has power in spiritual matters even over those who have been set highest among the secular powers, nevertheless he does not have such plenitude of power over them, even though it can be conceded by correct understanding that, as the holy fathers assert, the pope does have a plenitude of power. For he regularly has a plenitude of power with respect to all spiritual matters which must be dealt with and over which it is expedient that the head of the faithful has power. He even has a certain plenitude of power casually in other spiritual matters (as in temporal ones), which are superogatory and in which the faithful usually licitly do what they wish. For example, there could be a situation in which something is to be done and there is no one available. Let the one who has the relevant

---

[40] Gratian, *Decretum*, dist. 83, c. 3.

expertise for that particular matter have the power to dispose of such matters. If he does so in a just and useful way, others are bound to obey him; if not, they are bound to resist him.

Chapter 7

Having shown that the pope does not have such a plenitude of power as many attribute to him, two further points must be demonstrated. First, notwithstanding any papal statute, prohibition, precept, judgment, or proceeding, the prelates and the clerics subjected to the king of England must help him even from the goods of the church in his just war. Secondly, the pope cannot prohibit them from doing so by any statute, prohibition, precept, judgment, or proceeding.

There are some notable things to be said before all the evidence is brought forth. The first is that the prelates and clerics subjected to the king of England do not possess their temporal property, especially the surplus, by divine law, but by human law flowing from that same king. Augustine expressly bears witness to this when he writes in the sixth sermon of the first part on John and in the decrees (di. viii, c. *quo iure*). Speaking about the villas and other possessions of the church, he says: "By what law do you defend the villas of the church, divine or human? They would answer, 'We have divine law in divine scripture, human law in the laws of kings.' Whence does each possess what he possesses? Isn't it by human law? For by divine law, 'the earth is the Lord's, and the fulness thereof' [Psalms 23:1]. God made rich and poor from the same clay, and one earth supports both. Human law says, 'This estate is mine, this house is mine, this slave is mine.' Human laws, however, are the laws of the emperor. How? Because God distributed these human laws to the human race through emperors and kings. 'But what is an emperor to me?' According to his law you own the land. Take away the emperor's laws and who would dare say, 'This is my estate' or 'This is my house' or 'This is my slave'? But if, as men hold, they make the laws of kings, would you want to silence the laws so that you could rejoice? Again, laws can be reread where emperors have directed that those who, being outside the communion of the catholic church, usurp to themselves the name of Christian and are not willing to worship in peace the author of peace, so they may not dare to possess anything in the name of the church. But you say, 'What do we have to do with the emperor?' But I have already said that we are dealing with human law. The Apostle wished us to honor and obey kings, and he said 'Honor the king' [1 Peter 2:17]. Do not say, 'What are kings to me?' What are possessions to you then? Possessions are owned through the law of kings. You said, 'What are kings to me?' Do not say the possessions are yours because you have them by virtue of the law which you renounced."[41] From this it can clearly be seen that by human law, namely, that of the king, the possessions of the clergy are possessed by them from the lordship of the king of England. Indeed this can be easily proven in divine scriptures. God did not give to the ministers of the new law any special possessions, but ordained only that the lay people provide for their needs. Therefore, everything they have, especially the surplus, is conferred on them by kings and those subject to kings. Wherefore it is by the royal law that they possess the things they own.

The second thing of note is that anyone who makes a donation of his own possessions can set down any condition he wants as long as nothing stands in the way and it is not forbidden by a superior law. This is clearly held in both civil and canon law (Extra, *de conditionibus in matrimonio appositis*, c. *Verum*).[42] From this it can be inferred evidently that when the kings of England and their subjects assign their property and temporal possessions, especially the surplus, to the church, they can ordain how they should be dispensed with and how the clergy should use them. The clergy is bound at the price of salvation to respect such a condition, will, and intention, notwithstanding the prohibition, precept, or statute of anyone who is not accounted superior to kings in temporal matters.

The third noteworthy thing is that temporal possessions, especially the surplus, are given by kings and princes and other laymen to be used for holy purposes (*piae causae*). This is manifestly stated in many canons.

The fourth point is that a kind, humane, rational, and likely judgment should be made when there are no contracts and other legal documents expressly stating in what particular pious causes the temporal property (especially the surplus) given to the church is to be used. Just as in those matters dealing with the divine worship, "a kind interpretation" is to be made (Extra, *de privilegiis*, c. *In hiis*),[43] so in these matters dealing with piety, a kinder and more reasonable explanation ought to be made, so that it does not deceive anyone (*de regulis iuris*, c. *Quotiens*).[44] Thus, interpretation

---

[41] Gratian, *Decretum*, dist. 8, c. 1 (identical to Augustine, *In Ioannis Evangelium Tractatus* 6.25 [PL 35. 1436]).

[42] *Decretales Gregorii IX*, De conditionibus in matrimonio appositis, Verum (IV, 5, 4); also *Corpus Juris Civilis*, Digest 2.14.48 and Codex 4.38.3.

[43] *Decretales Gregorii IX*, De privilegiis, In hiis (V, 33, 30).

[44] *Corpus Juris Civilis*, Digest 50.17.200.

should be made in obscure matters so that things work out for the best, especially in the case of the common good, and that there be no unjust loss. Just as "a kinder judgment is to be preferred in doubtful cases" (*de regulis iuris*, l. *Semper*),[45] so too is it to be preferred in the matter of things set down unclearly. And the "good of princes," especially when it does not affect the rights of others, should be interpreted most broadly (*de simonia*, last chapter).[46] Just as the more useful reading is accepted in the case of ambiguity (*de iudiciis*, c. *Si quis intentione*),[47] so too is the more kind and reasonable reading to be rendered from something general and indefinite. Therefore, in all such cases the more reasonable and likely interpretation is to be accepted.

Chapter 8

Now that we have seen these things, we must prove that the prelates and clergy subject to the king of England are obliged to come to his assistance, even with the goods of the church, in his just war. For with respect to the possessions, especially the surplus, conferred on the church by the kings of England and their subjects, the will and intent of the donors must be respected, since anyone can make some agreement as he pleases with respect to a donation of his property, which must be kept by the donor and the recipient, according to the second remark above. But the will and intent of the kings of England and of their subjects in conferring their temporal property on the churches was that they be used in righteous causes, especially in causes that would spill over into the common good of everyone under the lordship of those kings, as can be seen in the charters and privileges which the churches receive and possess concerning these matters. If these documents should in a general way state only "righteous causes," for which these goods were given to the churches, the phrase must be understood in a more benign and humane, reasonable, and likely fashion, according to the fourth remark made above. But the defense of one's country and its royal laws must in no way be considered unimportant among righteous causes. Therefore, charters and privileges of this sort must be interpreted in such a way that they are extended to the defense of the country and the

---

[45] *Corpus Juris Civilis*, Digest 50.17.56.
[46] *Decretales Gregorii IX*, *De simonia* (V, 40, 16).
[47] *Corpus Juris Civilis*, Digest 5.1.66.

laws of its people. Wherefore prelates and clerics are obliged to come to the assistance of the king in the defense of the country and the laws of the people, something which is acknowledged to be for the good of everyone in the kingdom. For the prelates and clergy have been commissioned with the dispensation of the church possessions, and not with lordship over them. Furthermore, not only the property which is transferred to secular persons, but also that which is transferred to ecclesiastical persons — especially the surplus — is transferred with its condition, unless the person who has this particular power dissolves this condition. But the condition imposed on the property conferred on the churches was that it be used to aid the king in the defense of the country and the laws of the people. In no way is the property conferred on the churches by the kings of England free from this condition. Therefore, the clerics are obliged to use church property to come to the aid of the king in the defense of the country and the laws of its people.

It is not valid to say that church property has a general immunity from the kings of England and that consequently the clerics are in no way obliged to aid the king with the property of the church. As in a general promise everything forbidden and not expressly stated by the one promising is understood to be excepted, according to both canonical and civil laws, so too in a general concession of immunity everything forbidden and not expressly conceded by the one making the concession is held to be excepted from the concession. But not to aid the king in such grave circumstances is illegal, and kings would not give such special immunity to ecclesiastics. Therefore, this should be considered an exception to the general concession of immunity. Proof: Just as, as was proven before, a kinder and more reasonable interpretation must be made with respect to general donations or concessions to righteous causes, so too in the matter of the concession of immunity must a similar interpretation be made. It is reasonable and kind that the clergy help the king in his hour of need. Therefore, the general concession must be understood in this way.

Again, the canonical sanctions say that all privileges cease in times of need. For if both divine and human laws stop in times of need, and if need is cited as an exception to them (Extra, *de regulis iuris*, c. *Quod non est licitum*; *de consecratione*, di.v, c. *Discipulos*,[48] which is taken from the words of Christ [Matthew 12:3-8]), so much more surely should human privileges stop in times of need. Therefore, if the king now or hereafter

---

[48] *Decretales Gregorii IX, De regulis iuris, Quod non est licitum* (V, 41, 4); Gratian, *Decretum*, dist. 5, c. 26.

found himself in a situation of need, the privileges of immunity conceded to the clergy by kings would cease.

Hence, it is proven that the clergy should help the king with the property of the church in this case. For ecclesiastics are no more exempt with respect to the property of the church than they are with respect to their own persons or at least the persons of their servants. But in times of need the servants of the clergy ought not to be freed from the defense of the kingdom. According to Gregory (Extra, *de immunitate ecclesiarum*, c. *Peruenit*), when the need is imminent no man of the church should excuse himself from guarding the city, so that the city might be better guarded with everyone on the lookout.[49] Therefore, even the clergy are obliged to aid the king with the property of the church.

Again, the clergy should pay the wages of the soldiers guarding their possessions from the property of the church. This is borne out by many sacred canons. So much more, then, ought they to help in defending their lord in temporal things (to defend the kingdom and their rights), for through him they and the property of the church are defended. Proof: Because, just as "what affects everyone ought to be approved of by everyone" (Extra, *de temporibus ordinationum*, c. *Si archiepiscopus*),[50] so too what affects everyone ought to be guarded against by everyone. But an attack on the kingdom and the royal laws affects everyone in the country, clergy and laymen alike. Therefore, everyone ought to lend a hand in defending the kingdom and the laws of the king. Moreover, since the goods of the church are conferred on it for righteous causes, it is better to defend the country than to nurture poor people. For according to Tullius [Cicero] in his *Rhetoric*, through piety "a benevolent and diligent worship is given to the country,"[51] and consequently piety directs itself to the country. And in *Ethics* 1.1, it says that the common good is "better and more divine than the individual good."[52] From this it may be inferred that the good of the whole country is better and more divine than the good of the poor of that country. From this it is concluded that it is more pious to come to the aid of the whole country than to the aid of the poor of the country. For it is agreed that the clergy are obliged to help the poor with the property of the

---

[49] *Decretales Gregorii IX, De immunitate ecclesiarum, Pervenit* (III, 49, 2) (also St. Gregory the Great, *Registrum epistularum* 8.19 [PL 77. 921–922]).

[50] *Decretales Gregorii IX, De temporibus ordinationum, Si archiepiscopus* (I, 11, 6); but the wording is derived from *Liber Sextus* V, 12, reg. 29.

[51] Cicero, *De inventione* 2.53.

[52] Aristotle, *Nicomachean Ethics* 1094b8–11.

church. So much more, then, when the resources of laymen do not suffice, should they help the king in the defense of the country and the rights of the people.

Again, the clergy ought to help the king more for the sake of the care he takes of the country and all those in it than for the sake of his own person. But if the king is in need of the help of the clergy for the sake of his own person, they ought to help him not as any other needy person, but as someone more special than others in need. They ought to help him because of the care invested in his person, a care that extends to the clergy itself. They ought to help him because of the generosity of his predecessors as king who conferred goods on the church. The church ought to aid its patron when the need arises more specially than others in need (Extra, *de iure patronatus*, c. *Nobis*, and xvi, q. vii, *quicunque*).[53] Therefore, so much the more are they obliged to offer the necessary aid from the goods of the church if the king should need help from the clergy in the defense of the country and the rights of the people.

CHAPTER 9

It has been demonstrated that the clergy are required to offer the aid of subsidy even from the goods of the church to the king in his just war. Now it must be proved that they are obliged to do this, notwithstanding any papal statute, nor any prohibition or command, nor any sentence or proceeding, even if it were to come down from the supreme pontiff himself. As evidence for this, it should be known that it is not from divine right, but only from human right, that the pope has regular power over temporal things, especially the surplus, which have been gathered by kings and others of the faithful for the church, if the donors had conceded any power to him over the gifts; and consequently, he possesses only as much power as, and no more than, what the English kings, or those superior to them, gave to the pope over the ecclesiastical goods that they have given to the churches.

This can be shown in a number of ways. For, as was shown earlier, in Chapter 7, the clergy do not possess temporal goods, especially the surplus, by divine right, but only by human right, which is the right of emperor and king. Therefore, the pope does not have regular power over temporal

---

[53] *Decretales Gregorii IX, De iure patronatus, Nobis* (III, 38, 25); Gratian, *Decretum*, 16, q. 7, c. 30.

things given to the English churches, unless by the authority of the king; therefore, he has only as much as the kings have given to him, and no more.

Further, as is clear from what was demonstrated earlier, the pope does not have any regular power over temporal goods solely by the ordination of Christ, other than the power and right of seeking from the laity what is necessary for his sustenance and for the execution of his office; and if he has any other power, he has it from human beings. But the temporal goods given to the English churches by the English kings were not designated for the sustenance of the pope nor for the execution of his office; therefore, if he holds any ruling power over temporal goods of this kind, he does not hold it solely by the ordination of Christ, but from human beings, and from no one else other than the kings of England; therefore, the pope holds as much power over temporal goods of this kind as the English kings may have given, and no more.

Again, as is clear from the preceding, anyone can impose an agreement of law with respect to his own property, as he wishes, in a donation or endowment, and consequently he can ordain how much power the recipient, or anyone else, should have over it. But the things given to the English churches were first those of the English kings, and not of the pope; hence, when the kings gave them to the English churches, they were able to ordain how they should be expended and how much power the clergy and popes should have over them, nor should anyone have any power over these things, except what the English kings have bestowed upon him. Wherefore, if the English kings neither tacitly nor expressly gave any power over these things to the pope, then the pope has no ruling power over them. But I say "tacitly or expressly," because, if the English kings or others — whom, by virtue of their rights and in such an event, the English kings could not restrain — gave their consent, then if it at first had been ordained that the pope should have for himself the established power over the matters which have been and should be conceded to churches other than that of Rome; and if the English kings bestowed temporal goods upon the English churches, and they did not expressly ordain that the pope should have power in any way over temporal goods; then it follows that in some way they tacitly ordained that the pope should have power over these things, namely, that power which he is deemed worthy to have over the things which have been conceded to other churches. But they could ordain that the pope should have no more power over those things which they gave to the English churches than over the other temporal goods of their own kingdom, should the English churches, under such an agreement, be able to, and want to, receive the goods themselves. But if the churches, under the conditions of such an agreement, either were unable to, or did not wish to, receive the temporal goods themselves, and nevertheless the kings, under a lawful agreement, bestowed them upon the churches, it should be conceded that the pope has some power over temporal things of this kind, although only insofar as the kings give it to him: so that the pope may have power over temporal goods of this kind, which have been conceded by the English kings to the churches within the lordship of the same kings, only in virtue of the rights of the kings. The pope has only as much as has been granted to him through the privileges of kings.

This having been demonstrated, it must be proved that, when there is no papal statute, prohibition or command, or sentence or proceeding whatsoever obstructing them, the clergy are bound to give aid to the king in his just war from the goods of the church, especially its surplus. For, as has been shown, the pope does not have any power over the temporal goods given to the English churches, unless by human authority, and if the English kings have conceded it to him. But the English kings have not given to the supreme pontiff any power, by any statute, prohibition or command, sentence or proceeding, to forbid the clergy subject to the king to give aid to him in his just war. For, if the English kings gave such power to the pope through a special or even a general privilege, then either this is contained distinctly, explicitly, and in particular, in some special or general privilege, which belongs to the king and not to the pope, or it is held only implicitly and in general terms.

The first cannot be said: in the first place, because no specific intention can be found in any privilege concerning such power; in the second place, because if a specific intention were to be discovered in any privilege concerning such power, such a privilege is to be considered a non-privilege, because it would contain an obvious vice. It is vicious, unjust, and contrary to natural as well as divine law to transfer the whole treasury for the defense of the country and of the public rights from those who have enough from other sources to those who, not having other sources, are known to be wanting. Since therefore the laity, along with clergy and not without them, have enough for the defense of the kingdom and of the rights of the kingdom, it follows that such a privilege of whatever human power conceded to the pope in such a case should be reckoned a vice, and consequently the privilege should be held of no value; since a privilege is a private law (di. iii, c. *Privilegia*), a law is not a law unless it is just, a right is not a right unless it is just (di. i, c. *Ius auteum*).[54] Therefore, in no special or general

---

[54] Gratian, *Decretum*, dist. 3, c. 3; dist. 1, c. 2.

privilege, which is in fact to be reckoned a privilege, is it either in particular or explicitly expressed that the English kings gave the pope such power over the temporal goods that they bestowed on the church.

Neither can the second be said, namely, that the English kings gave such power to the pope through a general or special privilege, implicitly and under general terms. Because general terms placed in a privilege of this kind should not be increased, but rather should be restricted, so that it is not to be understood that such powers were conceded to the pope. As is clear from the fourth point above, in Chapter 7, in such matters the interpretation is to be made more reasonable and more kind. But it is also more reasonable and more kind that the pope should offer the aid of subsidy to the king, when he has such need, from the goods which his predecessors liberally bestowed upon the churches, rather than that he should deny him such aid; therefore, the general terms of his predecessors are to be restricted in such a way that the power of impeding such aid may be in no way conceded to the pope.

Furthermore, as was treated earlier, in Chapter 8, certain exceptions are understood in any general endowment, so that there may not be any specific expressions of things which are illicit, and which the endower should have in no way have specially conceded. But it is not licit to impede the clergy from giving support to the king during such time of need; rather it is impious and cruel, and displays open ingratitude. Even the kings who were predecessors of the king who now gloriously holds the government of the kingdom should in no way have conferred this, especially because, even if there is no evidence to the contrary, it should be presumed that they should have conceded nothing vicious or dangerous or prejudicial to the common good of the kingdom; therefore, the English kings did not give such power to the pope in general terms.

Again, contemptible privileges, and those which diminish the power and authority of others, are not to be increased, but restricted (Extra, *de decimis*, c. *Dilecti*);[55] this especially contains the truth when, notwithstanding any such restrictions, something is conferred through these privileges and if they were to be increased, it could detract from the common good. But the privileges conceded to the pope by the English kings concerning the holding of power over temporal things, especially the surplus, which the English kings conferred upon the English churches, are contemptible, because they diminish the rights of others. For through them the right of the king is dimin-

---

[55] *Decretales Gregorii IX, De decimis, Dilecti* (III, 30, 8).

ished, and even the rights of the clergy in the domain of that king, because, through privileges of this kind, the clergy would be made subject to the pope with respect to many things in which otherwise they would not be subject. They would have freer administration over these things if the kings were to concede less of such powers to the pope; for then they could do many things without the permission of the pope, indeed even against the pope's command, which now they cannot. Therefore, such privileges that have been conceded to the pope are not to be increased, but restricted.

But the way in which they should be restricted can be made clear from what has been written before: namely, in such a way that, for the sake of the common good of the kingdom and of those subject to the king, the pope himself should not be able to interfere, by any statute, prohibition, or command, procedure, or sentence.

Chapter 10

Clearly, as the truth of what was said before appears more evident, I should offer what may be replied to some objections that can be brought forth against these things.

For it seems that the clergy and prelates should not offer aid from the goods of the church to the king without the permission of the pope; for this is supported by Extra, *de immunitate ecclesiarum*, c. *Adversus*.[56] From this it is inferred all the more that if the pope prevents them from helping the king, they should obey the pope, and not offer aid. Furthermore, the pope has held neither power, nor any privileges, at any time from the English kings; therefore, everything that was said in the preceding chapter concerning the power and privileges conceded by the English kings to the supreme pontiff has been introduced into the present treatise uselessly and to no purpose.

Again, the pope alone can and should interpret the privileges of the supreme pontiff; therefore, if any privileges should be conceded by the English kings to the supreme pontiff concerning the things given to the churches and to anyone else, he himself, and no other, should seek to interpret them; and consequently, his interpretation of them should be maintained. If, therefore, he should determine that the clergy should not give aid without the permission of the laity from the goods of the church, it follows that

---

[56] *Decretales Gregorii IX, De immunitate ecclesiarum, Adversus* (III, 49, 7).

the English clergy should not give aid to the kings from the goods of the church contrary to the command or prohibition of the pope.

Thus, the "good of the prince" is to be interpreted most broadly (Extra, *de simonia*, last chapter);[57] therefore, should there be any privileges through which the English kings, in general terms, gave power to the supreme pontiff over the things which they gave to the churches, these privileges should be interpreted most broadly, so that if no express and special mention is made in them of the power of prohibiting the clergy from aiding the king with these same things, in any case whatsoever, then power should in no way be taken away from the supreme pontiff, but it is understood to be granted to him. For this reason, if it is in no way expressed in such privileges that the clergy should come to the aid of the king's wars, the pope can prevent them from coming to his aid in this event.

Furthermore, the goods of the church are the goods of the poor (xii, q. ii, c. *Gloria*);[58] therefore, they should not be expended in battles. Again, only four portions should be made from the goods of the church (xii, q. ii, c. *Quattuor*),[59] among which there is no mention of expending any temporal goods for battle; therefore, ecclesiastical goods should not be expended in battles.

Further, "the sentence of the pastor, whether just or unjust, is to be feared";[60] therefore, whether a sentence is brought forth by a canon or by the pope upon everyone giving subsidy to the king from the goods of the church, that sentence should be upheld; and consequently, they should not give aid to him against the express command of the pope, just as they should not act against his sentence.

Chapter 11

These things may be easily refuted. To the first objection, it can be said that the clergy should not give aid to the king from the goods of the church without papal permission, and unless the Roman pontiff is first consulted concerning those matters in which the pope has the power to obstruct the clergy from conferring subsidies for the purpose of alleviating the needs of

---

[57] *Decretales Gregorii IX, De simonia* (V, 40, 16).
[58] Gratian, *Decretum*, 12, q. 2, c. 71.
[59] Gratian, *Decretum*, 12, q. 2, c. 27.
[60] St. Gregory the Great, *In Evangelia* hom. 26.6 (PL 76. 1201).

others. On the other hand, in those matters in which the pope does not have the power to prevent the clergy from alleviating the needs of others, the clergy may give aid to the king and to others from the wealth of the church without the permission — indeed, against the command — of the Roman pontiff. It follows, moreover, that if the king should for any reason be in dire need, so that his life could not be saved unless the clergy were to give him aid from the wealth of the church (even if it were given liberally), the clergy ought to assist him before consulting the Roman pontiff, lest they petition the Roman pontiff and the king pass from this life before they receive an answer. Moreover, if the king were taken captive and the wealth of the laity would not suffice for setting him free, the clergy may be obliged to give the wealth of the church for his redemption before the supreme pontiff can be consulted, if it were the case that he who holds the king captive should desire to have him killed directly if the king's ransom were not immediately offered. Furthermore, if the English kings had ordered that the wealth of the church be conferred, because by that abundant wealth captives could be delivered or bridges constructed and whatever other common necessities and demands could be lightened, then the clergy, without such permission of the Roman pontiff, would be bound to spend those goods endowed upon them by royal generosity, nor would they be compelled to consult the Roman pontiff; for pacts and laws which are imposed by donors in their donation of things must be observed without exception.

Therefore, since the pope does not have the power of preventing the clergy from assisting the king when there is such a necessity, they are in no way obliged to consult the Roman pontiff in this case; and, if they were to consult him and he were to prohibit them from putting up the aid for the king, they ought not to obey him, either because such a prohibition is wrong or because in this matter the power does not extend to the pope. In those matters, however, in which the pope has the power of preventing the clergy from alleviating common needs or the needs of others, the clergy should not confer subsidies for alleviating common necessities and demands unless the Roman pontiff is consulted first. In such cases, moreover, in which the pope has such legislative power, it can be known by human judgment what the jurisdiction of the king is, or what cannot be instituted without the express or tacit consent of the king, as will become clear in the response to the second objection.

To the second objection, it can be said that if the English kings or even one of the inhabitants of their kingdom had not given, by themselves without other believers, any power or jurisdiction to the pope over the surplus temporal wealth which they gave to the churches, then the pope would have no regular power over those things, unless the English kings or the inhabitants of the realm, together with the other believers, had given such power to the pope, either through a general council or through some other form of assembly or by any other means, tacitly or expressly, or unless the pope had acquired such power from precedent and reasonable practice without any revocation on the part of the English kings and inhabitants. And for this reason it has been already said that every right that the pope has over the surplus wealth given to the church by the English kings is a right of kings, nor was it instituted without either the express or tacit consent of the kings; for the kings granted such a right expressly, either individually, or commonly with other kings set up in other regions, since, together in a general council or assembly with the English kings, they desired that the pope should have such power over those things which they had given or would possibly give to the churches. It must be the case that, on the one hand, the English kings agreed either expressly or tacitly to the ordination passed in a general council or in another assembly or by other means, to the effect that the pope should have such power over ecclesiastical goods; or, on the other hand, the pope acquired the power over such things legitimately from precedent and reasonable practice, without revocation on the part of the English kings.

Therefore, the objection becomes false when it states that the pope never had any power or privileges from the English kings. For any power which the pope has for legislation over the surplus ecclesiastical wealth that the English kings gave to the churches, he acquires from the English kings in any of the manners listed above. Moreover, if in general councils there are issued any statutes through which power is granted to the pope over those goods which the English kings gave to the churches, those statutes can in some way be called privileges given to the pope by the English kings through express or tacit consent. Therefore, all the statutes of general councils, and any other ones in which it is stated in general terms that the pope may have power over wealth given to the churches by the English kings, are to be interpreted and restricted in the same way as would be the privileges which the individual English kings under their own seals or otherwise gave to the pope concerning the holding of power over surplus temporal wealth which had been granted to the churches. And therefore those sayings are not empty which have been inserted in the preceding chapter concerning the power or privileges granted by the English kings to the supreme pontiff. Through these things it can be known how whatever statutes or decrees by which it is asserted that the pope has power over the wealth given to the churches by emperors, kings, princes, and any other believers, are to be interpreted and restricted; since they are to be interpreted in such a way that they exclude no piety and include no ingratitude or iniquity.

To the third objection, it may briefly be replied that only the pope may interpret the privileges that he himself concedes to others legitimately and properly when an interpretation becomes necessary for the express reason that the intention of the giver of the privileges is ignored. But the privileges that are granted by others to the pope himself must not and cannot be interpreted by the pope, but rather by the givers, when an interpretation is necessary because the intention of those giving the privileges is forgotten. If, however, the interpretation of such privileges is necessary for someone or some people because of their ignorance of the power which the pope has from divine or human law, such an interpretation pertains to those who have a truer, keener, more subtle, and more profound understanding of human and divine laws, even if they enjoy a lesser memory of divine and human laws. It pertains especially to them to judge — not by discriminating with authority and judgment, but by affirming with true doctrine and simple assertion — how much power the pope may attain over things given by the faithful to the church, which power comes from reasonable and customary practice (not by unreasonable or unprecedented practice), so that the pope would be able to exert regularly the power over such gifts to the churches, while the faithful who gave such things to the churches do not revoke it, but consciously allow it. As for the other ones, who understand divine and human laws less profoundly (although they may understand the truth through these things), they should be bound to follow anything of divine and human laws or human customs that might be remembered.

To the fourth objection, it may be said that the privileges and benefits of princes, insofar as special rights of princes are concerned, are to be interpreted most broadly so that they may not involve any vice, and so that those privileges which the princes had in no way granted specifically might be excluded; insofar as the common rights of others are concerned, they are to be strictly interpreted. And just as this applies to privileges, so it also applies to the power which one obtains through either the express or the tacit permission of the princes or through reasonable and customary practice: this must be most strictly understood insofar as the rights of others are concerned, especially where great harm could befall them. And thus, if the pope should have power over the things given to the churches by the English kings, through either express or tacit concession by those kings or through reasonable and customary practice, then it is to be understood that he has power [rightfully]. Likewise, he has no [rightful] power in a case in which he has not legitimately used such power. In such an instance when the power has not been made explicit in the concession or commission granted to him, he could generate great harm to the common good or to the rights of the clergy who are subject to the king. And thus, since the clergy could not be prohibited from aiding the king in such necessity without great harm — indeed, without great danger — to the common needs and even to the needs of the clergy who are subject to the king, it follows that the pope cannot make this prohibition. Should he make such a prohibition, it would be void and the clergy ought to resist him openly and in no way obey him as far as this is concerned, for they would sin mortally if they were to presume to obey him.

To the fifth objection, it may be replied that the goods of the English church do not belong only to the poor but rather to the entire community, including both poor and rich. They also belong to all those others from the same kingdom who are in such extreme necessity, or nearly so, that there can be no aid to them except through the goods of the church. And so, in accordance with the assertions of the holy fathers,[61] the ecclesiastical vessels and vestments may and should be sold for the release of captives — not only poor ones but also even rich ones — when they cannot be saved by any other means. And thus, the church goods should be given not only to the poor but also for the common good, namely, for the defense of the land and the public rights; in this event, the goods may and should be expended. And just as the pope may not decree that goods of the church should not be issued to the poor (either since this would be against the intentions of those who gave these same goods to the church, or since this would be against charity and brotherly love), so too he may not decree that these goods should not be expended for the defense of the homeland and of the public rights, either because this would be against the intention and will of the givers, or because this would be against the fervor and love of the common good and salvation — not only that of the laity, but also that of the clergy and of things that pertain to them.

To the sixth objection, it can be said that in earlier times it was customary in certain churches that only these four parts should be made from ecclesiastical goods. However, in one event they should be expended in another way; for, according to the true assertion of the fathers, they were to be expended for the release of captives. And thus, although goods of the church may not be customarily offered to the king, they are nevertheless to be placed at the king's disposal in the case of necessity for the defense of the

---

[61] Cf. St. Ambrose, *De officiis ministrorum* 2.28.136 (PL 16. 140).

homeland and of all laymen as well as clergymen who are resident in the land, and for the defense of their belongings and of the rights of the kingdom and of the king; and at his disposal they can be legitimately — even meritoriously — expended in just battles, if this action is directed by justice alone.

To the seventh objection, which is the last, it is replied that the sentence of the pastor who is true (not only according to the opinion of men) is to be feared, namely, that sentence which by its own authority and deed is not void so as to be unable to be conclusively judged. The sentence of the false pastor, however, no matter how good a pastor he is according to the opinion of men — even of the majority of Christians — is not to be feared. Even the sentence of the true pastor is not to be feared when the sentence is void by its own authority and deed, so as to be unable to be conclusively judged even though the sentence should not have been suspended by an appeal. Such, however, is the sentence of even the true pastor when it contains a gross error against justice, and when it is brought into a case in which even the true pastor has no power. Such, moreover, is the sentence of the true pope, when it is brought against the English prelates on account of their having assisted the king in the aforesaid case; for it contains a gross error and is brought into a case in which even the true pope has no power, as may be understood from the preceding statement, and as will become more evident from things that will be discussed below.

Chapter 12

Moreover, not only would such a sentence of the true supreme pontiff in no way constrict the English clergy in the aforementioned case, but even if the sentence imposed by the supreme pontiff were brought against the king himself on account of his claiming the rights of kings, it would have no validity whatsoever. Nor would it by any means bind the king, or even those adhering to him, unless perhaps it were due to the fact that some operate in bad conscience. Just as was mentioned earlier and is further brought out here, the sentence of even a true pastor against a right is void in a case in which he has no power, since it contains such a manifest fault or a gross error, and as it has absolutely no force, even though it should not have been suspended by an appeal. This can be clearly gathered from diverse sacred canons and glosses on them; and I will select a few from both. Extra, *de sententia et re iudicata*, c. 1 reads: "A sentence set forth against the laws or canons, although it should not be suspended by an appeal, can not, however, be maintained by its own authority";[62] on which the Gloss reads: "A sentence brought against the laws, that is, against the right of the constitution such as it is expressed in the sentence, is by its own authority void, and it is rescinded without an appeal. This is stated here, and later in the same canon, *Cum inter*, at the end, and in the same canon, *Inter ceteras*, and in ii, q. vi, c. *Diffinitiva*."[63] Wherefore in that decretal *Inter ceteras*, it is said: "When the sentence is said to be faulty, it is necessary to nullify it, and it must not be upheld if it contains a manifest fault,"[64] and the Gloss writes over the word "faulty": "Namely, since it has been written against a right, that is, against laws and canons, above in the same canon, c. 1, just as an error is contained in this same sentence, ii, q. vi, c. *Diffinitiva*, vers.: 'Again, if a sentence has been written against a right' ";[65] and there it says: "If a sentence is brought down against a written right, just as when a deceased man is said to have been less than fourteen years old and to have made an authorized will, then it has no force, nor is any help of appeal necessary against it";[66] and the Gloss says: "An error of the judge should not excuse the sentence."[67]

From these things and many others, it can be gathered that if the sentence of even a true pastor, which is brought against a right in such a case in which the same pastor, although a true one, has no power, then his sentence is void by its own authority and has no force whatsoever, since it contains manifest vice and intolerable error.

But if, because he was pursuing the right of kings or requiring a just subsidy from the English clergy, a sentence were to come down from the true and supreme pontiff against the English king, it would be against right. In such a case in which the pope, although true, has no power over the king, this also would contain manifest vice and intolerable error, according to what can be clearly seen from the preceding; therefore, such a sentence would be binding neither for the king nor for anyone else in any way, but would be void by its own authority and would have no force whatsoever.

---

[62] *Decretales Gregorii IX, De sententia et re iudicata* (II, 27, 1).
[63] *Glossa ordinaria ad Decretalis II, 27, 1, s.v.* "contra leges."
[64] *Decretales Gregorii IX, Inter ceteras* (II, 27, 9).
[65] *Glossa ordinaria ad Decretalis II, 27, 9, s.v.* "manifestum."
[66] Gratian, *Decretum*, 2, q. 6, c. 41.
[67] *Glossa ordinaria ad Decretum 2, q. 6, c. 41, s.v.* "contra ius."

Chapter 13

Clearly, in order that this argument can be made more apparent, I will take care to reply to some objections against it. And so it seems that this argument is deficient in many ways. For although a sentence brought down against a written right is void by its own deed so as to be unable to pass judgment, nevertheless a sentence brought against a right of a litigant does pass judgment, unless it should have been suspended by an appeal. For in ii, q. vi, c. *Diffinitiva*, after the words quoted above, it reads thus: "If, indeed, a sentence is declared against a right of the litigant, as when someone (previously) less than fourteen years old has completed his fourteenth year and thus is said to have made a legal will, one must seek the remedy of appeal."[68] But if this sentence should come down from the pope against the English king, in this case such a sentence would be only against the right of the king; therefore, it would not be void by reason of right itself. Again, "the opinion of a true pastor," which is not against written law or constitution, "is to be feared," because of what was said; with which Extra, *de sententia et de re judicata*, c. *Cum inter*, agrees, when it reads thus: "However, those considering that the law has been made from a sentence just as much for the litigants themselves, even if it had been brought against the law of the litigants, when it was not expressly brought against the authority of the constitution," etc.[69] Here, the Gloss over the word "constitution" says: "For this sentence neither passes judgment, nor is it necessary to make appeal on account of it."[70] From these it can be gathered that only that sentence which is against a written right or constitution is void by reason of right itself. But if such an opinion were brought by the pope against the king or those favorable to him, it would not be ...[71]

---

[68] Gratian, *Decretum*, 2, q. 6, c. 41.
[69] *Decretales Gregorii IX, De sententia et re iudicata, Cum inter* (II, 27, 13).
[70] *Glossa ordinaria ad Decretalis II*, 27, 13, s.v. "contra ius constitutionis."
[71] The text breaks off.

Table of Biblical Citations

GENESIS
1:16	179	23:17–20	161
1:27	43	31:32	161
3:19	106	31:37–38	161
4:10–11	87	39:5	161
18	92	41:35	161
18:20	87	42:21	103
19	92, 100		

EXODUS
2	87	20:1	136
2:23	87	20:3–4	136
2:23–24	135	20:17	75, 93, 124, 128, 129, 135, 138
3:7–8	135		
3:9	74	22:5	93
17:10	117	28:1–8	136
18:21	104	28:10–11	136
18:23	104	39:8	93
20	125		

LEVITICUS
18:30	103	26:3–6	136

NUMBERS
16:32–33	100

DEUTERONOMY
2:4–6	161	2:9	161

2:18–19	161	17:16	116
4:39–40	136	17:20	127
6:5	103	28	136
6:13	103	32:29	105, 138
11:26–28	135		

1 Samuel

3	83	12:25	83
4	83	15	83
12	83	15:26	93

2 Samuel

7	88	12:1–7	86
7:7	75		

1 Kings

9:11	161	20:31	100
12:14	91	21:2–19	96
19:15	161	21:28–29	89

2 Kings

12:13–15	89

2 Chronicles

36:22–23	161

1 Ezra

1:1–2	161

3 Ezra

8:28	137

Tobit

2:19–21	77	2:20–21	161

Judith

4:13	117	9:16	118

Job

1	75	1:21	106

Table of Biblical Citations

5:17	124	21:31	102
7:7	105, 122	24:12	74
14:10	119	27:19	113
15:34	134	36:6	80
21:12–14	131		

Psalms

2:8	165	68:29	132
9:13	74	71:13	100
9:17	74	73:13	162
11:6	74, 80	75:6	113
23:1	180	83:11	165
33:7	74	96:10	35, 126, 134
39:13	77	103:27	165
48:17–18	113	118:21	135
52:6	111	137:17	77
54:24	81	145:8	73
67:4	35		

Proverbs

1:24	83	18:3	112
1:24–25	110, 131	19:4	116
1:27–30	83, 110, 132	21:13	110, 131
2:14	110	22:1	76, 120
3:21–26	123	22:22–23	75
4:9	81	25:5	134
5:23	81	27:1	105
11:24	81	28:15	79
14:26	83	29:10	78
14:28	83		

Ecclesiastes

1:15	112	9:10	121
7:2	120	9:12	121
7:3	122	9:18	139
9:5	114, 121	10:17	99

Song of Songs

2:1	43	8:6	115

WISDOM

2:21	77	5:16–17	121
5:7–14	102	6:2–4	103
4:6	98	6:6	103
4:16	98	7:5–6	105
5:1–9	80	12:16	78
5:6–16	120	14:16	74

ECCLESIASTICUS

1:27	83	25:1–2	133
3:22	136	29:14	136
4:33	127	32:1	118
5:8–9	135	33:31	75
6:6	41	33:32	75
6:8	116	34:24	79
6:10	116	34:25–26	87
7:40	107, 108, 121, 122	34:26	75
7:5	125	34:27	79
10:1	88	35:16	101
10:3	88	35:18–19	101
10:8	83, 89	35:23	80, 101
10:12	105	35:17–19	80
12:8	116	40:13	79
16:3	117	40:13–14	114
21:6	74	41:1	122
23:20	112		

ISAIAH

1:2	99	56:10–11	133
1:15	83	57:21	137
1:23	134	58:1	77, 99
31:1	118	59:14–15	91
33:1	81, 124, 131	59:15	78
39:8	138	61:8	103
45:1	161	63:4	132
47:11	124	63:5	132
48:22	137		

JEREMIAH

1:10	165, 175	2:5	116

4:22	110	16:13	119
8:10	134	19	81
13:23	112	20	81

EZEKIEL

3:18–19	95	13:10	137
13:5	77	46:18	75

DANIEL

2:37–38	161	5	84
3	84	5:18	161

HOSEA

8:4	164

AMOS

8:10	82, 100, 131

MICAH

3:2–3	75	3:4	75

NAHUM

2:12–13	81

HABAKKUK

2:6	81	2:8	81
2:6–8	114		

MATTHEW

2:1	161	17:24	161
5:23–24	94, 125	19:27	162
5:32	173	20:25	163
5:45	100	22:37–38	134
7:12	123, 128	23:9	87
11:29	100	24:25	165
12:3–8	183	25:13	107
16:18	171	25:40	80
16:19	155	25:41	79, 80
16:25	98	26:52	174
17:19	139		

Mark
10:9	173

Luke
1:5	161	10:27	93, 134
1:26–30	111	16:19–31	132
2:1	161	16:28	79
3:12–14	161	17:26–29	100
6:25	82	20:21–25	162
6:31	123	22:25	164
9:25	98	22:26	164
10:7	38	22:38	173

John
6:20	112	18:11	174
8:34	82	19:11	161
14:12	132	20:22–23	171

Acts
3:6	163	16:37	161
8:20	165	17:28	26
15:10	156	22:25–28	161
15:22–23	156	24:10	161
15:28–29	156	25:10–11	161
15:31	157		

Romans
2:1	88	13:7	161
13:1	161, 164, 169	13:8	127
13:2	164	13:9	127, 138
13:4	168	14:17	130

1 Corinthians
3:8	119	10:31	26
6:3	176	11:29	94
6:4	162	13:3	126
7:20–21	161		

2 Corinthians
3:17	156	11:14–15	111

13:8	159	13:11	128, 130
13:10	159		

GALATIANS

1:10	111	5:12–13	156
2:3–5	156	6:9–10	119
4:13	156		

EPHESIANS

5:6	101	6:5	170
5:24	170		

PHILIPPIANS

2:10	26

COLOSSIANS

3:20	170	3:22	170

1 THESSALONIANS

3:5	137	4:10	112
4:3	112	4:12	112, 124
4:6	112		

2 THESSALONIANS

3:5	133	3:5	133

1 TIMOTHY

1:14	112	6:1–2	161
2:4	160	6:7	84
6:1	170, 177		

2 TIMOTHY

2:21	134

TITUS

1:16	133

HEBREWS

12:6	124	13:14	121
12:14	138		

JAMES

1:17	26	4:4	102
1:25	156	5:4	78, 87
3:16	133	5:19–20	156

1 PETER

2:13	169	2:18	161, 169
2:14	175	3:10–12	138
2:13–14	161, 168	5:3	162, 164
2:17	180		

1 JOHN

2:4	123	4:16	132
3:1	87	4:20–21	123
3:10	94	4:8	95
3:17	124, 132	4:20	94

REVELATION

18:7	102	19:16	32

Index of Names

Abel 87
Abiram 100
Abraham 169
Ahab 89, 96, 97
Ahaz 89
Alexander the Great, King of Macedonia 18, 25, 29, 39, 42, 50, 61, 89, 121-122
Amalek 117
Ambrose, St. 73, 116, 117, 162
Anna, wife of Tobit 77
Antioch 156
Aquinas, St. Thomas 3
Aquitaine 27
Arabic language 18
Aragon 98
Aristotle 6, 12, 17, 18, 20, 22, 25, 28, 29, 50, 103, 148, 151, 184
Arius 98
Augustine, St. 69, 75, 76, 79, 84, 87, 89, 101, 113, 133, 144, 149, 157, 161, 171, 180
Avignon 147
Bacon, Roger 6, 18
Barnabas 156
Bernard of Clairvaux, St. 3, 69, 133, 163, 166, 167, 173, 174, 175, 176

Bloch, Marc 8
Boniface VIII, Pope 142
Boyle, Leonard 66
Bracton, Henry de 1, 3
Burley, Walter 6, 11, 12-13
Cain 87
Canterbury 66, 67, 141, 144
Cassian 73
Cassiodorus 76, 103
Chester 27
Chrysostom, St. John 163, 166, 167, 168
Cicero, Marcus Tullius 17, 148, 151, 184
Clement V, Pope 162
Cornwall 19
Curia Regis 9, 35
Cyprian, St. 73
Dathan 100
David, King 86, 88, 89
de Montfort, Simon 5
Dispenser family 22, 101
Duns Scotus, John 6
Edward the Confessor, King and St. 99, 112, 113
Edward I, King 21, 64, 98, 137, 143
Edward II, King 5, 22, 27, 64, 65, 68, 72, 101, 143, 144

Edward III, King 6, 19, 20, 21, 22, 24, 27, 64, 65, 68, 71, 72, 103, 145, 146, 148, 153, 154
Egypt 87, 103, 118, 135
Eli 83, 89
Elijah 97
England, kingdom of 1, 2, 5, 6, 8, 13, 14, 17, 23, 28, 63, 68, 83, 96, 99, 106, 113, 129, 141, 142, 145, 149, 151, 152, 153, 154, 180, 181, 182, 183, 186, 191–192
English language 16
Ethiopia 162
Eugenius III, Pope 163, 164, 165, 173, 175
Europe 141, 142
Ferster, Judith 17, 22
Forhan, Kate L. 20
Fortescue, John 1, 8, 23
France 96, 98, 99, 123, 130, 142, 148
Franciscan order 146, 147
French language 40, 69
Frontinus 17
Gabriel 110
Gascony 98
Gaul 56
Gaveston, Piers 22, 98, 101
Gehazi 89
German language 16
Germany 56, 146
Giles of Rome 18, 142
Gratian 20
Greece 6
Gregory the Great, St. 69, 74, 76, 97, 107, 115, 132, 162
Hanson, Donald W. 7
Henry II, King 96
Henry III, King 3, 5, 75, 98, 110

Hostiensis 144
Hugh of St. Victor 101
Hull 66
Innocent III, Pope 96, 155, 158, 172
Ireland 27
Isabella, Queen 71
Isidore of Seville 69, 88, 102
Islip, Simon 66
Israel 87
James, M. R. 19
Jeraboam, King 91
Jeremiah 176
Jerome, St. 144, 162, 166
Jesus 85, 112, 123, 154, 155, 156, 158, 159, 161, 162, 165, 166, 167, 168, 169, 170, 171, 172, 173, 174, 177, 178
Jews 157
John, King 7, 96
John XXII, Pope 146, 147
John of Salisbury 17
John the Almoner 121
Joinville, Jean de 69
Joseph 93
Judas Barsabas 156
Justinian, Emperor 26
Lambeth, Council of 67, 78
Lancaster, Count of 106
Langtoft, Peter 143
Lateran Council, Fourth 142–143
Latin language 17, 18, 40, 69
Lot 92, 100
Locke, John 1–2, 4
London 66, 92, 95
Louis IX, King and St. 69, 123, 130, 139
Ludwig of Bavaria, King 145, 146, 147
Lutterell, John 147

Index of Names

Machiavelli, Niccolò 17, 21
Magna Carta 78
Marsiglio of Padua 148
Martin of Braga 20
Mary, mother of Jesus 27, 30, 110–111
Mauricius, St. 128
Meopham, Simon 66
Michael of Cesena 147
Moisant, Joseph 66
Mortimer, Roger 71, 101
Moses 117, 135, 138, 157
Munich 146
Naboth 96, 97
Nathan 86, 90
Nepotionus 162
Noah 100
Norway 99
Occam, Surrey 146
Ockham, William of 6, 20, 22, 146–148, 149–152
Origen 163, 167, 168
Oxford, University of 6, 18, 19, 66, 146, 147
Paris, University of 6, 19
Parliament 9, 12, 13, 35, 64
Paul, St. 156, 159, 160, 176–177
Paull, Yorkshire 66
Pecham, Archbishop 78
Persia 50
Peter, St. 155, 156, 159, 166, 167, 168, 169, 171, 172, 173, 174, 175
Philip II, King 127

Philip III, King 123
Philip IV, King 142
Pisa 147
Plato 20, 25
Pompey 58
Ponthieu 27
Prestwich, Michael 8
Privy Council 36
Reading 66
Rhine River 146
Richard I, King 96
Richard II, King 7
Rome 56, 88, 143, 144
St. Mary's Church, Southwark 146
Salisbury 66
Sallust 58
Scotland 63, 64, 68, 98, 99
Seneca 69, 74, 100, 119, 122, 123
Sertorius 58
Silas 156
Spain 98
Stephen, King 3
Vegetius 17, 20, 21
Wales 63, 98
Walter of Milemete 16, 19, 20, 22, 23, 27, 69, 142
White, A. H. 8
William I, King 7
William of Pagula 20, 22, 66–68, 69–72, 142, 145
Winchelsey, Robert 143
Windsor 66, 68, 87, 88, 89, 91
Winkfield, Berkshire 66